Economics and Freedom of Expression

Media Structure and the First Amendment

And though all the winds of doctrine were let loose to play upon the earth, so Truth be in the field, we do injuriously, by licensing and prohibiting, to misdoubt her strength. Let her and falsehood grapple; who ever knew Truth put to the worse, in a free and open encounter?

Milton, Areopagitica

Economics and Freedom of Expression

Media Structure and the First Amendment

Bruce M. Owen

Ballinger Publishing Company ● Cambridge, Mass.
A Subsidiary of J.B. Lippincott Company

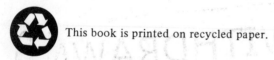

This book is printed on recycled paper.

International Standard Book Number: 0-88410-044-8

Library of Congress Catalog Card Number: 75-26645

Printed in the United States of America

Library of Congress Cataloging in Publication Data

Owen, Bruce M
    Economics and freedom of expression.

    Bibliography: p.
    Includes index.
    1. Mass media—Economic aspects—United States. 2. Liberty of speech—United States. I. Title.
P96.E2509   301.16'1   75-26645
ISBN 0-88410-044-8

For
Josetta, Peter, and Brad

Contents

List of Tables

List of Figures

Table of Cases

Foreword

Five years of working on various subjects in the economics of the mass media have inevitably exposed me to the monuments of jurisprudence in the field, and since these monuments have often appeared misplaced or badly constructed, I have been compelled to put together some suggestions for improvement. This book is therefore addressed to lawyers, jurists, and policy makers, as well as to economists interested in the organization of the mass media industries. I would have been more comfortable addressing the latter group alone, except that it did not seem to me that one could usefully discuss the subject of media performance without reference to the First Amendment and those government policies, presumably grounded on that Amendment, which have shaped media structure.

I apologize in advance to lawyers and jurists for the layman's failure to give full sympathy to the weight of precedent and to the limits of judicial legislation in my criticisms of major court decisions. I do recognize the difficulty that precedent puts in the path of judicial reform, but I have not been trained to take it very seriously. As a result, my comments on these decisions may seem unduly harsh. But just as it is often true that lawyers can see gaps and errors in economic reasoning (usually the result of inappropriate assumptions), so I hope that it will be acknowledged that an economist can sometimes see the source of error in judicial reasoning.

As its title implies, the theme of this book is that an understanding of the economic structure of the mass media can aid in our search for greater freedom of expression. The key word is structure. The bias of lawyers, both as legislators and as jurists, is to remedy inequities by imposing behavioral sanctions and constraints on the process by which decisions are reached. The bias of an economist is to seek an organizational structure that will provide internal incentives to decentralized decision makers, which will lead to actions having some desirable attributes such as efficiency and fairness. The latter bias is, I submit, often more conducive to freedom. From this point of view, much of the regulatory and legal structure of the media is very badly constructed indeed.

At this point in the history of mass communication, western societies seem to have developed a fairly robust set of public policies toward the printed media. Although there are minor discrepancies—such as the contrast between British and American treatment of official secrets and judicial proceedings—the prevailing policy is laissez faire. Within broad limits people can print and read what they want without prior restraint, although they may have to face the consequences of their expressions.

It is noteworthy that this system of public attitudes toward the printed media has taken more than four centuries to evolve. But now these policies have been challenged by rapidly changing technology in the form of electronic communication. Governments have been reluctant to extend the principle of laissez faire to the new media. Indeed, most governments in the West have simply nationalized these media. One of the things that I argue in this book is that this is neither necessary nor desirable.

The electronic revolution was not the first in communications. Leaving Gutenberg aside, there was an analogous event in the nineteenth century, when the application of mechanical power to presses, rapidly falling transport prices, and increased literacy vastly increased the audience for printed media. The social implications of the nineteenth century revolution in communication were not, in their magnitude (and to some extent in their nature), very dissimilar to the present situation. That the response of governments to those earlier events was different may be largely attributable to a differing climate of opinion about proper scope of government intervention. In any event, the current state of affairs is hardly unique, and the debate about mass media policy would be considerably enlightened if we stopped regarding the electronic revolution as sui generis.

A careful examination of the economic and technical assumptions upon which our present policies toward the electronic media are based reveals a most distressing failure of policy makers to understand the nature of the problems they are addressing. Many of these false assumptions have been pointed out before. Here, I will attempt to argue from what seem to be the correct assumptions towards a set of policies that are consistent with economic and First Amendment objectives. Some similar but perhaps less drastic statements can be made about the printed media.

To the extent that public policies and official attitudes are determined not by logical analysis of the facts and legitimate policy objectives but by emotional preconceptions, one despairs of making much progress in effective reform. I do not think that we need to be four centuries about the business of reconciling electronic technology with libertarian principles. Yet we are today sufficiently off the track that it could well take a very long time to set things right.

ACKNOWLEDGEMENTS

I am extremely grateful to the Hoover Institution on War, Revolution, and Peace for supporting me as a National Fellow from grants supplied by the William Volker Fund and the Smith Richardson Foundation during the time this book was being written, and for supporting my able research assistant, Abbott Lipsky. Marianna Scherrer provided efficient and patient typing services through endless revisions of the manuscript. I owe a considerable debt to those scholars and friends whose work I have drawn upon or who have sacrificed their own time to help me formulate these ideas. I must single out Moses Abramovitz, Paul David, Richard Epstein, Henry Geller, Henry Goldberg, David Lange, Willard Manning, Frank McCabe, William Meckling, Charles Meyers, Thomas Moore, Roger Noll, William Rivers, Marc Roberts, James Rosse, Mike Spence, and Tom Whitehead for special thanks. Since I have not always been able to accept their advice, none of these persons is in any way responsible for my remaining errors.

Economics and Freedom of Expression

Media Structure and the First Amendment

Chapter One

Introduction and Overview: Freedom and Power

[F]reedom of speech does not exist in the abstract. On the contrary, the right to speak can flourish only if it is allowed to operate in an effective forum—whether it be a public park, a schoolroom, a town meeting hall, a soapbox, or a radio and television frequency. For in the absence of an effective means of communications, the right to speak would ring hollow indeed. And, in recognition of these principles, we have consistently held that the First Amendment embodies, not only the abstract right to be free from censorship, but also the right of an individual to utilize an appropriate and effective medium for the expression of his views.

—Justice Brennan, dissenting in
*Columbia Broadcasting System, Inc., vs
Democratic National Committee,*
412 U.S. 94, 193 (1973)

TO BEGIN

This monograph is about the ways in which mass media economic structure and public policy affect freedom of speech and press. An understanding of the economic structure of the media is essential (though not sufficient) to public policy seeking to enforce basic First Amendment objectives. This chapter is devoted to the discussion of a series of interrelated issues that must form the background for the study of individual media in subsequent chapters. There is, so far as I can discover, no way of dealing with the issues in this chapter in a "linear" fashion, at least without being very long winded indeed. Accordingly, the reader will find in the following pages a series of ideas and arguments that may not begin to fit into a coherent whole until they are applied to specific media later on.

Lest any reader be misled, it is well to state at once those issues which, while they involve freedom of expression, are not dealt with in this monograph. These issues include personal (nonmedia) expression, rights of assembly and petition, sedition, privacy, obscenity, pornography, libel, and religious and academic freedom. While these issues—particularly privacy and libel—are obviously of great importance (and indeed, occupy the bulk of Emerson's [24] treatise on the First Amendment) they are not issues about which economics has a great deal to say. The issue that really provides the background for the present work is the constitutional and political role of the media in American society.

It is the press—broadly defined—that provides the greatest part of the flow of information and expression in society, and the press is essential to the "effectiveness" of more personal forms of expression in the social and political sphere. Thus, speeches and demonstrations are well known to be affected by, as well as to affect, news media presence, and much of their impact, if any, is due to this relationship. (E.g., the notion of a "media event"—that is, an event created by or for the media while pretending to be of spontaneous and independent origin and significance.) People, either as citizens or as consumers, spend an enormous part of their lives consuming media output, and it is worth asking at least the traditional economic questions about the structure and performance of the industry producing this output.

The reader is entitled to an explicit forewarning of the author's maintained hypotheses (or prejudices), at least those of which he thinks he has made conscious use. Briefly put, there is a libertarian, antipaternalistic underpinning to the present work, consistent with a literal interpretation of the First Amendment: "The Congress shall make no law . . . abridging the freedom of the press." This literal or "strict constructionist" interpretation is, however, modified or compromised to this extent: the spirit of the First Amendment will be taken to mean not merely a negative constraint on the power of government, but a positive obligation to intervene in various carefully defined ways when freedom of expression is threatened by private agglomerations of power. That is, I would permit—indeed encourage—intervention by government to remedy structural or institutional conditions which "constrain" unnecessarily the freedom of expression through the media. This extension of the First Amendment is consistent (but not identical) with the theory of such cases as *Associated Press* v. *United States*[1] where the Court found that the First Amendment did not bar antitrust activity against the media:

> It would be strange indeed however if the grave concern for freedom of the press which prompted adoption of the First Amendment should be read as a command that the government was without power to protect that freedom. The First Amendment, far from providing an argument against application of the Sherman Act, here provides powerful reasons to the contrary. That Amendment rests on the assumption that the widest

possible dissemination of information from diverse and antagonistic sources is essential to the welfare of the public, that a free press is a condition of a free society. Surely a command that the government itself shall not impede the free flow of ideas does not afford non-governmental combinations a refuge if they impose restraints upon that constitutionally guaranteed freedom. Freedom to publish is guaranteed by the Constitution, but freedom to combine to keep others from publishing is not. Freedom of the press from governmental interference under the First Amendment does not sanction repression of that freedom by the private interests. (*Associated Press* 326 U.S. at 20).

A very great deal can be accomplished, particularly in broadcasting, simply by regarding the First Amendment as a statement of laissez faire, provided it is acknowledged that the antitrust laws in their present form are as applicable to the media as to other businesses. Some of the notions in this book go beyond this, and suggest particular institutional restructuring that might require legislation particular to the media. Although these results might conceivably be reached through antitrust, some of them might not be. In most, if not all, of the cases considered, laissez faire is an acceptable alternative, and the improvement to be gained from going further is certainly a debatable trade-off with the philosophical argument against direct structural legislation.

The theme of this book is provided by the quotation from Justice Brennan which appears at the beginning of this chapter. *Effective exercise of First Amendment rights requires freedom of access to the means of transmission at competitive market prices.* Such a right is quite distinct from the right to insert messages in already existing edited collections of messages; the latter "right" may amount to a license to destroy mass communication, while the former is crucial to the free exercise of speech through the media. The distinction rests on an understanding of the economic and technological relationships among the stages of production within the present media, an understanding which seems heretofore to have escaped First Amendment scholars and jurists.

FREEDOM AND POWER

I am preoccupied in this book with questions of "power" and "freedom," which are likely to be annoying to economists. Much of what follows is about the manner in which we have acquired too much private economic and public regulatory power and, therefore, too little freedom in some of the media industries. But first I must explain what is meant by "economic power" and why this leads to a reduction in freedom of expression in the media.

Power is a slippery concept. Some say that power exists only when it is not exercised, since to exercise it is to lose it. In this sense, power *is* freedom—the freedom to do or to not do something, presumably at some affordable cost. If there is no choice, there is no power and no freedom. A monopolist whose market is protected from entry by law has the power to set price, and to set price in a manner that achieves any objective he likes. Maximization of profit is only one such objective. Just as there are degrees of monopoly power, limits on the range of action, there are limitations on the objectives that can be achieved; therefore power is almost always a matter of degree. Although I shall use the word rather freely, none of the firms in this industry has a true economic monopoly, i.e., 100 percent of their market. By monopoly power, then, I mean a worrisome degree of discretionary power, including the power not to maximize profits.

We must ask why it is undesirable for a firm to have monopoly power in this market. First, the monopolist can, in order to maximize profit, exclude certain ideas that would be produced in a competitive environment. He may even do this in order to appear "responsible" to a licensing authority, and thus to retain his legal monopoly. Or he may do it because a multiproduct monopolist finds it unprofitable to produce products that are too close substitutes. Second, the monopolist may exclude ideas he simply doesn't like even at a cost in terms of profit foregone. No one else will be in a position to do so.

Presumably, monopolists may have views on political, social, or economic issues which they are willing to pay to advertise or to prevent others from advertising. The monopolist of the media is in a fortuitous position to exercise these whims, since there is by definition no reasonable price any one else can pay to stop him. Finally, it may be that the profit function which depends on the ideas broadcast is flat or nearly flat in the relevant range, allowing the monopolist to exercise his whim without cost. If there were more than one or a few firms in the market, the opportunity for diversity, from the point of view of the audience, would be greater.

The greater the power of the monopolist, the less the freedom of other potential speakers. Freedom of expression must therefore mean something like equal freedom of all speakers, though the freedom of anyone may be less than that of the monopolist, since no one can prevent others from speaking. I believe this notion of freedom is approximated by an economically competitive market for ideas. Such a market imposes the constraint on freedom, that messages be worth something to their audience, so that they will pay to hear them. But the sum required need only be large enough to cover costs, and in equilibrium may be no larger.

There is a school of thought which suggests that a monopolist will supply all the products demanded in the market place, only at a higher price. This theory suggests that from the First Amendment standpoint, monopoly is not necessarily a factor leading to a decline in diversity of sources of opinion. We must reject this. First of all, it is not clear that a monopolist does produce the same range of product choice produced by competition (Spence [87], and the appendix to Chapter Three). Moreover, there is considerable doubt that the takeover, capital market check on failure to maximize profits (as, for instance, when a media monopolist unprofitably excludes certain political views) works very well in the newspaper industry (where family ownership is still very common) or in broadcasting (where all controlling stock purchases must receive FCC approval). Finally, monopoly does in any event charge a higher price, and this in itself is hardly defensible from the point of view of access, where price may very well be crucial. We will return to the issue of power after we have examined some of the theories justifying freedom of expression. Before we can do that, however, it is necessary to explain the marketplace metaphor.

The Marketplace Metaphor

The "marketplace of ideas" is a metaphor with more than one interpretation. The one that will occur to most noneconomists is suggested by the epigraph from Milton's *Areopagitica* at the beginning of the book. That is, "ideas" compete for intellectual domination over men's minds, and presumably truth wins just often enough to keep the game interesting. The sense in which I wish to use the term is, however, rather different from this. In particular, I want to take the "marketplace" notion quite literally.

There is a market in which information and entertainment, intellectual "goods," are bought and sold. The media comprise an important part of this market, though not by any means the whole of it. It happens that to operate effectively in this market, either as a buyer or as a seller, one must usually deal with intermediaries, such as printing presses, broadcast transmitters, and post offices. It will be clear, then, that by "monopoly in the marketplace of ideas" I do not mean that circumstance in which one idea has, by its intellectual or emotional force, gained ascendency over men's minds. I mean, rather, a state in which one firm or institution has an economic monopoly, generally achieved by controlling access to the means of transmitting messages.

Such a monopoly has two vices: the first is that the quantity, quality, and variety of goods produced may be inefficient in the economic sense; the second is that the Miltonian process may not work properly, and ideas that are not the truth may come to dominate the intellectual market as a result of the systematic exclusion of messages that do not suit the economic or political interests of those who control access to the media of transmission. Even if the second vice does not obtain (as, for instance, when the government as the monopolist explicitly seeks popular truth), there is arguably a case for assuming that the competitive Miltonian process is a desirable end in itself. Indeed, the notion that "truth will conquer" has in nearly all the writings on this subject from Milton to Mill been put forward by way of apology for the more fundamental proposition that personal freedom of thought and expression is a desirable end of social organization.

What justifies freedom of expression? What, for instance, was the original motivation for the First Amendment? Historically, suppression of dissent had taken the form not only of newspaper and book censorship, including prior restraint, but also economic sanctions (see Collet [8]). These have the effect, other things being equal, of reducing the power of nonestablishment groups, whether religious or political. The American revolutionists suffered from the effects of these tactics, and they presumably sought to prevent their use in the future. It is important to note at once the economic context that faced the framers of the First Amendment in 1791. Their experience suggested a set of "communications media" that was comprised of a number of small enterprises. Particularly as regards pamphlets and books, there seemed to be no difficulty of entry, and the resources required to achieve access by this means to the populace were not great.[2]

In 1780 there were about 37 newspapers published in the former colonies, most of them weekly or twice weekly. The first daily appeared in 1783. By 1790 there were eight dailies and 83 weeklies. A great deal of political expression also took place in printed pamphlets and books, often published by the same printers who published newspapers. Thus, we can regard the First Amendment as having at least one implicit assumption, that competition in the marketplace of ideas will be conducive to political freedom in a democratic system. It is then a small step from the condemnation of monopoly by government in this marketplace to a general objection to monopoly by any private institution. The founding fathers were quite naturally preoccupied with constructing checks on government power; but the spirit of their endeavor, the search for freedom, surely extends to private power as well.

We can now identify at least six motivations for seeking freedom of expression. First, it can be regarded somewhat pathetically as a simple revolutionary reaction to the oppressions of colonial government. Second, it can be regarded as a means of guaranteeing that truth will emerge from decentralized political and philosophical debate, giving in the colonial context an opportunity for the adherents of each religious faction to prove the validity of their own vision. This is what I have called the Miltonian process. Third, a more modern view, freedom of expression may serve as a safety valve for dissenting groups, a substitute for violence. (Personal expression alone may be inadequate to the purpose if there are barriers, political or economic, to mass dissemination of those expressions.) Fourth, open debate and a free press may serve as a check on the power of government, by revealing corruption or malfeasance among government officials. Fifth, a free press serves as a means of producing an informed and alert citizenry, a prerequisite of elective democracy, Sixth, freedom of expression may be a valuable end in itself, an improvement of the human condition.

The objections raised against freedom of expression are generally made by those who know they possess the truth and are in a position to impose that truth on others. Being in power is not, however, a prerequisite for denial of the usefulness of freedom of expression (see Wolff, et al. [100]).

The political role of the press is said to be founded on antagonism toward government. This doctrine has permeated First Amendment discussion for many years. The theory is that a skeptical, even cynical, press which questions government activity at every level will help to maintain virtue in political life. This model of the press suggests not merely the exposure of corruption in government, but the use of the press to keep the public continuously informed regarding substantive public decisions that ought to affect the electoral process.

It is important to note that this model of the press does not necessarily require competition. The press here is merely a conduit for information essential to informed voting. In order to find a role for competition, we have to ask what incentives are otherwise present for vigorous performance of this role by the press, and what abuses might arise within the press itself in the absence of competition. If the press is to function as a check on government corruption and a source of public information, it must have incentives to do so effectively and consistently.

The principal incentives it might have are those provided by competition, provided that this "role" has a high survival value in the marketplace. (Competition rewards firms that best satisfy consumer demand; if consumers do not want this information, competition will not provide it.) It seems pretty clear that the public does relish scandal, and that government corruption has sold a lot of newspapers. We can count on the press to perform this role so long as it must in order to survive in the retail marketplace.

Of course, if tastes are not taken as given, the press may wish to cultivate a demand for news of misgovernment. A monopoly press does not have the same vigorous incentives to perform this role, or at least has a great deal more discretionary power in deciding on the extent and degree of its coverage. It is not difficult to imagine situations in which the profit seeking owners of a monopoly press can gain by selective performance, and even by implicit cooperation with the politicians whom they are supposed to watch. Certainly it has always been supposed that an "establishment press" has this characteristic vis à vis scandal in the social and economic establishment itself. Whether or not a publisher "censors" the news, reporters may be reluctant to say unkind things about the country club set to which the publisher and major advertisers belong, or about their own peers.

This brings up a major issue regarding freedom of expression. The "watchdog" theory of the press, however recent, has much to recommend it, as the Watergate scandals have illustrated. But there is a school of thought which holds that courageous exercise of this function requires that the media be large, wealthy organizations with the resources necessary to "subsidize" investigative reporting. If so, there is some conflict between this theory and the "more is better" theory of freedom of expression with respect to the number of editorial gatekeepers competing in the marketplace.

It is certainly true that the monopoly media were responsible for the decisions to publicize the Watergate scandals, but it is not clear that this took any extraordinary degree of courage. The original stories in the *Washington Post* by

Woodward and Bernstein do not appear to have required the massive resources of a great organization; it is far from clear that these or other reporters employed by a more competitive press would not have broken the story just as soon. (A close reading of Woodward and Bernstein [8] suggests that competition did play a role in hastening the publication of the story.) Indeed, it might have broken sooner if newspaper editors and their electronic counterparts had felt more competitive pressure and less sense of "social responsibility."

The "countervailing power" theory of the role of the press must, it seems to me, be rejected.[a] It requires a belief in the efficacy of conscious moral action by institutions with at least sometimes contrary incentives, and it depends unduly on the frail reed of human nature. Neither the profits nor the prophets of the press are themselves "elect." We are far better off with a system in which it is assumed that everyone is following his own self-interest; behavior is then predictable and can be discounted appropriately. When an institution sets itself up as the moral and ethical protector of "truth," and claims to stand above the incentives affecting its own self-interest, more than a few citizens may be seriously misled, and even those who are not will have difficulty interpreting the direction and extent of the inevitable biases.

The basic economic issue however is whether the press has economies of scale in the dimensions involved in investigative reporting. If so, then there is a countervailing power argument for a degree of concentration in the press. Unfortunately, investigative reporting seems to be done, on the national level at least, by newspapers which are both competitive and large, making empirical tests rather difficult. Little reporting of this kind is done by the network television oligopoly, no doubt in part because of disincentives provided by FCC regulatory policies. Casual empiricism does not suggest any systematic relationship between newspaper size and vigorous local investigative reporting. Periodicals seem to do the most investigative muckraking. But there is, apparently, no systematic study of this point in the literature. Given the presumptions of the First Amendment tradition, the burden of proof of the countervailing power hypothesis must lie with its proponents.

The proper performance of the social and political role of the press ought not to be a matter of "courage" but a matter of survival. Whenever there is great discretion[b] in the performance of the press, there is danger of abuse and an imperfection in the theoretical structure on which the First Amendment is based. Given human nature, the process cannot safely depend on "fearless" editors, nor can it depend on "responsible" editors; it must depend on editors concerned for their competitive survival in the marketplace.

---

[a]By "countervailing power" I mean the notion, popularized by Galbraith [31], that large monopolistic institutions are necessary to deal effectively with the corresponding power of, in this instance, government. See Schumpeter [82].

[b]The editorial process by definition involves the exercise of discretion. But in a world of competition the resulting output must stand the test of the market. The editor who makes unprofitable discretionary choices will not survive.

The positive argument for the preceding position need not depend on the apology that truth will necessarily prevail. In the first place, a pluralistic debate is unlikely to reach a broad or long lasting concensus. In the second, what emerges can hardly be independently verified as "the truth." That truth will result from unfettered debate is therefore an untestable hypothesis. Freedom of expression, in the sense of freedom from government intervention and freedom from fortuitous economic monopoly, can be justified on more fundamental grounds in which it is the process of free debate, not the result of that debate, that has ethical merit. I shall not try to reproduce here the moral arguments for freedom that have been so well put elsewhere, as in Nozick [59], but the underlying assumptions involve a belief in individual human dignity and therefore consumer sovereignty.

Clearly the demand side is of enormous importance, and we can trace many of the failures of the First Amendment system[c] to imperfections in its theory of demand. There does not seem to be any difficulty in the area of scandal and corruption. The public's appetite for scandal seems nearly insatiable, although Watergate may have strained the outer limits. (There is, of course, no guarantee that the degree of exposure of malfeasance is "optimal.") But for other kinds of information—particularly technical information relating to government actions that affect the public as individuals only slightly—demand is not so great. Much of the activity of the federal and state governments comes under this heading, and this makes possible a great deal of special interest legislation and anticonsumer interest regulatory activity. Special interest legislation favoring farmers, for instance, is likely to get covered in the local agricultural state press, whose readers are benefited, and not in the rest of the country, which pays the bill. The reasons for this are fairly obvious.

If there is a deficiency in the First Amendment's theory of demand, one must raise serious questions about the rest of the theory and its implications. For special interest groups the theory works well. Particular industries, trades, professions, and societies are generally well served by specialized publications that provide quite complete and thorough reports on government activity affecting the interests involved. Such organs are often crucial to the organization of lobbying efforts by these groups. It is often, if not always, true that the gains scored by such organized activity come at the expense of the general public. It is not entirely clear that the media catering to the general public fail to provide relevant information on these issues: perhaps it's that the public is well aware of and content with the situation, or resigned to it.

The First Amendment theory of the press was formulated, of course, in the days of newspapers. The world is different now. The electronic media—radio and television—have in large part supplanted the newspaper as the source of news and opinion (and entertainment) for most citizens. Does the end of the Guten-

[c]I mean the "system" which has the press serve as a check on government activity.

berg revolution imply that our constitutional theory of the press is outmoded? Do we need a new theory for the electronic media? These are serious questions, to be addressed after we have examined the economic context of the media.

THE DEMAND FOR MASS MEDIA MESSAGES

The traditional and most useful taxonomy of economic effects is the distinction between supply and demand. Before we can explore these two sides of the media marketplace, we must ask what commodity is being supplied and demanded. This is a difficult point, since the output of the media is neither one-dimensional nor concrete. The most obvious answer is to say that the media supply "information."

The term information has acquired a rather clear mathematical meaning as a result of studies in the theory of communication, which is concerned with such questions as how to code signals efficiently, and how to maximize the information flow in a given channel of communication.[3] Information is defined, in that literature, as an event that changes an individual's a priori probability distribution regarding alternative possible realities. For example, when you are walking home in the afternoon, you do not *know* whether your house is on fire or not. Presumably, your a priori expectation that it is not on fire is rather high. But smoke on the horizon provides a signal that may reduce the probability with which you hold this expectation, and fire trucks headed down your street may reduce the probability drastically. Both events or signals have provided information. An event does not contain information if it does not change your a priori subjective probability distribution of any possible reality.

These notions do not seem to help very much in dealing with the media, at least at first glance. After all, much of media output is "entertainment" or "opinion." Relatively little is "news" of the kind that fits into the decision theory paradigm. But what is "entertainment?" Clearly we must look at these ideas from the point of view of consumption behavior. Here, the social psychology of media consumption may help us sort out the nature of the commodity. Unfortunately, most of the social psychology research in this area is concerned with attitude change and persuasion, particularly propaganda.[4] These studies are useful in advertising research, but they do not seem to shed much light on the consumption of entertainment, although one theorist (Stephenson [89]) has constructed a "play theory" of mass communication. They are also troubling to an economist who is used to assuming (no doubt quite unrealistically) that tastes are exogenous to the economic system.

One idea prominent in the psychological literature is the "dissonance" theory of communication (Festinger [28]). Briefly, people tend to discount messages that are at variance with their a priori expectations. Thus, persuasion requires use of devices to overcome this resistance to cognitive dissonance, such as repetition. "Reinforcing" messages or signals, on the other hand, are "accepted" by consumers and valued highly even though they do not impart much information, precisely because it gives satisfaction to have one's opinions "confirmed." Now it is perfectly rational not to change one's opinion on a matter simply because one dissonant signal has been received. And it is understandable that the psychological cost of changing a belief system in any significant way may lead people to "reject" (put a low value on) dissonant signals.

Presumably the same reasoning explains people's tendency to put a high value on "reinforcing" messages. These considerations may very well explain why the economic value of information may have a great deal more to do with its relationship to people's belief systems than with its "objective" content measured in decision theory terms. Whether this approach is sufficiently robust to "explain" entertainment or "play" demand is another matter. The empirical work on persuasion and attitude change does suggest that it is extraordinarily difficult to make people believe things they are not already inclined to believe.

It seems clear that it will not be fruitful to proceed very much further on the psychological level here. Henceforth we shall take it for granted that people have a "demand" for news and entertainment, and that this demand is affected by such standard variables as price and income, and that different people like different things. Since it is essential to the political theory of the First Amendment, we shall also assume that people demand information about their government and its behavior. This will be demanded in varying degrees of detail as individual economic interests and tastes warrant. Finally, no distinction will be made among news, opinion, and entertainment. This last assumption requires some justification.

Why not treat news separately from entertainment? First, news is sometimes consumed because it *is* entertaining—otherwise it would be difficult to explain yellow journalism, political cartoons, "happy talk" TV news shows, or movie magazines. Second, much entertainment contains political and social commentary which is crucial to the First Amendment system. And surely the most powerful and subtle vehicles for attitude change and persuasion, as well as reinforcement, are dramatic and literary works. These arguments suggest that from the point of view of First Amendment theory, any distinction among communicated messages by "type" is fruitless, and indeed dangerous. The courts have generally accepted this view, with the exception of pornography and obscenity cases, and with the important exception of "commercial" speech: that is, advertising messages as a class seem to have a much lower degree of First Amendment protection than most other utterances. On the other hand, they are viewed kindly by the media.

The demand for mass media messages surely depends upon the social and cultural environment in which people live, since this environment conditions the "usefulness" of the information received. This effect will help to determine the structure of the media themselves, since the media affect the attractiveness of the message, à la McLuhan [49] (see also Innis [39]). Of course the present work is hardly broad enough in scope to encompass this set of issues in a way that can lay any claim to comprehensiveness; nevertheless they are important, and will be brought into the discussion from time to time. Suffice it to say that media technology is not exogenous to the socioeconomic system. Social conditions are no doubt different in the electronic era from what they were in the age of print, but it may be very difficult to separate cause from effect with respect to the role of the media themselves in this change.

THE STAGES OF PRODUCTION OF
MEDIA MESSAGES

There are three stages of production on the supply side of the media marketplace. These are: (1) The creation of messages, (2) the selection or editorial process, and (3) the transmission of messages to the audience. This has more than taxonomic significance, for each stage has different economic characteristics.

1. *The creation of messages* takes place in the writing of a news story, in the process of authoring an article or book, or in the production of a TV program or movie. In this process there is great heterogeneity. The frequency distribution of messages with respect to their "creators" is very nearly flat. There is great competition, despite the fact that creative talent is relatively scarce. There are few barriers to entry, in the sense that nearly anyone can sit down and write a novel or a screenplay or a news story; but getting it published or produced is another matter.

2. *The editorial process* is performed by newspaper editors, publishers, TV directors and program executives, motion picture studios, and the like, and may be subject to control by capital market decision makers as well. Economic organizations at this stage decide which of many potential messages will in fact be transmitted to the public—which messages the public will be allowed to choose from. This "gatekeeping" role is enormously influential if editors have monopoly power. They do not have this power if they are simply responding to consumer demand, where their survival as economic entities depends on their selecting just the right mix of messages. Probably the best examples of this are the magazine trade and the book trade.

But sometimes, for various reasons, editors do have great discretionary power. Then there exists a wide range of choices available to them, all of which are compatible with economic survival. Newspapers and television are examples of media with some degree of this power, and it is here that numbers play an important role, though they are not the whole story. Sometimes this power is channeled by implicit or explicit professional codes which move the journalist or editor in the direction of "leading" the public's opinion, and which impose standards of responsibility. These are a rather unsatisfactory response to the problem of monopoly power.

The editor who competes with other editors for survival serves as a surrogate for the consumer. He must be able to assess with great accuracy the tastes of his readers or viewers. This job may be equally difficult for the general publication and the highly specialized limited circulation media. Often the editor must worry not merely about his audience's tastes but the kind of audience desired by his advertisers. Clearly different content will produce different audiences, and it is a truism that not all audiences are equally valuable to advertisers.

3. *The transmission stage* of mass communication involves "broadcast" of the messages selected by the editors. This can take the form of printing presses and delivery boys or the U.S. mails, or the electromagnetic spectrum, or movie theaters. The technology of the transmission process has been subject to enormous change over the years, in marked contrast to the creative and editorial stages. In this century even printing technology has changed drastically, to say nothing of the invention of phonograph records, tape recorders, motion pictures, radio, television, and cable television. These technological innovations have had a profound effect on media structure and costs, as well as derived effects on consumption patterns.

For our purposes the crucial point about technological change in the transmission stage is that it has frequently been the occasion for new legislation and new judicial interpretations of the First Amendment. If the First Amendment can be fairly characterized as libertarian and antipaternalistic in spirit, then more recent acts of government have been the opposite. One of the questions we shall try to answer in this monograph is whether this change is justified by the technology or social context of the new media.

The three stages of mass media message production are all related. Different media have structured the relationship among the stages in ways that are dictated partly by the demands of technology and partly by the forces of economic self-interest. Sometimes the government mandates a certain relationship. As we shall see, it is in the relationships among these stages that much of media structure and behavior can be explained.

SOURCES OF CONCENTRATION

In the next three sections we shall explore the economic sources of concentrations of private power in the media.

Vertical Integration

Figure 1-1 provides a stylized view of the three-stage production process for five major media. Reading across the figure, it is apparent that there are marked

	TV	*Newspapers*	*Magazines*	*Books*	*Movies*
Creation	program packagers and their factors	news source reporters syndicates	writers photographers	authors	writers producers directors talent
Editing	networks, stations	editors publishers	editors publishers	publishers	studios
Transmission	transmitters spectrum	press trucks newsboys newsstands	press mail newsstands	press bookstores mails	distributors theaters (Also TV)

Figure 1-1.   Stages of Production

similarities among the first two stages in different media. Neither creation nor editing requires much capital investment (except for movies); both are labor intensive. Entry is easy (conceptually, treating the stages as independent). There ought to be a great deal of competition in these stages.

In contrast, the transmission stage is characterized by heavy capital investment costs, economies of scale, licensing, and other barriers to entry. These effects are particularly important for broadcasting, newspapers, and motion pictures. They are less important for magazines and books, largely because postal service is independently supplied, and even subsidized. The economic conditions for private power in individual media are clearly present in stage three. They are not present in stages one and two. Yet we find great concentration at stages one and two in some media. Why is this? Clearly it must be an effect of the non-neutrality of stage three.

Consider the media where concentration is absent at stages one and two: magazines and books. For these media the transmission stage (printing, mailing, bookstores, bookclubs, newsstands) is independently owned: there is little or no vertical integration. By contrast, for broadcasting and newspapers, the owners of the concentrated transmission stage are vertically integrated: they control editing and sometimes creation. Consequently the number of competing message sources and competing editorial services is reduced. Competition is constricted by virtue of the power of the most concentrated stage to control access and content.

The owner of a newspaper press does not act like the post office; he does not accept all requests for transmission at published rates, although for advertising matter something close to this does happen. He actively controls transmission, editing, and to some extent creation. Thus in an important sense it is vertical integration of control in some media that is responsible for private monopoly power in the marketplace of ideas, given the increasing degree of concentration in the transmission function occasioned by scale economies, licensing, and other causes. Behind this, of course, lies the technical or economic source of concentration in the transmission stage, which effects are explored below. In addition, there may be technical or economic reasons why certical integration is necessary in some media. It may be hard to imagine a daily newspaper publisher acting like a common carrier, for instance, largely because this may interfere with the economics of the editorial process, or because of externalities within the newspaper. It is somewhat easier to imagine TV stations as common carriers like the postal service, and we shall explore this idea later.

The important point is that given the perhaps necessary or natural concentration of the transmission level, vertical integration may be responsible for concentration in the crucial creating and editing stages. After all, provided that the transmission media are neutral—that is, do not discriminate systematically among messages or speakers on the basis of content—there is no other reason to suppose that there would be significant concentration at the earlier stages. For those media (magazines and books) which are characterized by neutral transmission media, there is extensive and vigorous competition at the earlier stages, despite the fact that "public goods" are being sold. It is only in the broadcast, newspaper, and motion picture industries that economies of scale, licensing, or other conditions give rise to individual firms with discretionary power to control content. We shall return to this point again and again, since the elimination of vertical integration is often the key to policy changes that might enhance freedom of expression.

The preceding argument is not meant to imply that the concentrated transmission stage acquires control over vertically related processes for predatory reasons. The reasons for vertical integration may be quite innocent, or even dictated by technological or economic necessity. It is easy to see why, for instance, a newspaper would hire reporters rather than buy news stories from independent freelance journalists. First, there is an element of timeliness that does not allow much opportunity for dickering over terms and conditions of sale. Syndication is much more common and competitive for nonnews items.

Second, the "product" is in this case one which has to be in effect "consumed" by the buyer in order for him to make a bid; but the news story is not easily protected from piracy as a result of such transactions, since the event involved, once known, can usually be independently verified and reported. For less timely material, the author or creator can and does exercise greater control, but ideas are practically impossible to appropriate. While freelance reporters do exist, their existence depends on conventions of "gentlemanly behavior" on the part of buyers, or (in the case of news wire services) the absence of much competition.

Backwards vertical integration by a monopsonist (the monopolist of transmission in his role as a buyer) may be motivated by a number of factors. A monopsonist can gain from vertical integration by eliminating the deadweight efficiency loss of monopsony buying.[d] Second, depending on various conditions in the supplying industry and the output markets of the monopsonist, the monopsonist can in some circumstances appropriate some portion of the rents generated by fixed factors in the competitive supply industry. Finally, manipulation of prices of the input can be managed by partial integration, and this can have an effect on competitors of the integrating firm if it is not a monopsony but simply a dominant firm.

Thus there are circumstances in which optimal integration is less than complete integration, and other circumstances in which it is optimal to integrate gradually rather than all at once.[e] Finally, in an industry such as television, individual programs as inputs are rather risky—their audience productivity is not known with certainty in advance. Under these circumstances the monopsonist or oligopsonist may be able to reduce costs by vertical integration or other equivalent measures that have the effect of pooling these risks, something an independent competitive producer of programs cannot do.

In general, then, partial or total vertical integration by a monopsonist or oligopsonist may well be profitable. In many circumstances it is also efficient, in the sense of reducing industry costs. The implication is that barriers to vertical integration, (proposed often in this book) may result in efficiency losses. These can be eliminated in principle by regulation of the monopsonist himself, although in practice this may not be feasible. The efficiency gains from vertical integration may, depending on the elasticity of demand for the final product, be rather small compared to the redistributive and noneconomic effects.

Economies of Scale

If the source of power and concentration in the first two stages is vertical encroachment from the concentrated transmission stage, what is the source of power in the transmission stage? Typically this power derives from economies of scale in transmission. There are two sorts of scale economies. The first we shall call "first copy" costs. These costs are incurred no matter how large the audience: they are the same for one reader or viewer as for ten thousand or ten million. Obviously, the larger the audience, the lower the pro rata (average) first copy costs are. This effect is illustrated in Figure 1-2. It is essentially a "public good" effect, and we will return to it in the next section.

The second sort of scale economy is found in the technology of distribution itself. It may be cheaper to produce and deliver the 100,000th copy of a newspaper than the 50th. Put another way, a newspaper of 100,000 circulation may have lower average total costs than one of 50,000, even leaving first copy costs aside. An extreme case is that of a TV station, where an additional viewer

---

[d]A monopsonist buying from a competitive industry takes account of the effect of his marginal purchases on the price of inframarginal units of the input. This leads him to purchase less of the input than he would use if it were internally produced.

[e]I am indebted to Martin Perry for much of the preceding analysis.

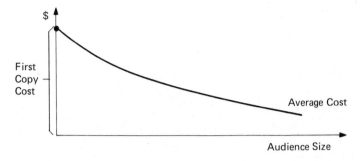

Figure 1-2. First Copy Costs

within the signal area costs the station literally nothing, in the partial sense. (It may cost a relatively significant sum to improve the attractiveness of a program sufficiently to *induce* the marginal viewer to watch.) This effect is illustrated in Figure 1-3, showing declining marginal cost of circulation.

So long as marginal cost is declining, so must average costs decline. The effect of this is clear: the larger the audience the greater the competitive advantage. Large newspapers[f] will tend to drive out smaller ones; two smaller newspapers can both gain by merger; a new motion picture distributor must have great difficulty obtaining a viable foothold in the industry; a UHF station that can only reach some of the homes in its market will do poorly compared to a VHF station that can reach all homes.

Scale economies of one kind or another are responsible for much of the concentration we observe at the transmission stage of mass media, but they are not the only cause. (In broadcasting, government policy is at least equally important.) Moreover, it must be remembered that scale effects are not and cannot by themselves fully determine the extent of competition. They must be taken in context with the "extent of the market" and the characteristics of consumer demand. Just one illustration of this point: if newspapers have economies of scale, why is there not only one newspaper in the United States? The reason is clear: demand for newspaper content is geographically specialized; this specialization of demand eventually offsets the scale effects, and determines the geographical extent of local newspaper monopoly.

Scale economies have mixed effects on consumers. Given the structure of the market, economies of scale mean increased consumer welfare as the extent of the market grows, simply because costs and therefore prices fall. (Even a monopolist lowers his price if his marginal costs fall.) But the presence of scale economies tends to produce noncompetitive markets, which are characterized by inefficient monopoly pricing and perhaps a deficient rate of technological

---

[f]As we shall see, the most important scale economy in daily newspapers may be with respect to the number of pages, rather than circulation.

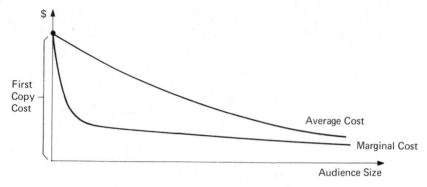

Figure 1-3. Declining Marginal Costs

innovation. Depending on the magnitude of the scale effects and the elasticity of demand, consumers (and advertisers) may or may not derive a *net* benefit from this trade-off. This is the sort of problem with which the antitrust authorities must constantly deal. But in the present context the presence of monopoly power due to scale effects has an additional negative effect: it constricts access and freedom in the marketplace of ideas, and this in turn generates pressure for government intervention that may extend to content.

PUBLIC GOODS AND MONOPOLISTIC COMPETITION

A "public" good has the characteristic that one person's consumption does not reduce the amount available for others. By this definition, a TV broadcast is a public good while bananas are not. Most goods have some element of the public good in them; there are few pure private goods and few pure public goods. But media messages are close to being pure public goods, although they are often embodied in a private good, such as the physical newspaper, book, magazine, or a TV set. (In television, both the program and the signal are public goods.)

Public goods have enormous economies of scale in consumption; marginal cost for an additional reader or viewer is almost literally zero beyond the transmission cost. This phenomenon is simply the first copy cost discussed in the previous section, and resembles all fixed costs in its effects. Note that the first copy cost does presumably influence how many people will want to receive the message, but not how many can.

Truly competitive production of public goods is either impossible (price competition will drive prices down to equality with marginal cost, which is zero) or likely to be inefficient, relative to the social optimum.[g] On the other

[g]See the Appendix to Chapter Three.

hand, media messages are almost by definition "differentiated"—no two are identical.[h] This product differentiation attenuates the debilitating effects of price competition. If there are a large number of firms producing goods sufficiently differentiated to make them only imperfect substitutes, we refer to the market as being monopolistically competitive. The creation and editing stages of mass media production can therefore (absent concentration) be described as the monopolistically competitive production of public goods.

One characteristic of monopolistic competition is that entry (of new products) and competition (in price and product space) keeps profits of individual firms down to "normal" levels. There are no profits in excess of normal returns. Until recently not much was known about the problem of firm location in product space in monopolistic competition. Recent work has demonstrated that firms in a monopolistically competitive equilibrium tend to produce too few products of a certain type, relative to the social optimum. The products that tend not to get produced are those with low price elasticities of demand. These are generally associated with small groups of customers who place a high value on products with specialized characteristics. There is a bias toward production of "mass consumption" products; this is caused by the presence of fixed costs. On the other hand, it can be demonstrated that media structures characterized by relevant forms of monopoly do even worse in this respect. What this means is that specialized, minority tastes are not well served.

We will return to this issue below in the context of our discussion of television. But the public good problem is quite a general one in the mass media, and it has certain implications for freedom of expression. One of these implications is that there may be a tendency toward underproduction of messages generally, simply because of the difficulty and cost of excluding "free riders." The law of copyright is a sort of second best solution to the public good problem in communication. There are two interests at stake: the need to provide an economic incentive to producers of messages, and the inefficiency that results from charging a price above the marginal cost of making the message available. It is inefficient to exclude a consumer from consumption of such a good by means of a price which exceeds that consumer's reservation price. This does not preclude charging a positive price for the good, but it may imply a need for price discrimination.

A second implication is that efficient solutions are unlikely to be available without direct government intervention in the process of defining message sources and content. We are constrained from this by the First Amendment itself. In any event, the information requirements for an efficient solution are so heavy—and the incentives for people to give false information are so great—that government intervention in practice is certainly not guaranteed to leave

---

[h]Copyright laws are intended to prevent them from being identical, and represent an interesting social response to an economic problem which was only defined by economists much later.

anyone better off, even in economic terms. For related reasons the private, price discriminating monopolist solution to the public good problem must be rejected in the present context.

Despite its demonstrated biases, monopolistically competitive production of public good messages may be a tolerable second-best situation from the First Amendment viewpoint. This is so at least in part because the character of consumer demand is apparently sufficiently heterogeneous that the worst conceivable cases of market failure are not observed in practice. A really dominant plurality of consumers with nearly identical tastes in media content could have very serious implications for the robustness of expression, given the incentives facing producers in this market. As things are, the more serious problems are found on the supply side, and even here the pathologies are traceable to influences external to the creating/editing process which is at the heart of First Amendment concern.

DIVERSITY

Most people seem to think that diversity is a good thing, but it is not obvious why this should be so. In the area of freedom of expression, "diversity of viewpoints" is often used synonymously with freedom itself, or as a measure of the success of the safety valve theory, and this has resulted in much judicial mischief. After all, a totalitarian state might, if it wished, offer the public access to a diversity of viewpoints, even though no one had any freedom of expression.

Similarly, a monopolist might choose to produce a wide range of opinions for his audience. This would go some ways toward relieving the effect of monopoly on consumers, or on the audience, but does not provide effective freedom for speakers. The First Amendment clearly is meant to apply to speakers, and while it may be based partly on the theory that freedom for speakers is good for the audience, this does not justify the substitution of government or monopoly supplied diversity in place of freedom for speakers.[i]

It is conceivable, on the other hand, that a completely "free" society could be so homogeneous that there was no diversity of ideas or opinions, expressed or unexpressed. As we shall see below in the context of broadcast regulation, the courts have concluded that the government has the obligation to provide the public with a diversity of viewpoints, but have rejected the notion that there is any private right of access to the media in our society.

Even from an economic point of view, diversity has little normative content. There is no necessary relationship between the extent of diversity of media content as conventionally measured (see Levin [46] and Land [42]) and con-

[i]This is a fundamental error of the Supreme Court's decision in *Red Lion Broadcasting Co. v. FCC* 395 U.S. 367 (1969).

sumer welfare. This is particularly true if there are economies of scale. There is certainly no presumption that people would be better off with a choice of blue, orange, and yellow aspirin at $1.00 per bottle than they are with white aspirin only at $.50 per bottle. They might be, but we cannot say for sure without knowing the structure of preferences.

Finally, diversity of content is terribly hard to measure. In broadcasting, the standard approach is to think in terms of "program types" (such as westerns, situation comedies, quiz shows, etc.). In print media, one uses "content analysis" (essentially categorizing and counting adjectives and nouns).[j] These methodologies are infirm, since they are not grounded on any theory of consumer psychology or perception.[k] It is simply not true that one situation comedy is a perfect substitute for any other, for many people, or that one "pro Labor" word is equal to another and exactly equal to minus one "pro Management"' word.

If we wished to measure diversity from the economic point of view, we could try to partition individual items of content into categories such that the *cross-elasticity of demand*[l] within categories was high, and cross-elasticity among categories low. This would be an empirical matter, not a conceptual one. But whatever its interest as an ethical or humanistic concept, diversity is really a red herring for our purposes. When it refers to content it has no necessary relationship either to freedom or to economic efficiency and consumer welfare. If, on the other hand, it refers to the sources of media messages, then it may be a measure of freedom of access, provided that the society itself is heterogeneous. But we might as well go directly to the main issue, which is ease of access to the media of expression, for speakers, and ease of access to alternative independent sources of information for the audience.

ACCESS

There is a close relationship between freedom of expression and ease of access to the media for individuals. Ease and flexibility are definitions of freedom. If one or a few persons control who shall speak and who shall not, there is no freedom of access or expression. If access to the media is controlled by a multiplicity of persons or by a set of neutral rules,[m] and if it is not structured in

---

[j]For an example of this methodology see Ephron [23].

[k]At least, an explicit theory; they do contain an implicit theory, but it is very naïve.

[l]The noneconomist's patience at this point has surely been exhausted. The term refers to the effect on the quantity demanded of good X resulting from a change in the price of good Y. Obviously, if X and Y are close substitutes this effect will be greater than if they are unrelated.

[m]It is hard to define a neutral rule. Many rules are neutral with respect to content per se but nonneutral with respect to the economic, social, or other characteristics of speakers, and thus the messages they are likely to want to deliver. For example, first come, first served discriminates against people who value their time highly or who don't like queues.

a way that makes expression by some groups much more difficult than for others, then there is relative freedom of expression. But there are a number of thorny problems that remain.

First, freedom of access to the media means little if there is no audience. Second, the cost of access (in a private system) can hardly be zero, because the cost of transmission is greater than zero. This means that people with "too little" money are denied some degree of freedom of expression, just as they are denied some degree of freedom in other economic activities. Third, if the number of media channels is limited, some rationing device such as prices or queues must be employed, and it is hard to think of "fair" rationing devices. Finally, effective economizing behavior by consumers leads to their selection of editors or editorial services which screen out in advance unwanted messages.

A right of access to such edited collections of messages would be an intolerable burden on the consumer, leading to a complete breakdown of mass communication. Access, if it is to be a useful concept, must mean the opportunity to utilize the *means of transmission* for the conveyance of messages. That is, the ease or degree of access is determined by the economic and institutional conditions surrounding transactions between speakers and the owners of the transmission stages—the airwaves, the presses, and the mails. Access cannot usefully mean the opportunity to insert messages into the editorial process of another. This distinction is no doubt confusing when, as with television and newspapers, the owners of the means of transmission also own their own editorial and creative services, but the distinction is nevertheless conceptually clear and essential to the formation of appropriate policy. Moreover, it is a distinction that would greatly aid in clarifying the meaning of the First Amendment in its application to modern media.

Clearly, freedom of access to the media cannot mean *free* access—access at a zero price—for this would have two consequences, both likely to be intolerable. The first would be a demand for media capacity that could not be satisfied without government subsidies—and with subsidies comes intervention.[n] The second would be an "overload" of consumption capacity such that few messages would be received. The cost to consumers of exercising choice would be raised to the point that far fewer choices would be worth making.

I am not saying that it is undesirable to allow as many people as wish to, to manufacture (say) automobiles, of all descriptions. What *would* be intolerable is a "right" on the part of anyone to attach accessories to the automobiles of any manufacturer, forcing the manufacturer to sell them as a unit with the car. Such a right would simply reduce the value of automobiles, and certainly increase their prices, with the result that few would be sold. Freedom of access

[n]A trivial example: a government subsidized TV channel would surely have rules against pornography. Less trivial examples are likely. If the subsidies and their rules were really controlled by elected officials rather than bureaucrats, we could perhaps argue their workability; reality is different.

cannot be taken to mean the right to insert messages "in the midst of" a package of edited messages for which some one else has built up a paying audience and good will. To accept this as a right would in effect destroy the incentive to invent and compete in the market for edited packages of messages.

Of course, the extent to which a right of paid access is undesirable depends on the consequent changes in the economic integrity of the product. This will be different for different media, and will depend on the "rules" surrounding the right. For instance, a right to buy newspaper space in units not smaller than one page, or TV time in units not smaller than one hour, may have significantly different effects than when smaller units are involved; similarly, much depends on the extent to which editors retain control of placement or scheduling. These considerations suggest that it would be unwise, for instance, to legislate a "right" of free (zero price) access to newspapers, magazines, or TV channels as presently conceived. But they do not bar the right of paid access to the means of transmission.

Freedom of access must mean a general right to put before the public (not force on the public) messages that can only be delivered effectively via the mass media. Such a right exists with respect to the postal service for magazines, although it is not entirely unrestricted (various publications have been denied second class privileges on political and moral grounds). Because it does exist, and because the transmission stage of this medium is not vertically integrated, there is great competition in the magazine industry. Note that freedom of access in this context clearly means the right to publish and mail a periodical (or book), not the right to insert messages in any already existing publication. Happily, this freedom of access for "speakers" seems to result in a significant degree of freedom of access by the audience to a range of independent sources of information and opinion.

Freedom of access in this sense is restricted, in the newspaper industry, by the economies of scale of publication, and by the peculiar editorial characteristics of a newspaper. While one can conceive of a common carrier newspaper printer which provided this right for message creators,[o] one can also imagine significant economic harm being visited on newspaper readers as a result, depending on the rules and on the equilibrium size and content of the newspaper which results. This trade-off may nevertheless be worth making.

Freedom of access in television might be satisfied by the establishment of a private market in spectrum, so that "anyone" could buy enough to start a new station. It might also be satisfied by a right of paid access to existing channels, or by some modification of the present structure of concentrated control.

There remains a fundamental difficulty with our concept of freedom of access, and that is that the price of access need not (should not) be zero. At a nonzero price, some messages will be excluded. What kinds of messages will

[o]"Shopper" newspapers consisting entirely of commercial and classified ads are close to this.

be excluded from the marketplace by a nonzero access price? The first kind are messages that are valued by consumers at less than their cost of creation and transmission, and which no person or group is willing or able to subsidize. The second kind are messages that consumers would value (and pay to receive) more than their cost, but that creators cannot produce because of the biases of monopolistic competition in product space (see the Appendix to Chapter Three).

The first sort of message ought not to be produced at all, from an economic point of view, but might conceivably be desirable from a political standpoint. The second sort represents a real market failure, and the cost of this failure may fall heavily on persons and groups at the lower end of the income distribution scale. A great deal of the activity of eleemosynary institutions can be regarded as an effort to remedy this problem, and it is conceivable that some government subsidy programs, properly structured and administered, could also alleviate it. To the extent that the problem results not merely in inefficiencies but also in *inequities* (these being, of course, a subjective and ethical matter), we can regard it as a reflection of the underlying inequities of wealth and income distribution.

Messages excluded due to the nonoptimality of monopolistic competition in product (as well as price) space are likely to be associated with demands from relatively small groups of consumers with rather intensely felt wants. The market failure is due to the inability of competitors fully to respond to the consumer's valuation of such products. On the other hand, if the groups involved are sufficiently small or identifiable, their members may be able to form coalitions for the purpose of satisfying these unmet demands.

Finally, it should be noted that the price of access as a barrier to freedom of expression may be of significance even if the media are free from concentrations of power leading to monopoly prices: that is, it may simply be too expensive to create and transmit messages even if the media themselves are competitive and efficient. This would mean that the socially correct level of production of messages (taking account of political considerations) was greater than the economically correct level of production. It is difficult to tell whether this would be the case and still harder to say what to do about it.

THE RIGHT TO HEAR VS. THE RIGHT TO BE HEARD

Supreme Court interpretations of the First Amendment in the context of the mass media are not frequent. In recent years only in *Miami Herald Publishing Co. v. Tornillo*[5], *CBS v. DNC,* and *Red Lion* has the Supreme Court dealt in any depth with the issues we are discussing. The *Red Lion* decision was remarkable for its theory of the "right to hear" via the broadcast media, a "right" which the court did not choose to extend to the print media five years later in *Tor-*

nillo. We will discuss the *Red Lion* decision later in the chapter on television, but the concept of a right to hear is worth a word or two at this point.

In *Red Lion*, the Court said that the public has a right to hear, or be informed, on certain issues (those which are "controversial" and of "public importance"). The Court saw the mechanism of this right being exercised through government intervention in the behavior of private broadcast licensees. Broadcast licensees have highly circumscribed, if any, First Amendment rights themselves.

The *Red Lion* decision says, in effect, that the government has an obligation to promote conditions that would have the *same end effect* as freedom of expression (that is, an informed public), and that this obligation must be exercised through direct regulation of the content of the electronic media. But freedom of expression is important not (just) for its effect on the public's information, but as a process which is an end in itself. This is the essence of the wrongheadedness of *Red Lion:* the same principle could have been served by structural remedies.

The new right to hear is clearly distinct from the right to be heard, which I shall take to be synonymous with a reasonable interpretation of a right of access. Arguably, freedom of expression, reasonably defined, might not result in the fulfillment of the public's passive right to be informed. This raises certain rather dangerous questions about the responsibilities and powers of the state.

A great deal of the substance of this controversy is attributable to the peculiarities of institutional conventions surrounding economic transactions. A simple example is postal service. In the eighteenth century, and well into the nineteenth, it was conventional for the recipient to pay postage on letters and other mail. Indeed, it was not until the 1880s that prepayment of postage on newspapers became effectively mandatory, although rates were higher on C.O.D. mail long before that date. Under such an institutional arrangement, the locus of choice is shifted in large part from the sender to the receiver of the message. Institutional arrangements of this sort can have a profound effect on media content and on choice.

It is doubtful that the First Amendment really contains an implied "right to hear" distinct from freedom of expression. The whole concept of such a right, and its exercise, runs counter to the most basic notions of freedom of expression, precisely because the institutional arrangements implied by the first right requires subjugation of the second. To be sure, the First Amendment must be taken to mean the absence of government control of the content of information or messages the consumer receives, and this is a right to hear or a freedom from censorship, which affects recipients. But the right to be informed by the state, particularly when the implementation of this right restricts freedom of expression, is not reconcilable with the constitutional doctrine. It is possible that alterations in the institutional structure of transactions (such as the postage question, or, in another context, the pay TV question), can shift the balance of choice between producers and recipients of messages, and thus require trade-offs between the right to hear and the right to speak. It is doubtful, however, that such issues can be treated in general terms.

ECONOMIC FREEDOM

Economic freedom[p] for consumers can mean only the degree to which they are able to achieve satiation of their wants.[q] A number of constraints exist. Wealth and income constraints are present for nearly all consumers, and these can be traced to much more general and basic conditions in the economic order. Economic freedom is also constrained by the existence and tastes of other consumers, given economies of scale, fixed costs, or other nonconvexities in the production process. A consumer with unconventional tastes will be more constrained in his choices (less well off, less free) than one with conventional tastes, because the production process in general discriminates against him. On the other hand, the competitive private enterprise system is ideally suited to maximize consumer freedom, since it responds only to consumer wants. Absent the many imperfections that in fact exist, a competitive private enterprise system would give consumers greater economic freedom (qua consumers) than any other system of resource allocation. The story may be quite different for consumers qua workers, however.

Economic efficiency—making consumers as well off as they can be, given available resources and the distribution of their ownership—is consistent with a competitive system of private enterprise. The proof of this proposition[6] has been one of the greatest achievements of economics, and its political implications are worth a moment's reflection. What it means is that decentralized individual decision making, involving only the calculus of personal gain, results in an overall state which is the best that can be achieved for everyone. Moreover, there exists such a state for every conceivable distribution of the ownership rights in resources, or wealth, so that there is no necessary "inequity" attached to the efficiency of decentralized decision making. Personal economic freedom in the conventional sense is *not* constrained by the system of allocation. Of course, there remain those "imperfections" that can and do make the system work at less than its theoretical efficiency.

Leaving aside what are essentially confusions about the relationship between capitalism and inequity of wealth and income distribution, the "socialism vs. capitalism" controversy boils down to the question of whether the private enterprise system can be patched up well enough to work tolerably, or whether it should be scrapped. In this debate it is common, but irrelevant, to compare

[p]I have been and will continue to use the word "freedom" without strictly defining it. For one economist's definition, see Moore [56].

[q]Satiation occurs when additional consumption would not add to one's subjective well-being. The concept is relativistic and personal.

ideals. It is relevant, however, to ask whether consumers are to decide for themselves or whether the state is to decide for them. (See Nozick [59].)

Against this freedom for consumers, we can contrast the utter lack of freedom for competitive producers. To be sure, producers are free to enter or leave the market at will, and to produce "what they like." But the mechanism of an efficient, competitive private enterprise system (to the extent it really works) will reward the firm or producer with economic survival only in highly constrained circumstances. Any deviation by the firm from efficient prices, outputs, locations, product choices, speed of reaction to innovation, or changes in consumer tastes will result in its instant economic nonviability. There is no real freedom for producers in a private enterprise system that is competitive in the sense required to maximize consumer freedom. Producers achieve freedom from this survival mechanism only at the expense of consumers, and they achieve it by acquiring in one way or another some degree of monopoly power.

How can there be freedom of expression in such a system? A message can be created and produced only if it survives in the economic sense. Producers have only the freedom to try to survive. The market guarantees that after the dust has settled all economic messages will be produced, and that all uneconomic ones will fail to survive. But this very freedom to enter the market, to test consumer response, which is guaranteed by the competitive mechanism, may be all that is essential to freedom of expression (from the constitutional viewpoint) provided consumers demand the right information about political matters. Surely the framers of the constitution did not have in mind an absolute right to survival in the marketplace for all potential purveyors of ideas.

An immediate difficulty is that messages by their very nature do not fit the assumptions of the competitive model. Messages are inherently differentiated, not homogeneous,[r] and competition in their production must be imperfect or "monopolistic." And as we shall see, monopolistic competition in product space does not result in the "right" mix and number messages because of the fixed costs of production and nonhomogeneity of tastes. More serious, it may well be precisely those messages that are of critical importance in the political sense which are squeezed out by imperfect competition. Monopoly is no remedy for this, luckily, and government intervention would be of little help to the economic issue because of its information requirements. An efficient solution may not be available. On the other hand, there are many areas in which we have not achieved even a second-best solution, so there remains room for improvement over the present system, provided we accept the structure of the producing industry itself as a valid and practical policy instrument.

Improvement must generally take the form of reducing monopoly power. Here, the political and economic goals coincide, for monopoly denies both

---

[r]Perfect competition, whose virtues were outlined above, requires inter alia that there be many producers of each good, and the output of one producer be indistinguishable from that of another.

political and economic freedom to consumers in the marketplace of ideas just as in the marketplace of goods. The acquisition and maintenance of monopoly power denies freedom to other producers as well, and thus directly impinges on freedom of expression in message production. When private firms join with government to establish and maintain such power, as they do in broadcasting, there is ample room for improvement in the system of freedom of expression and economic freedom as well.

The critical point about monopoly power in the media is that it gives the media owner some power to decide what people shall see and hear, and what they shall not. The diversity of sources of information is constricted, and there is no source of marketplace relief for egregious behavior, such as entry of new firms. If the owners of the media are then drawn from a class with similar backgrounds or similar economic interests, there will be a systematic tendency to bias media content in certain predictable ways. This may even be possible without economic loss, since such subtle (or potentially subtle) factors as political slant in content may not affect the economic value of messages to consumers. (Consumers can and do place an "economic" value on political content in general; this is subsumed in the proposition.) This is particularly likely to be true of entertainment programming.

Even if this is not the case, the monopoly media owner has power in the discretionary use of his excess profits, and he can afford to spend these profits in ways which further the economic, political, or social interests of his class. He can simply exclude even those who can afford to pay for access. He can choose to behave uneconomically to the extent permitted by the barriers to entry in his market and by the structure of control of his firm. He can defy the discipline of the market system, which works hand in hand with the system of freedom of expression. That he often fears and respects his power and seeks to act responsibly is of little moment. Why should we be content with a "responsible" monopolist? Competitive media owners, whatever their class, do not have this power if they are to survive in the marketplace.

THE ROLE OF ADVERTISING

Advertisements are simply a special class of messages which convey signals about products or services. They deserve special attention because of their role in the economic process of resource allocation and because of their prominent place in the financing of the media (see Table 1-1).

In many important respects advertisements are indistinguishable from other media messages. They are valued by consumers (many people read newspaper ads more regularly than editorial content). They are sometimes entertaining, sometimes informative. They are sometimes exaggerated and untruthful, but so is much nonadvertising content. They are distinguishable mainly by virtue of their role in allocating other goods and services, rather than being end prod-

Table 1-1. Volume of Advertising, 1867–1970 (millions of dollars)

Year	Total	Newspapers	Magazines	Radio	Television	Direct Mail
1867	50					
1900	546					
1909	1,142					
1920	2,935					
1930	2,607					
1935	1,690	762	136	113	0	282
1940	2,088	815	198	216	0	334
1945	2,875	921	365	424	0	290
1950	5,710	2,076	515	605	171	803
1955	9,194	3,088	729	545	1,025	1,299
1960	11,932	3,703	941	692	1,590	1,830
1965	15,255	4,457	1,199	917	2,515	2,324
1970	19,600	5,745	1,323	1,308	3,596	2,766

Source: *Historical Statistics of the U.S.* p. 526; *Statistical Abstract* 1973, p. 759.
Note: Total includes outdoor and miscellaneous advertising not reported separately.

ucts in themselves. To the extent that they are not valued by consumers, such messages must be accompanied by other material that is, or there will be no audience. Thus "popular" (economically viable) editorial content is sometimes produced in order to facilitate the consumption of advertising, as in sugar coating a pill. This is an accurate description of commercial broadcasting. It is just as often the case, however, that advertising enhances or complements the value of editorial content.

Why do advertisements appear in some media and not in others? Books and motion pictures seldom carry advertising. On the other hand, broadcasting depends entirely on advertising revenue, and such revenue is very important for newspapers and magazines. The answer lies partly in timeliness—books are read over an extended period after publication, and most advertisers change product types or styles sufficiently often to make the book medium unsuitable for this reason. A more important answer lies in the superiority of some media over others as advertising vehicles. Compared to movies and books, other media are simply better vehicles, with larger audiences, faster response times, and/or lower costs.

Without advertising revenue most of the mass media would be unable to survive. Advertising revenue accounts for 100 percent of commercial broadcast revenue, and more than 50 percent of newspaper and magazine revenue (see Table 1-2). This is the principal reason that this class of messages is worthy of special consideration. As to the influence of advertisers on freedom of expression, there is a great deal to say, but little concrete evidence to cite.

It has often been alleged by program and news personnel in broadcasting, and by their counterparts in the print media, that advertisers have a good deal to say about editorial content that affects their interests. The counter culture

Table 1-2.　Sources of Revenue for Mass Media, 1967 (millions of dollars)

	Revenues		
Medium	*Consumers*	*Advertisers*	*%Adv.*
Television	0	2275	100
Radio	0	907	100
Newspapers	1654	3896	70
Magazines	1121	1547	58
Motion pictures	3476	0*	0*
Books	2255	0*	0*

*Negligible.
Source: *Statistical Abstract*, 1973, p. 500, 502, 506, 755.

would presumably suggest an inherent establishment bias in the media for similar reasons. If true, such allegations suggest systematic discrimination against a certain class of ideas, and this is antithetical to the First Amendment principle. Actual evidence of such influence is however scarce. More likely, media owners and employees practice self-censorship in the sense that ideas likely to offend seriously an important advertiser simply are never seriously proposed for publication or broadcast. This process is insidious. It is, however, merely a reflection of underlying imperfections in the structure of the media, since a competitive media would not have the power *not* to offend advertisers.

This is a delicate point. A firm on the margin of existence may, by alienating an advertiser, go out of existence. But unless the advertiser is important to *all* media, some other medium will convey the harmful information anyway. So the advertiser finds no advantage in ceasing to patronize a medium which carries unfavorable information about him, except to the extent that it may be awkward to juxtapose the two messages. So in the competitive case, it may be true that an advertiser can "discipline" a media firm. But this does not restrict the flow of information.

From a purely economic point of view, advertising is a mixed blessing. It is a blessing because its presence permits the production and transmission of certain messages, and the existence of certain media, that for various reasons could not exist on the basis of subscriber or consumer revenue. Certainly it would have been more difficult to develop TV and radio if advertising were not available, because of the substantially greater transactions costs involved in collecting money from consumers. Even though consumers pay for TV programs indirectly through their purchases of advertised products, they pay less than they would have to pay if they purchased the same programs directly in the present system.

But advertising is also a bane, especially in broadcasting, because it requires the media to respond to incentives that have little to do with consumer interests. This point will be made in more detail in our discussion of program bias effects in Chapter Three. The basic problem is that the advertiser buys audiences while the consumer buys content. Generally, the consumer's value of content exceeds the advertiser's valuation of the consumer. This leads to decisions about the type and quality of content which are inefficient, at least, and possibly non-neutral from the First Amendment standpoint.

INTERMEDIA COMPETITION

While newspapers compete with each other, they also compete with television; intermedia competition for audiences and for advertisers is a matter of some consequence in certain parts of the media marketplace. Historically, of course, the electronic media have eclipsed parts of the print media either because of their superior audience appeal, or becasue of their advertising productivity, or both. Meanwhile, one electronic medium (radio) has been eclipsed by another (television), which in turn seems threatened by a third (cable television). These Schumpeterian [82] processes have accelerated in recent years, despite the efforts of the media themselves to seek government protection from the march of technology. The protection thus afforded is, in historical perspective, a short respite.[5] We will discuss intermedia competition and cross-media ownership more fully in the chapter on television.

ECONOMICS AND PERSONAL EXPRESSION

Although this book is concerned with expression, and particularly the expression of political ideas, through the mass media, it is important not to understate the significance of other forms of communication. We live increasingly in an information economy—one in which a large fraction of the productive sector is engaged in producing and consuming information. There are a number of things that economists can say about this process, although the study of the economics of information is itself a very young science. Much of the social concern with privacy of information about persons or with security of corporate information can be traced to problems of signalling on the one hand, or the nonappropriability of information as a public good on the other. There is a significant degree of economic content, therefore, in copyright, privacy, freedom of information, credit terms disclosure, and similar laws. Although an examination of these issues would take us far afield, they are vital issues to which economics is just beginning to make a contribution.[7]

---

[5]Since many or most politically important events are short lived phenomena, this long run optimism is hardly grounds for complacency.

Chapter Two

Newspapers

The free press is the omnipresent open eye of the spirit of the people, the embodied confidence of a people in itself, the articulate bond that ties the individual to the state and the world, the incorporated culture which transfigures material struggles into intellectual struggles and realizes its raw material shape. It is the ruthless confession of a people to itself, and it is well known that the power of confession is redeeming. The free press is the intellectual mirror in which a people sees itself, and self-viewing is the first condition of wisdom.

—Karl Marx (1841)

INTRODUCTION[a]

This chapter is concerned with both the economic structure and the economic history of the newspaper industry, and with their relationship to issues of public policy affecting freedom of expression through the press. Newspapers are our most important historical media link with the framers of the Bill of Rights. In tracing the economic history of newspapers from colonial times to the present day, we will want to ask whether there have been changes in structure or role that should lead us to question the relevance of the First Amendment to present-day newspapers.

It is probably wise to say at once that the description of the changing structure of the newspaper medium that follows, though it necessarily traces the

[a]The material in this chapter owes an enormous debt to Professor James N. Rosse, whose research into the economics of newspapers has proved essential to the author's understanding of this fascinating industry. Some of this research is unpublished, but see Rosse [75], [76], [77], [78], [79].

causes and consequences of declining numbers and increasing scarcity of newspaper voices in the present century, should not necessarily be taken as an overall decline in freedom of expression. As we shall see, monopoly papers may be more tolerant of ideas than competitive ones, and in any event one must consider all media taken together before reaching such a conclusion.

NEWSPAPER ECONOMICS

Newspapers supply not one but many different services. They are a source of news, opinion, and entertainment to their readers, and a source of audience exposure to their advertisers. The demand and supply relationships among these many different outputs are neither simple nor obvious, and they all interact to determine the structure of the newspaper firm.

Newspaper readers demand news, opinion, and entertainment of many different kinds. The newspaper firm is able to supply different services because the newspaper as a unit lends itself to joint production. Most newspapers have sections or pages devoted to relatively specialized subject matter: national news, local news, editorials, sports, women's, and comic sections are not unusual. In addition, readers have a demand for advertising that may be as important or more important than their demand for editorial content. Indeed, advertising may be the most important single variable in explaining newspaper structure. A great deal of newspaper space advertising supplies information—on products available, sales, prices, etc.—which is highly valuable to consumers. This is perhaps most obvious in the case of classified advertisements.

Similarly, advertisers' demand for newspaper space is a function of the number, location, and kinds of readers, as well as the price charged for the space by the newspaper. Thus the "demand" for newspapers is jointly determined by the interaction of readers' and advertisers' demands. The more advertising there is (other things being equal) the higher will be the demand by readers; the more readers (other things equal) the higher the demand by advertisers.

On the supply side, the technology of production is of greatest interest. The cost of publishing a newspaper is comprised of several elements. These are: (1) editorial costs, or the cost of acquiring or generating all of the nonadvertising content of the newspaper; (2) other first copy costs such as typesetting; (3) printing costs, which vary directly with circulation; (4) distribution costs associated with the process of getting the newspapers from the printing plant to the reader; and (5) other miscellaneous costs, such as overhead, the advertising sales departments, and the subscription promotion department.

Each of the costs of publishing a newspaper varies with certain qualitative or quantitative dimensions of the newspaper and its audience: circulation, number of pages, population density, geographical extent of the market, editorial "quality," frequency of publication, and the like. Table 2-1 provides an overview of the magnitude of these costs, and revenues, for a "typical" newspaper of 100,000 circulation in 1966. (Actually, a newspaper of 100,000 circulation is very large.)

Table 2-1. A "Typical" Newspaper, 1966 (Based on a morning-evening-Sunday newspaper of 100,000 circulation) (dollar figures in thousands)

			e^*
Advertising Revenue	$5,315	76%	1.16
Subscription Revenue	1,640	24	1.09
Total Revenue	6,955	100%	1.14
Expenses			
Administration and Depreciation	1,157	20%	.97
Advertising Department	453	8	1.03
Circulation and Mailing Department	772	13	1.13
Editorial costs	932	16	1.12
Composing and Engineering	868	14	1.03
Press and Steno typing	381	6	1.14
Newsprint and Ink	1,302	22	1.53
Total Expense	$5,864	100%	1.10
Total Profit (before tax)**	$1,091	–	1.46
Advertising inches published, annual	2,283,630	58%	.75
Nonadvertising inches published, annual	1,672,538	42	.48
Total pages published, annual	22,992	–	.60

*Elasticity with respect to circulation.

**This figure is not meaningful except as a percentage return in investment; data on investment are not readily available.

Source: Based on unpublished research by James N. Rosse.

The numbers in Table 2-1 were derived from a simultaneous equations regression analysis of combined cross-section and time series data. Thus the "elasticity with respect to circulation" data reported in the last column of the table take account of all the interactions described above, rather than partial effects. (*Editor and Publisher* magazine also publishes annual financial profiles of newspapers of various sizes.)

Newspapers, of course, compete both with one another and with other media for readers and for advertisers. To understand the structure of the newspaper industry, one must examine all these interactions, along with the technology and cost of production. It is worth remarking again that advertising is critically important to this understanding. Note that the typical newspaper in Table 2-1 gets 76 percent of its revenues from advertising, and devotes a commensurate quantity of space to it. Geography is also essential, both because of the important role of distribution costs (and timing) and because the demands of advertisers and subscribers are geographically specialized. That is, there is a demand by readers for local news, and by advertisers for local audiences, specific to the regions from which their own customers are drawn. These factors trade off against economies of scale in certain dimensions of the publication process to produce the particular locational and competitive structure of newspaper firms existing at any given time.

A stylized example may help to explain how this mechanism works. Suppose that the higher the circulation the lower the cost of producing a newspaper, per copy. This means that in a given area competition between two or more newspapers will either drive one out of business or lead to a merger, other things equal.[b] But the resulting monopoly cannot extend itself geographically without limit, because as it does so distribution costs may rise, marginal advertising revenue may fall, and subscriber interest (demand) will decline as the newspaper increasingly reaches readers who are not "local." The result will be a pattern of regional monopoly newspapers. Of course, the real world is more complicated than this; we describe these complications in later sections. The point is that there is a tension between economies of scale in some dimensions of the process of producing a newspaper, and various geography related effects on both the demand and cost sides that limit expansion. In general, the effects relate to specialization of tastes; in the U.S. newspaper industry, demand for local news and local advertising dominates the outcome. Together, these effects determine the actual structure of the industry.[c]

That there are economies of scale in producing a newspaper almost goes without saying. "First copy" costs are the best example. The cost of producing the nonadvertising or editorial content of a newspaper is not directly related to the number of copies sold; neither are composing room costs and similar items. Hence, the average cost per copy attributable to these items falls as circulation increases. On the other hand, it must be remembered that these costs are not totally independent of circulation; for instance, reducing editorial costs will reduce the quantity and quality of the editorial content, and hence the demand by readers. Thus we find that editorial costs are greater in larger newspapers than in smaller ones—even more than proportionally greater.

Another dimension in which there are economies of scale is the number of pages: it costs less to go from 34 pages to 36 than from 32 to 34, other things equal. This means that "general" newspapers can drive "specialized" newspapers out of business, by incorporating the specialized content and specialized advertising as a supplemental part of the general newspaper, at least under certain conditions.

Newspapers, nowadays, tend to have a certain geographical structure. For reasons to be explored below, there is almost never more than one newspaper firm in a given city. But cities vary in size, and large cities have newspapers which have considerable suburban and regional circulations. Even smaller cities often have areas in which they overlap with a neighboring daily. It is not uncommon to find local suburban dailies coexisting under the umbrella of a large met-

[b]Provided, of course, there is not a kind of audience segmentation by taste which is impossible to satisfy within a single newspaper. A city that seems to violate this assumption is New York, where the *Times* and the *Daily News* appeal to rather different readers. Similar examples are available—for instance, Chicago's *Defender*.

[c]See the Appendix to Chapter three for a theoretical model applicable to these considerations.

ropolitan daily. The extent of competition among these firms of overlapping circulation is sometimes considerable.

The large metropolitan daily is at a disadvantage because of transportation costs and delays and the presence in the newspaper of community specific news; this can be overcome at a cost by suburban printing plants, by special suburban editions, and by the presence in the larger paper of features unavailable to the local daily. The large daily in this situation is also most subject to competition from TV and radio stations. On the other hand, the metropolitan daily with larger circulation is likely to have some cost advantages over the suburban papers. The equilibrium effect of these factors determines sizes and locations of newspapers; this trade-off seems to have been moving more and more against the metropolitan daily. Equilibrium forces in the newspaper industry are probably attentuated by the tendency of newspapers to be family owned enterprises. This tradition has perhaps kept many papers alive longer than would otherwise have been the case, and may also have killed off some newspapers before their time.[d]

The rather extensive discussion of economic history in this chapter is undertaken partly to try to build a link between the historical context of the First Amendment and modern conditions, and partly because the changing structure of the newspaper industry over the past two centuries provides first-class examples of economic effects on media political roles. The next three sections explore the economic history of the American newspaper industry from 1690 to the present day. The Appendix to this chapter provides background data for these sections.

NEWSPAPERS IN THE EIGHTEENTH CENTURY[e]

The press is the only private business to receive explicit protection in the Bill of Rights. Presumably this reflects a judgment by the framers of the First Amendment that the press served its function best when it was free from government regulation. The economic history of the colonial publishing industry can give us some understanding of the basis for this judgment by helping us to evaluate, if not to test, the hypothesis that freedom of expression is consistent with unregulated competition when the press is characterized by small scale technologies and ease of entry.

The first part of this section outlines the major factors influencing the development and structure of the American publishing industry up to the time of the adoption of the First Amendment in 1791. We then focus on the ability of the press to act as a forum for public debate, which is the most interesting aspect of press performance. In particular, we try to generalize about the ability of the

[d]Recently there has been a trend toward public ownership of newspapers. It is too early to tell what effect, if any, this will have on newspaper behavior.

[e]This section is co-authored by Abbott B. Lipsky, Jr.

individual to have his views printed, and how it was affected by the economic conditions of the industry. Ease of access to the press has several dimensions: (1) economic and other costs necessary to have one's views printed and distributed; (2) opportunities for the individual to have his views appear in publications —newspapers in particular—having established readership; (3) conditions of entry in the publishing industry.

Tracing the economic history of the colonial publishing industry is simplified by the fact that printing technology appears to have remained constant over the entire period. Since Gutenberg's time, the flatbed press had been improved only by a few minor changes in construction and the substitution of some metal for wooden parts (see Lee [44], p. 20). Experienced workers could attain a maximum output of 2,400 impressions in a ten-hour day. A minimally equipped one-press shop of the period used three or four type fonts, each of which needed replacement after several years of normal use. Press and type (not manufactured domestically until 1769) were of comparable cost: estimates of the total value of press, type, and other equipment (excluding the real estate necessary to house the shop) are few, but they indicate that the fixed cost for a one-press shop was about £85 sterling. (This figure was approximately equal to a journeyman's wages for one year.) Wroth [101], who has compiled the few figures available, concludes that fixed costs for a given scale of plant remained approximately constant throughout the eighteenth century.

Operation of the press required two men, thus setting the minimum labor requirements of the shop.[f] The master printer's four main sources of labor were immigrant journeymen, apprentices, members of the printer's household, and unskilled laborers. Journeymen were compensated at roughly four times the rate for day laborers of the period. Wroth surmises, on the basis of available commodity price data, wage rates quoted in Benjamin Franklin's records for the year 1754, and wage rates prescribed by one of the first journeymen's associations in 1799, that the journeyman's real wage was approximately constant during the entire eighteenth century.

There is no evidence that journeymen successfully organized or bargained collectively with master printers, although a journeymen's strike in New York in 1778 met with some success, and a similar strike among Philadelphia journeymen in 1786 appears to have thwarted the announced intention of the master printers of that city to lower wages.

Another equally important source of labor was the apprentice, who worked subject to an indenture usually entered into at an early age. The indenture bound the master printer to provide accommodation, nourishment, and instruction in the trade, and the apprentice to serve his master until "he should attain the status of manhood."

---

[f]The implied capital-labor ratio is very small compared to that of present-day printing establishments, especially newspapers.

Next to labor, the printer's most important variable input was paper, most of which was imported until the 1760s. Imports were generally cheaper than paper of domestic manufacture, but American mills became increasingly important because fluctuating demand and the long voyage from England frequently strained inventories in the colonies. The domestic industry showed marked progress over the colonial period, and by 1791 Alexander Hamilton was able to say, in his *Report on Manufactures*, that "Manufacturies of paper are among those which are arrived at the greatest maturity in the United States, and are most adequate to national supply."

Two significant constraints on paper manufacturing in the colonies were official attitudes toward colonial industry, and the rag supply. Although paper shortages were frequent, it does not appear that paper prices were ever so high that new flax fibers were used directly in paper making, indicating that their value was greater when used to make clothing. Manufacturers were forced to rely solely on the collection of scraps of worn-out linen, offering a certain price per pound for rags brought to them. Printers often acted as agents to receive these rags, and published appeals encouraging rag collection. Rewards in addition to the normal offering price were sometimes given to the most successful collectors in times of extreme shortage.

Paper making, among many other manufacturing enterprises, was generally discouraged by colonial authorities in order to encourage trade with Britain. Although Boston was by far the leading city in press output, the first paper mill in Massachusetts was not built until 1728, which was 90 years after the arrival in Cambridge of the first press in the colonies. In that year the General Court was persuaded to grant a monopoly to a partnership of local merchants (including a publisher). That colony was without a competing mill for another 40 years.

The situation of the paper making industry changed significantly after passage of the Stamp Act in 1765. Although the Act was quickly repealed, it was soon followed by the Townsend Act of 1767, which imposed import duties on paper and other important basic commodities. The colonies responded to this measure with the nonimportation agreements, and imports of paper were soon completely cut off. Imported paper began to trickle in later, but the supply was again cut off in 1775 when the Revolutionary War began.

Clearly these events encouraged domestic manufacture of paper. Connecticut's first mill was built in 1766, subsidized by the legislature with a bounty on each ream produced. A New York newspaper publisher was allowed to construct that colony's first mill in 1768. North and South Carolina both subsidized construction of mills in 1775, and the legislature of Maryland made an interest-free loan for construction of the first mill there in 1776.

During the war, increased demand for paper to be used as cartridge paper in ammunition, for military communications, and for the printing of currency—together with the confiscation of paper making equipment by the British and disruption of coastal and interior travel—contributed to a severe paper shortage.

Several colonial legislatures exempted paper makers from military duty so that they could practice their trade, and where possible, paper making equipment was evacuated from settlements threatened with British occupation.

Elaborate measures were taken to conserve existing supplies. Newspapers managing to continue publication used any available stock, and the use of margins disappeared. Torn sheets were carefully patched, and smaller type was used. Printed matter was often used as cartridge paper, and margins were used for military communications. After the Revolution imported paper faced a high tariff, and domestic production expanded rapidly. There were perhaps 100 mills in the United States when Hamilton made his assessment in 1791.

The character of the colonial publishing industry was determined in part by the nature of the demand for its output as well as by governmental and ecclesiastical control of the press. In the first settlements the common background of the inhabitants, common observance of religious and other social events, and the proximity of the few settlers to each other provided maximum opportunity for face-to-face communication. Information that was not in the direct experience of the colonists, originating within the settlement or elsewhere, was easily transmitted to all inhabitants without the need for the written word, let alone the printed word.

Increases in the size and heterogeneity of the colonial population decreased the ease with which news propagated through the settlements, and a specialized written news medium appeared, the newsletter.

> This letter was prepared either by a writer who wandered from one coffee house to another to pick up the news, or by the postmaster who handled the few copies of newspapers which came from abroad, and who had contact with the captain and passengers of incoming ships. As soon as the requests for this paid letter service became too numerous to be handled by pen, the writer was forced to employ a printing press (Shaw [84] p. 410).

The last sentence of the passage just quoted may be misleading, for the colonial weekly or biweekly newspaper was rarely published by someone other than its printer, and with one exception, no printer made the publication of a newspaper his exclusive business.

One likely explanation is that acquisition of a print shop generally left the printer with excess capacity in several dimensions. First, once the printer had incurred the fixed cost of the shop, he was well equipped to produce all types of press output. Second, operation of the press required two workers, and it was not always possible to keep them continuously employed. Third, the printing apparatus was not large, and most colonial printers had room to trade other goods in their shops. Many were booksellers, many sold writing paper and other household items (some of which they also advertised in their newspapers), and several printers sold goods which they had accepted as payment in kind for newspaper subscriptions.

Entry of the type described by Shaw was restricted to the first newspapers of Boston, the earliest in the colonies. The first continuously published American newspaper appeared in Boston in 1704, published by the postmaster, John Campbell. Seven successive Boston postmasters published newspapers, two of them continuing to publish competing newspapers after leaving office. All these newspapers eventually were taken over by their printers. In 1727 another Boston newspaper was begun by a nonprinter, whom Isaiah Thomas [91] describes only as a "young gentleman." (In 1733 it too was given to its printer.) At least until the Revolutionary War, every newspaper in Boston, Philadelphia and New York, with two short lived exceptions, was published by its printer.

An individual wishing to enter the publishing industry could do so in one of several ways. First, he could go through an apprenticeship and become a master printer himself. This type of entry never occurred during the period except in the regular course of a printing career begun at an early age. Second, he could hire a printer and furnish him with a shop. Instances of this type of entry were also rare. Third, an individual who desired to print his own views could induce the publisher of a newspaper with established readership to include his views.

Only one example can be found of entry by a nonprinter by means of acquiring a printing establishment for the purpose of publishing his own views. The printer William Goddard entered a partnership with Thomas Wharton and Joseph Galloway in order to publish the *Pennsylvania Chronicle and Universal Advertiser* in 1766. The contents of the newspaper were undoubtedly under the control of Wharton and Galloway. This enterprise survived only a few years.

Perhaps the most famous example of the third type of entry, "entry by influence," was the publication of the *New York Weekly Journal* by John Peter Zenger. This paper was little more than a serial diatribe against the administration of New York's Governor Cosby and his successor. Thomas thought that the paper was financed by the Governor's opposition, and according to Mott [57], another opposition party member was de facto editor. The Zenger case is also an illustration of the constraints on content imposed by local authority. More or less rigid control over the press was exercised in all the colonies, and there can be little doubt of the effect of this control on printers interested in commercial survival.

The relationship between advertising revenues, circulation, and commercial success of newspapers appears to have been much the same in colonial times as it is today. John Campbell's *Boston Newsletter* was composed mostly of reprints from foreign newspapers available to him as postmaster. It contained a few advertisements, mostly of the "lost and found" variety, and in 1719 it had achieved a circulation of only 300 in a town of about 12,000, although its readership was certainly much greater. The more successful newspapers of

Philadelphia gave advertising a more prominent position in the papers' format, emphasized diverse and interesting (if uncontroversial) content, and solicited commercial advertisements valued by readers. The rapid growth of daily newspapers in the last two decades of the century can probably be attributed in part to increased advertising demand.

The character of the American press changed considerably after 1765. The Stamp Act and the Townsend Act, because they had a direct effect on the availability and cost of paper, were bound to arouse the printers' enmity. After passage of the Townsend Act, newspapers published extensive accounts of legislative proceedings, town meetings, lists of "grievances," and letters to the editor protesting the Act, presumably reflecting the printers' outrage as much as reader interest in these issues.

Contributed articles supporting and opposing British authority came to be of some importance in the newspapers of the day, and coverage of American political news increased, although foreign news was still dominant. Circulation, which had remained in the range of several hundred to a thousand copies per issue, reached as high as 3,500 for some issues. The printer himself continued mainly as a conduit for other sources of news and opinion, but it was impossible for him to remain neutral in the struggle, though some honestly tried. By the time of the outbreak of hostilities in 1775 almost every newspaper in the colonies could be clearly identified as either Patriot or Tory.

The question occurs, if there was effective control of the press by colonial authorities, how could anti-British views be published? The short answer is that repression of these views was not politically feasible, for the same reasons that the Stamp Act could not be enforced in the colonies. In addition, no grand jury of that time would indict Patriot printers, so that public prosecution of "seditious" printers was difficult.

Mott calculates that there were 37 newspapers published in the colonies on the day of the battles of Lexington and Concord. By 1781 there were 35, but in the interim seventeen of the original 37 had ceased publication, and another 33 had appeared, of which only fifteen survived. The decade following saw an extraordinary growth in the number of newspapers. About 60 papers appeared during the mid 1780s, many of which soon stopped publication. Nevertheless, in 1790 there were 92 newspapers in the United States. This total included ten semiweeklies, (of which only three had existed in 1780) and eight dailies, the first of which appeared in 1783 (see Appendix Table 2A-1, page 64).

Mott describes another very important change in the character of the press in the period 1783-1791:

> Whereas nearly all newspapers heretofore had been set up as auxiliaries to printing establishments and had been looked upon merely as means which enterprising printers used to make a living, now they were more and more often founded as spokesmen of political parties. . . . Up to this time, conducting a newspaper had been chiefly a matter of selecting, without much

initiative, the conventional items of newspaper content, and printing and distributing them. Newspaper conductors were, in the main, mere printers and publishers, and they so regarded themselves. But now we have one newspaper after another coming forward as the expression of the personality of an "able editor" who may or may not be a printer himself; . . . Mott [57], pp. 113-114).

It thus becomes important to bear in mind that the most recent experience of the framers of the First Amendment was with a highly partisan press that offered easy access to the means of reaching an audience, and whose members were steadily growing. And this trend continued: in the decade 1790-1800 the number of newspapers increased from 92 to 235. In all, 450 newspapers were started in the period 1783-1801.

It is reasonable to suppose that this rapid increase in the number of newspapers can be explained by printing technology, improved conditions in the paper industry, and changes in demand. Recall that the technology of the print shop was constant over this period, and that the total cost of a one-press shop was also constant. The cost of a shop was modest: a steadily employed and frugal journeyman could save the necessary capital to start his own business in several years. Increases in the size, heterogeneity, and literacy of the population, rising real income per capita, improvements in transportation, and increasing volume and variety of trade all contributed to rising demand for press output, and to an increasing supply of news.

There may also have been a shift in tastes that contributed to demand, occasioned by wide interest in American political issues such as the Jay Treaty and the adoption of the Constitution. It is very difficult to say how much of the growth in newspapers was due to this increased demand for news and how much to increased demand by advertisers and by readers for advertising. The subject is worth further study by economic historians. We put it forth as a hypothesis that a large part of the answer lies in the growth of demand for commercial and trade information, as evidenced by the emergence of a number of daily commercial advertisers in this period.

From a strictly economic standpoint, the number of firms in the industry is not a quantity of prime interest, provided that the number is not small enough to be a significant determinant of firm behavior. There is little evidence that collusion occurred among colonial printers; one exception being the abortive attempt by the printers of Philadelphia to lower wages in 1786, mentioned above. One author mentions that there were several attempts to "establish rules and regulations for the benefit of the trade" (Thomas [91], v. 1, p. 238), and, one may assume, for the detriment of competition among printers, but he also notes that the attempts had not proved successful. There were competing print shops in all the larger settlements after about 1730, and in Boston much earlier, but there are not enough data available to determine whether printers behaved collusively in any sense.

However, to the student of the First Amendment, the number of firms in the publishing industry and the number of newspapers have an independent significance. If the press is to perform its function as a forum for public debate, the effectiveness of that performance depends on the diversity of sources of views expressed and on the ease of access by "speakers." Even while the newspaper publisher behaved only as a conduit for news and opinion during the Revolutionary period, the overwhelming majority of newspapers identified strongly with one political group or another. This trend continued into the era of Federalists and Republicans, and the press continued to be highly partisan until the end of the nineteenth century.

If we accept the idea that each newspaper expressed one point of view to the virtual exclusion of all others, the diversity of opinion in the post-Revolutionary press was related to the number of opinion sources. Thus the relatively small minimum efficient scale of the eighteenth century print shop had much to do with the character of the press in the period just before adoption of the First Amendment. Whether the First Amendment was actually adopted with the idea of preserving the press as it then existed is more debatable; one constitutional scholar argues that this theory of the First Amendment was a later fabrication of Federalist judges responding to Republican pressure applied to Federalist printers and editors, (see Levy [47], pp. 245-248).

Communications technologies dominated by significant scale economies at relevant output levels were unknown to the framers of the First Amendment. In their experience, economic competition was consistent with the political function of the press because of the small scale technology of printing and the rapid rate of entry in the industry in the decade preceeding 1791. It is impossible to answer the question whether these men would have acted differently if they had been faced with a media structure such as we have today. One can say, however, that they had not the slightest notion of a "responsible" or balanced or fair press. Their experience was with a highly partisan press, but one in which there was great accessibility to the means of reaching the public with new ideas. No one thought of legislating a "right of access" to the pages of newspapers, at least in part because of the relative ease of access to the presses themselves.

NEWSPAPERS IN THE NINETEENTH CENTURY

The period from 1790 to 1850 is remarkable for the rise of the daily newspaper (see Appendix Table 2A-1), which in this period became an important if not the principal source of news in the larger cities, for the application of mechanical power to presses, and the invention of the faster rotary press. The rise of the "penny press" phenomenon after about 1840 has been linked by many observers with the sudden discovery of advertising as a source of revenue. This is unlikely. Advertising, on the little evidence available, seems all along to have been of some importance to newspapers. No doubt this importance gradually increased over the period, but there is no reason to suppose anything sudden happened in the 1840s. More likely, the penny press was simply a marketing innovation, presaging the more massive and more successful efforts of Hearst and Pulitzer 50 years later.

In 1810 there were only nineteen copies of daily newspapers for every 10,000 people; by 1880 there were 718—still not a remarkably large number when compared to the present 3,000 (see Appendix Table 2A-5). In 1810 there was one daily newspaper *firm* for every 278,000 people; by 1880 newspapers had increased so that the ratio was 52,000 (see Appendix Table 2A-8). This was a period in which the newspaper was still basically individualistic and political—the creature of an individual editor/publisher, devoted to his personal views and those of his friends. Technology did change, but it was only a quantitative change. Presses became bigger and faster—the rotary press of the 1840s was certainly a breakthrough—but the largest daily newspaper in 1880 had a circulation of only 150,000 (see Appendix Table 2A-4).

The invention of a process for making cheap wood pulp newsprint spread this new and cheaper paper rapidly through the industry after 1870. In interpreting the falling price of newsprint (see Appendix Table 2A-10), it is well to remember that prices fell generally in the 30 years after the Civil War; however, newsprint prices seem to have fallen more rapidly than the general price level. After 1880, and continuing for about 40 years, truly revolutionary changes took place, not merely in the structure and technology of the daily newspaper but in its social and political role (see the Appendix Figures). In this remarkable period, a number of things seem to have happened simultaneously. The effects were dramatic: individual newspaper circulation became very large, and the number of newspapers in each city began to decline (See Appendix Table 2A-15). Yellow journalism and muckraking were born, and the era of the editor began to die (see Hofstadter [37], pp. 186-198, and Innis [39], p. 174). Chains and mergers became important, newspapers began to grow rapidly in physical size, and aggregate circulation began to approach saturation of the potential audience (see Appendix Table 2A-5). These changes dwarf those later effects, thought to be so serious, from the advent of television.

Circulation and Politics

To understand what happened in this period it is necessary to understand how journalists and publishers rode the bandwagon of the progressive era into giant circulation, and how they in turn influenced the politics of that era. But is is perhaps more important to seek out those technological and economic forces that allowed publishers to behave in this way. A careful, systematic analysis of this subject could and should occupy another book; here we can only outline an impression of what seems to have happened.

If we define market penetration of newspapers in the following rather objectionable way, some interesting results emerge. Suppose every copy of a newspaper is read by two people and that 50 percent of the population for various reasons cannot read a newspaper (for example, because they are children). Suppose further that circulation numbers are reduced by one-fourth to account for some readers subscribing to more than one newspaper. Then we can calculate market penetration by multiplying aggregate daily circulation by three and dividing by population. If we do this for 1860, the result is a market penetration of 14 percent; for 1880 the figure is 22 percent. But by 1920 the penetration rate had reached 79 percent, from which it gradually rose, by 1940, to 99 percent. (By 1970 it had fallen back to 92 percent.) The assumptions, of course, are without serious foundation, but they are not wholly implausible. Alternatively, consider Appendix Table 2A-5, wherein it is shown that newspaper circulation per household increased from .36 in 1880 to 1.16 in 1920.

The crucial point is that in the 40-year period beginning in 1880, penetration of the newspaper market approached saturation. In the large cities this happened much faster than in the country as a whole. Newspaper publishing in this period began to be a zero sum game in circulation, as readers had increasingly to be enticed from other papers, rather than from the population of nonreaders. This fact alone may explain why it was possible before this period to have more than one competing newspaper in a city, but not afterward. In the earlier period, the opportunity to take advantage of economies of scale in publishing a newspaper was demand limited: more than one newspaper survived because they did not need to compete for the same, or at least exactly the same audience. Here is Bennett, writing in 1835:

> There are in this city [New York] at least 150,000 persons who glance over one or more newspapers every day and only 42,000 daily sheets are issued to supply them. We have plenty of room, therefore, without jostling neighbors, rivals or friends, to pick up at least 20,000 or 30,000 for the *Herald* and leave something for those who come after us.[1]

But this changed; new subscription starts had to come increasingly from the subscriber lists of other newspapers, and this meant that economies of scale were no longer limited by the extent of the market for a specialized editorial product. Put another way, newspaper publishers before this period found it much more profitable to seek specialized audiences by publishing relatively specialized content and trying to attract nonreaders, rather than trying to be more general in order to attract readers of other newspapers. But as the population of nonreaders declined, publishers came into direct competition for one another's readers, forcing changes in their content.

Similar effects may have been taking place with respect to advertisers as business became less localized, transportation improved, and national consumer markets grew in importance. After 1870, national advertising agencies such as Ayer began to appear. This hypothesis is borne out by the data on subscription prices, which rose in the period before 1880 in real terms, and then declined drastically over the next 40 years (see Appendix Table 2A-12). This decline is even more dramatic when one considers the growing physical size of newspapers. Big city newspapers in 1880 had four pages; by 1900 they had eight, and this had probably doubled again by 1920. All this must be taken in the context of economies of scale in printing and distributing newspapers, and the steadily increasing capital costs of entry.

This change was reflected in the nature of the newspaper itself. Editors could no longer afford to put the stamp of their personal biases on the entire range of editorial content; they had increasingly to include content of appeal to diverse groups. The editor as an institution receded into the background. The publisher's success formula was to take advantage of scale economies with respect to the physical size of the newspaper by including content that was specialized to serve subgroups of the population, and at the same time to generate demand for circulation by broadening (and perhaps lowering) the appeal of the basic news content of the newspaper. The newspapers in their search for mass audiences interacted directly with the political environment of the day: boosterism, muckraking, progressivism, yellow journalism, even a war promoted by a newspaper publisher. Newspaper publishers scrambled for huge circulation because that was the key to profit and survival, and the newspaper ceased to be the instrument of an individualistic editor or his political cronies.

The forces on the demand side that contributed to this phenomenon are difficult to isolate. Literacy and urbanization were of course increasing, the first less dramatically than the second. Educational levels in the population were also increasing. But underlying this seems to have been a deeper force. Perhaps publishers began to emulate the men who populated their advertising columns, and created their own demand for the newspaper product. (Certainly Hearst acted as if this was his goal.) Perhaps there was simply an exogenous shift in consumer behavior, toward the notion that newspaper reading was a desirable thing.

If newspaper reading as a consumption good has value in part because of its creation of a community of knowledge among social groups, then the passing of critical point in readership may accelerate the trend toward saturation. Once a certain critical proportion of one's friends and acquaintances is known to obtain their conversational gambits from a given newspaper, it may become "necessary" to subscribe one's self. In any event, newspaper reading rather suddenly became a majority rather than a minority pastime.

Before the rise of Hearst, Pulitzer, Scripps. and the like, newspapers existed to incite passion in their readers, and they did just that: newspapers were almost by definition controversial. Hearst and Pulitzer were in a sense working in this tradition, but they turned the moral crusades of the earlier generation of editors from the path of eccentricity to the path of profit. After the success of their excesses, personal journalism was no longer possible in the daily field. It is very difficult to say to what extent the vast changes in the structure of the industry in this period were due to the invention of what was in effect a new marketing strategy.

There were contributing factors on the supply side. Press technology did not run into any roadblocks, and the presses kept getting bigger and faster as the demands put upon them grew (see Appendix Table 2A-4). The linotype machine in the 1890s increased the speed and decreased the cost of composition, probably allowing an increase in the number of pages per edition while raising the capital costs of entry. But these things had a cost and that cost was increasing specialization of the printing departments in newspaper production, and a decreased ability to use temporarily idle or excess capacity for job printing.

The effect was to put even more pressure on newspapers to reach for circulation, and to remove a source of subsidy which had previously helped to preserve competing newspapers. Morning and evening newspapers began to merge in order to gain the economies of joint use of a single mechanical department. Newspaper publishers since colonial times had depended to some degree on job printing, and they still do (see Appendix Table 2A-14); this period simply reduced the extent of that dependence.

Improved local transportation and communication facilities also contributed to the growth of circulation. Telephone and telegraph communication made it possible to gather suburban news for inclusion in the metropolitan dailies, making them potentially regional. Improved local transport systems such as the horse-drawn streetcar and later the electric trolley made it possible to distribute the metro paper in the suburbs and in satellite cities. It was even possible in this period to establish printing facilities in areas remote from the editorial offices in order to take advantage of transportation connections.

The period after the Civil War was characterized by the growth of department stores with wide geographical markets; these became important advertisers. Finally, the innovation of rural free delivery of mail was of considerable importance in bringing the urban newspapers to the countryside after 1890.

All these forces came together in a way that doomed the multinewspaper city and simultaneously set up the modern structure of the newspaper industry. It probably happened most rapidly in the smaller cities, where segmentation of the audience by specialized political tastes was least viable. It did not happen anywhere overnight. But the effects were profound. The first true mass media were born.

NEWSPAPERS IN THE TWENTIETH CENTURY

This history of newspapers in the present century is a story of economic adjustment to the structural forces generated in the period 1880-1920, and of reaction to the inroads of the new electronic media. The equilibrium structure of the newspaper industry after about 1900 is described below as an "umbrella model" (see Fig. 2-1 below). Briefly put, we have been undergoing a transition from multinewspaper cities to one-newspaper cities, while simultaneously the major dailies of the largest cities have been hardest hit by competition from the new media.

Although the decline in direct newspaper competition and in the number of firms is quite dramatic, it is easily exaggerated. In 1973 only 5.4 percent of newspaper firms had direct competition in the same city, but these firms produced 32 percent of total U.S. newspaper circulation. By contrast, in 1923, 60 percent of the firms had direct competition, and they accounted for 89 percent of total circulation (see Appendix Table 2A-17).

The size distribution of firms in the industry has changed remarkably little over the last 50 years (see Appendix Table 2A-18). The distribution is highly skewed. The largest 25 percent of all firms have been producing about 80 percent of U.S. total daily circulation at least since 1923, but the median firm size has grown from 4,000 copies per day in 1923 to 12,000 in 1973. The entire size distribution has simply shifted gradually toward larger circulations. In 1923, 68 percent of all firms had evening-only publication schedules. Although this proportion declined over the ensuing 50 years, evening-only newspapers still account for 56 percent of all firms. But evening papers are much smaller, on average, than morning issues. The reason for this is fairly clear: evening newspapers face much tighter time constraints in terms of transportation and delivery than do morning papers. As a result, the geographical area they can feasibly serve is smaller.

Labor unions have presented a peculiar problem for newspaper firms in this century. Unionization has followed craft lines, resulting in a multiplicity of jurisdictions within each plant. Large newspapers often deal with ten to seventeen independent unions. The result is that technological innovation which took the form of labor saving machines in one stage of the production process was often successfully delayed by the particular craft workers affected. Publishers often lacked the flexibility to transfer workers among departments. While big city printing unions have often been militant, it is difficult to assign blame to them for the failure of larger dailies to innovate or for the demise of multi-newspaper cities. Most of the electronic innovations of the past decade seem to have originated in the smaller dailies for reasons only partly explained by union difficulties, and the wage demands of the big city unions have not by themselves been a major source of the demise of competition. It is probably fair to say, however, that strikes and other union activity have accelerated and precipitated newspaper failures that were on the horizon in any event.

Since 1953 newspapers have been under serious pressure from television. This pressure has been most evident in the significant declines in circulation of papers in the largest cities, but is reflected in the overall statistics by an absolute decline in national circulation per household (see Appendix Table 2A-20). Still, newspapers receive greater total advertising revenue than do TV stations. Newspapers accounted for 45 percent of all advertising expenditure in 1935; by 1970 they accounted for 29 percent, and TV for 18 percent. Smaller newspapers do not receive such direct competition from the electronic media, and have also been the recent beneficiaries of new cost-saving technology not readily available to the larger dailies.

Electronic technology has revolutionized the newspaper production process in the last ten years. The use of computers to perform typesetting functions has been extended backwards into electronic innovation in the editorial process, and there have also been signs that computer related printing technology may soon be applied to the presses themselves. Partly because of favorable labor union contracts, this electronic revolution has worked its way gradually upwards from the smaller to the larger newspaper firms. Our only true national newspaper, *The Wall Street Journal*, uses microwave relay and even communication satellites to send copy to its regional printing plants.

These innovations raise at least two interesting possibilities for the future. The first is that computerization of the whole newspaper production process may make it possible for one production facility to produce more than two daily newspapers in a city — that is, more than one morning and one evening edition. The second is that distribution costs and time delays may be so much reduced as to make national daily newspapers possible in the general news field. Such newspapers have existed for many years in Europe, in large part because European nations are geographically and culturally more compact.

Table 2-1 above presented some financial data for a "typical" newspaper of 100,000 circulation. It will be seen that while such a newspaper may be "typical" of large city newspapers, and therefore of most of the total circulation of newspapers in the United States, it is by no means typical of the daily newspaper firm. The typical newspaper publishes only an evening edition, and half of all newspapers had, in 1973, circulation under 12,000 copies per day; even the mean evening newspaper has a circulation of only 26,000. In terms of sources of news, one must not be misled by the large number of firms that still exist. Sixty-six percent of total daily circulation is now, and has been for the last 50 years at least, produced by the largest 10 percent of all newspapers—in 1973 by the 157 newspapers with daily circulation over 76,000, or in 1923 by the 198 firms with circulations over 32,000.

Finally, it is worth mentioning that the number of cities with a local newspaper has continued to increase—from 1,302 in 1923 to 1,519 in 1973 (see Appendix Table 2A-16). This means that while electronic media have begun to drive out the regional and national news and advertising service provided by large city newspapers, local coverage has actually increased in geographical extent.

Professor J.N. Rosse [77] has developed a model of newspaper structure and location that he calls the "umbrella" hypothesis (Fig. 2-1). The essence of the model is the recognition that while few cities have more than one daily newspaper, these newspapers nevertheless compete with each other and with other newspapers. There is generally in each region of the country a major city newspaper whose circulation market reaches out far beyond the boundaries of the central city, sometimes for hundreds of miles. These are "level 1" newspapers. Of course, circulation density falls off as distance from the major metropolitan area increases, and is particularly low in "level 2" cities. Level 2 cities may be regarded for this purpose as satellites of the major metropolitan city, and each

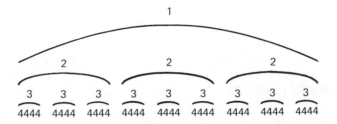

Key:
Level 1   newspaper in large metropolitan center
Level 2   newspapers in satellite cities
Level 3   local dailies
Level 4   weeklies and other specialized media

Figure 2-1. The Umbrella Model

of these will have a newspaper of its own, also with a circulation area beyond the city boundaries. (An example of a level 1 city is San Francisco. Oakland and San Jose would be level 2 satellite cities.) The daily newspapers in the level 2 cities throw up umbrellas of their own. These cover newspapers in level 3 cities, which are quite local in circulation. These in turn must contend with even more specialized and localized media, such as weeklies, shopping throwaways, and the like.

Newspapers in the secondary and tertiary level cities do not compete with each other, except possibly on the fringes of their circulation areas. But each newspaper must compete with other papers in layers above and below it. Advertising revenue is the key to understanding this relationship, along with specialization of audience interest. The level 2 and 3 newspapers exist, despite economies of scale for the metro daily, because the metro daily cannot include local interest news and advertising matter for each of the cities outside the metro center. The metro center daily gets advertising revenue from its own city and from regional and national advertisers. The more local papers depend on local advertising by stores located in their immediate area, for whom an ad in the metro daily would be wasteful.

Level 1 newspapers are the ones most subject to competition from electronic media, whose circulation area coincides with their own. As a result, since the advent of television, the circulations of major metro newspapers have steadily declined, while the circulation of lower level papers has increased (see Appendix Table 2A-21). The metro dailies are simply pulling back to their area of natural advantage, the central city, leaving the regional market increasingly to radio and television.

All this is of course in marked contrast with the situation a hundred years ago, when newspapers competed head-on in the central cities. The implication is clear. Newspapers face a great deal more economic competition than their characterization as "local monopolies" implies. They are indeed local monopolies, but competition at the fringes and between layers provides a degree of market discipline. There is no good evidence that the local monopolies enjoy monopoly profits, at least on average.

HAVE THINGS CHANGED?

How has the changing structure of the newspaper industry, by itself, affected freedom of expression? It is extraordinarily difficult to answer this question. Before about 1900 the daily newspaper was read by a minority of the population, but an influential minority—the "opinion leaders." In this century newspapers have become a mass medium, but they have simultaneously become fewer and less directly involved in political issues. The editor of a colonial or nineteenth century newspaper would never dream of allowing access to his paper by persons with political or philosophical views contrary to his own. The modern publisher does this all the time, in order to gain circulation. Still, the modern editor and publisher control the identities of those who are allowed to reach the public, and they have some range of discretion, particularly on matters of purely local interest.

In modern times, the mass media represent the only practical link between those who would speak and the public; in earlier times the newspaper could be and was circumvented with relative ease, either by direct recourse to speech or by the use of pamphlets, broadsides, and the like. It is thus true that editors as "gatekeepers" are very much more powerful than they used to be, but at the same time there have evolved rather strong economic limits on the exercise of that power; some of these limits have been institutionalized in journalistic codes and notions of press responsibility.

But these institutionalizations may be in themselves harmful. The political and personal newspapers of the 1710-1880 period had only individualistic ethics; no one except the true believer was tempted to take what was printed as gospel. The modern press pretends to a level of integrity and responsibility which is at least misleading, but which may well convince some readers. Thus a population unaware of the economic incentives that condition the content of the newspaper, even if they doubt the divinity of the reporter and editor, stands a fair chance of being misled. On the other side, it is probably a lot harder today to reach everyone in a local community with a message than it was 100 or 150 years ago, or at least there are fewer ways of doing it. Against this it must be said that it is certainly a lot easier to reach everyone in the nation with a given message; few practical means of doing so existed in the earlier period.

ANTITRUST IN THE NEWSPAPER FIELD[2]

For the reasons described, head-on competition among newspapers in the same town is a disequilibrium situation, one that will eventually be succeeded by merger, failure of one paper, or a joint operating agreement, tantamount to merger. Antitrust action aimed at preserving competition in this sense is simply doomed to failure, at least under preelectronic technology. But antitrust activity can be important in preserving competition within the umbrella structure, and in preserving intermedia competition. This section briefly describes the areas in which there has been antitrust activity.

The two cases involving head-on competition are *Citizen Publishing Co. v. United States*[3] and *Times-Picayune Publishing Co. v. United States.*[4] The first involved a Justice Department attack on two newspapers in Tucson, Arizona, which had agreed to form a joint operating company to centralize production and advertising sales; editorial staffs and policy were to be kept separate. (There are about 25 such arrangements nationwide.) The Antitrust Division obtained a summary judgment in its favor, which was upheld by the Supreme Court. This led more or less directly to the so-called Newspaper Preservation Act (1970). The Act exempts such arrangements from the antitrust laws, putting newspapers for this purpose into the same category as labor unions and sports leagues, which enjoy antitrust immunity. As noted above, this probably doesn't matter very much; antitrust cannot in any event preserve same city head-on competition among newspapers. But the passage of the Act attests to the political power of newspaper publishers and their representative, the American Newspaper Publishers' Association. It is not a good policy precedent.

The *Times-Picayune* case involved combination rates. It is very common for newspapers with a morning and evening edition to charge a rate for advertisements to appear in both papers which is considerably less than the sum of the separate lineage rates, and even in some cases less than the price for one; the effect is to force "all-or-nothing" choices by advertisers, a form of price discrimination. (Of course, costs are lower for joint advertising as well.) However, when this happens in cities where one of the two editions faces competition from an independent firm, the practice is obviously disadvantageous to that firm. Such was the case in New Orleans. The Supreme Court said that the practice was legal. Again, in terms of its effects on the long term structure of the industry, this is probably not an important decision. The contrary result might have postponed the inevitable a few years longer.

The cases in the areas of wire services and syndication of feature material *are* more important because they affect the "intraumbrella" effectiveness of competition. The wire services were begun in the Civil War era, taking advantage of the telegraph. The Associated Press has always been a cooperative: member newspapers share with each other local news of national interest. UPI is owned as a profit seeking venture by the Scripps interests, but it otherwise operates in much the same way. Both services have been accused of employing restrictive practices to discourage competition with their member newspapers, usually by charging very high fees for new memberships in cities where there are already member newspapers. This practice was held to be illegal in view of the antitrust laws in the *Associated Press* case (1945). This case is of enormous importance for its precedential value not only in the narrow substantive area involved, but in setting forth the notion that the government can and should, under the antitrust laws and consistent with the Constitution, intervene to protect and preserve competition in the marketplace of ideas, in ways which do not involve direct regulation. (See the quotation from *Associated Press*, supra pp. 2-3).

AP and UPI are by no means the only wire services, but they are the most important for newspapers. Broadcast media also depend upon them heavily: radio stations, particularly, typically do little more than "rip and read" the news from the wire service. On the other hand, the wire services' editors have fairly strong incentives simply to report "everything." The gatekeeping role of the services is not a very strong one, in part because of the diversity of the needs of their clients, and in part because of the incentive for speed in reporting the news, which tends to suppress the opportunity for the exercise of editorial judgment. Finally, there are a number of practical substitutes for AP and UPI, especially for metro papers. These considerations, together with the fact that the news hole available for wire service stories in the typical newspaper is in any event large enough to allow publication of one-tenth or less of the material available, suggests that wire service oligopoly is probably not a very serious problem in the marketplace of ideas.

The business of producing syndicated features (comics, political columns, advice, etc.) is apparently quite competitive. Most large metro newspapers syndicate their major features, and there are in addition perhaps hundreds of independent syndicators.[5] Some features are, of course, more popular than others: it is said that *Peanuts* can make a significant difference in circulation all by itself, for instance.

There are two practices in this market which have been seen as anticompetitive. The first is packaging features for sale on an all-or-nothing basis, a practice akin to block booking in the motion picture industry. The second is the common, but by no means universal, custom of selling such features on a "territorial exclusive" basis. This simply means that a newspaper which buys a feature has the exclusive right to publish it in the marketing area defined in the contract. Newspapers at layer 1 in the umbrella model, the large metro papers, may thus buy up rights to packages of features that extend for a hundred miles or more from the central city. Some of these may not be published. This denies the feature to newspapers in subordinate layers.

Sellers of features presumably benefit both from the lower transactions cost of dealing with just one buyer per region and from an ability to extract from that buyer some part of the scarcity rent thus created. It may be true that this helps to preserve the geographical extent of the major regional newspapers, and that it is thus actually beneficial to competition, given the growing strength of newspapers in lower layers. The Antitrust Division has an action under way to test the lawfulness of this practice.[g]

[g]See "Boston Globe Agrees to Share Material From Syndication with Papers in Its Area," *Wall Street Journal*, 3/6/75, p. 9.

Another area affecting competition within the umbrella structure, as well as intracity competition, is the issue of distributors. Newspaper distributors are responsible for getting the newspaper from the printing plant to readers' homes and to newsstands and dealers. They are sometimes just employees of the newspaper, and sometimes independent businessmen. A newspaper distributor owns trucks and hires newsboys; in principle, there is nothing to prevent him from distributing more than one newspaper. Independent distributors thus provide the opportunity for newspaper competition. When the distributors are employees of the newspaper, a substantial barrier to entry is created, since any newspaper wishing to penetrate the area must duplicate this distribution network. Newspaper publishers prefer to deal with the distributors as independent businessmen rather than as employees for a variety of managerial reasons; were it not for the prospect of inviting entry, there would probably be no question about dealing with independents. Sometimes, a newspaper attempts to write exclusive contracts with independent dealers. Antitrust policy should seek to preserve independent, nonexclusive distributors, for the reasons put forward in the last section of this chapter, below.

The final area of possible antitrust activity in the newspaper industry involves cross-ownership of broadcast stations and newspapers. This form of horizontal concentration is harmful to economic competition among media on the regional level (down to level 2 cities), and is also of course harmful to competition in the marketplace of ideas. This issue is discussed in detail in Chapter Three. Newspaper chains are a matter of considerable concern to many libertarians (see Rucker [80] , Chapter 2). It is not clear, however, that they pose a very serious threat either to economic competition or to freedom of expression. At least, they are a second order problem when compared to the issues we have been discussing. Their existence is probably attributable more to the peculiarities of the tax laws and the transferability of management skills than to a desire to reduce competition.

PUBLIC POLICY ISSUES

The fact that newspapers face competition from other layers in the umbrella model, and from other media, provides a source of market discipline. In particular, editorial packages must be "correct" in order to reach a profitable number and type of readers. Probably there is not very much room for discretion in this regard. But this does not mean that, when it comes to particular issues of public importance, editorial policy cannot be monopolistic in the usual sense. The resident of a layer 3 suburb has a number of alternative sources of news and entertainment, but only one source of coverage of local issues, such as local elections or city council meetings. The local newspaper can have a significant effect on the outcome of these issues, not only by its editorial page policy but by its editorial decisions regarding coverage of candidates and events.

The same statements can be made about local news and local issues for the other levels of the umbrella model, with the exception that electronic media provide some check on the editorial discretion of the metro newspaper. Still, the electronic media must be regional in interest, and have little time or resources available for coverage of local political issues in the central city. The problem is of course aggravated when the local newspaper also owns one of the local stations.

The public has the greatest number of sources of news and opinion when it comes to national issues; the least on local issues. With respect to national news there are essentially five sources: ABC, CBS, NBC, UPI, and AP. Local newspapers and broadcasters almost always depend on these sources in reporting national news. There are of course other sources, including other wire services and sending reporters to Washington, but these simply are not very important in practice, at least for the average evening newspaper of 26,000 circulation. National opinion is more widely dispersed as to sources (that is, there are many syndicated columnists and periodicals), but syndicated columnists must pass the gatekeepers of the local newspapers, and they are not on television. Periodicals do not reach very large audiences—or at least most of them do not.

What can be done about local newspaper monopoly? There are several alternatives: (1) do nothing, because the problem just is not serious enough to warrant intervention; (2) regulate the press, perhaps with a "fairness doctrine" like that used for broadcast stations; (3) legislate a right of direct access for editorial announcements and other matter—e.g., make the newspaper into a public utility; (4) restructure the newspaper institution so as to allow greater freedom of access through vertical disintegration of the stages of production.

Let us examine these in turn. It is not easy to make the case for intervention, since the effects of local press monopoly on freedom of expression are not clear cut. We have explored the case, above, for supposing that the extent of economic discipline on a local newspaper's choice of editorial product is quite severe. On the margin, local newspapers must be responsive to reader interests; but do they need to be responsive to nonmarginal readers? A reader in the center of the city is not easily lost because of inept editorial policy. Moreover, in some dimensions profit may not be much affected by editorial decisions because readers on the margin are insensitive to them. When this happens, the paper has some degree of discretion, and it can afford to exercise its whims despotically with respect to the inframarginal readers. When it comes to coverage of national events, this may simply not matter: readers who want access to such material do have other options, although they may be relatively costly. But in local issues it may matter a great deal, not just to readers but to people who would reach those readers and who have no other reasonable alternative.

The political candidate who is ignored (not covered) in a local election will have to spend a great deal of money to overcome this display of antagonism by the local newspaper. The PTA group which is trying to reform the school curriculum may win or lose, depending on the presence of reporters at the school board meeting where the proposals are presented. Letters to the editor, even if published, are a poor substitute for news coverage. And no one can do anything about it—the editor's decision is final and there is no appeal. It is too expensive to reach people, at least regularly, in any other way. Thus, there is some cause for concern about local newspaper monopoly, and something to be balanced against the costs of intervention.

The alternative that seems to occur to many people who have thought about this problem is government regulation, modelled on our present regulation of broadcasting. I will not discuss this very extensively, because broadcast regulation is analyzed in the next chapter, and because licensing of the press and government regulation seem to be ruled out prima facie by the First Amendment. Government regulation, even in theory, seems far worse than local monopoly. It may be bad for the local editors of 1,500-odd monopoly newspapers to decide what their readers shall see; but it would be far worse for a single commission in Washington to make or affect these decisions, or to legitimize local decisions by the award and renewal of a license, as now happens in broadcasting.

The notion of a right of access for paid editorial announcements has a great deal more appeal, since it does not appear necessarily to require government licensing or regulation (see Barron [6]). The newspaper would be required to publish a schedule of rates for editorial matter, just as it does for advertising matter, and accept all comers at those rates. There are, however, some difficulties. (For the legal objections, see Lange [43].) The first is that the content of these insertions will not, presumably, be of indifference to readers; thus, they will affect circulation quantity and quality. The effect of this will be to alter advertising revenues, in reaction to circulation changes. Given competition among newspapers and with other media, this may quite simply drive the newspaper out of business. Also, publishers are legally liable for the content of their newspapers. If it is true that the editorial content of a newspaper is rather strictly limited in order to be consistent with economic survival, then giving up a significant degree of control of editorial content will be inconsistent with survival. But we really do not know whether the premise is true or not.

The second problem with a statutory right of access to newspapers is that the Supreme Court has recently said it is unconstitutional. The state of Florida had a law requiring newspapers to publish replies to editorial attacks on political candidates. In *Tornillo* the Supreme Court struck down this law as violating the First Amendment. *Tornillo* reaches the correct result—that there should not be a right of free access to the editorial process—without fully analyzing the structural issues, and without recognition of the distinction between the editorial process and the transmission process. Access to the editorial process is both uneconomic and unconstitutional. The process to which a right of access might usefully be mandated is the transmission process, not the editorial process. What may be needed is a system of access to newspaper printing presses, as opposed to the pages of newspapers already existing.

Thus the fourth and final possible solution to the problem of local press monopoly is an alteration of the institutional structure of the industry. Publishers employ editors and stereotypers and pressmen and (often) truck drivers and distributors. They integrate in this way because it is more profitable (less costly) to do so than to contract for such services with independent suppliers. But it is in some of these functions that we find the economies of scale responsible for local newspaper monopolies. Could these transmission stages be split off? And if so, would this allow greater freedom of access to the newspaper reading public?

The distribution function is in many cases already independent—that is, newspaper firms contract with independent distributors to deliver newspapers and service circulation business in local subareas. There are economies of scale in this function as subscriber density increases. It is not obvious why this function could not be employed simultaneously by two or more competing newspapers. The same thing is true of the press and typesetting functions. These could be centralized and independently owned, serving two or more newspapers—for example, weeklies are already published this way. If this institutional change were made, then the only economy remaining would be with respect to the public good character of editorial content—and there is nothing to be done about that!

The result might be that a number of different organizations could exist, each producing a newspaper of more or less competitive editorial content, and each using the facilities of a central printing and distribution service. It is fairly clear that the sports section or the women's section could thus be produced and sold independently and successfully; subscribers would simply tell their distributors which packages they wanted. What is not so clear is the extent to which this would result in head-on competition among firms producing the same sorts of editorial content. Could there be two competing sports sections? Or two competing local news sections? One does not know the answer. But it would nevertheless be true that access and entry (being now virtually synonomous) would be greatly enhanced. The political party or PTA coalition can regard the prospect of starting up a competing newspaper as not entirely hopeless, simply because the capital costs of entry would be considerably reduced. Some notion of this can be gained by remembering that only about 16 percent of a newspaper's expenses are associated with producing nonadvertising content, or by the fact that a morning-evening combination newspaper has 13 percent lower costs than separate firms of the same circulation.

The Common Carrier Idea

The notion that newspaper printing plants might usefully be treated as common carriers is advanced here in the most tentative way possible, for the reasons stated. It is an interesting idea, worth careful consideration. But there is an additional problem that might as well be discussed here, since this is merely the first of several suggestions that transmission media be made into common carriers.

The problem is that common carrier status acknowledges a "natural" monopoly and imposes two distinct constraints on that monopoly.

The first constraint is that of required nondiscriminatory access, a powerful bar on refusals to deal. This is required for First Amendment purposes. The second constraint is on profit and price levels. This has traditionally been thought necessary in order to prevent monopoly pricing, which is bad even when it is nondiscriminatory (or, sometimes, especially when it is nondiscriminatory.) The difficulty is that there is a substantial body of opinion, and some evidence, suggesting that profit regulation does more harm than good. That is, such regulation either provides an incentive for firms to be inefficient in their technical production decisions, or is accompanied by economic protectionism designed to slow innovation through entry, or both.

Whether the results of profit regulation are worth their costs depends on the particular conditions in each industry. Nevertheless, it is my own view that the media industries are probably unsuitable for profit regulation. It seems better to regard the common carrier policy as a sort of strong antitrust remedy, rather than as a weak form of utility regulation. It does not seem at all unreasonable to impose the access conditions of common carrier status, where necessary, without also imposing regulation of profits and prices. Surely there are industries, of which this may be one example, where competition is sufficient to make profit regulation unnecessary, while competition is nevertheless not strong enough to be an effective safeguard of individual liberty. Laws barring racial discrimination by otherwise unregulated enterprises may be a useful parallel example.

The common carrier alternative is attractive because it affords the opportunity for increased access and freedom without requiring government regulation, although it does require government restructuring, either by legislation or by antitrust action. There is no guarantee that the result will be a marked improvement, however. Also, one must assume that the change would cost something in terms of efficiency; publishers now own their presses for some reason, and one somehow doubts that it is only because they wish to deny access to others.

On balance, a restructuring of this type may be a desirable policy objective; it certainly is if we take the newspaper industry out of the context of changing technology. The advent of such potentially important new technologies as cable television and computerized pressrooms may make the problem less serious by substituting a new means of transmitting messages to the public on the local, as well as the national level. On the other hand, it is precisely these technologies that may make the proposal workable.

The crucial point is that there is a way of increasing freedom of expression and competition in the newspaper field that does not depend on compromising the editorial integrity of the newspaper itself. In newspapers, as in broadcasting, the key is the vertical structure of production and access to the means of transmission.

Appendix to Chapter Two

ECONOMIC HISTORY OF THE NEWSPAPER INDUSTRY: THE NUMBERS

The statistics on newspapers are quite unreliable, this being partly the result of ambiguities in defining the term "newspaper," and partly the result of widely differing levels of coverage and accuracy in the statistical reports available. Accordingly, all the numbers put forward in this appendix must be regarded as at best rough and ready; certainly these data should not be regarded as having any more usefulness than the indication of broad trends, over extended time periods.

The data have two systematic biases. First, there is a tendency to count as "newspapers" things that do not really fit the modern meaning of that term. This is exascerbated by a tendency to count morning and evening editions of the same newspaper as separate newspapers. Thus the numbers in this section that refer to "newspaper firms" are almost certainly overstated. The second systematic bias is in circulation statistics. Newspaper publishers have always had an incentive to exaggerate their circulation in order to increase the demand for advertising space in their publications. Before the creation of the Audit Bureau of Circulation (ABC) in 1914, all data on circulation, even from census sources, must be regarded as inflated.[a]

The first successful newspaper, a weekly, was published in Boston in 1704. The number of newspapers increased steadily during the colonial period, reaching 29 in 1770 (see Table 2A-1 and Fig. 2A-1). The first successful daily newspaper appeared in 1783. Figure 2A-1 reveals that both daily and weekly newspapers grew steadily in numbers from their beginnings until about 1900, when significant decline set in, continuing almost to the present day. Figure

[a]None of these comments applies to the Rosse data for the years 1923, 33, 43, 48, 53, 58, 63, 68, 73.

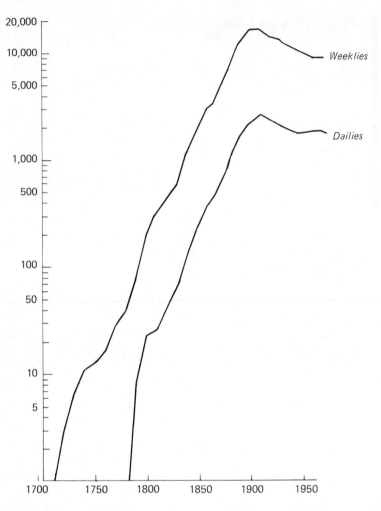

Figure 2A-1. Number of Daily and Weekly Newspapers, 1704-1973
Source: Table 2A-1 series 1 for dailies, series 3 for weeklies 1880-1933, series 1 for other years.

2A-1 and most subsequent figures are drawn on a log or ratio scale; anything growing at a constant rate shows up as a straight line.

Newspaper circulation for dailies (total copies per day) is shown in Table 2A-2 and Figure 2A-2. This series shows growth at a fairly steadily decreasing rate over the whole period from 1810 to 1970 (this may not be true of the 1810-1850 period, but data for these years are very gross estimates.) Circulation of daily newspapers grew faster than population until about the last half-century.

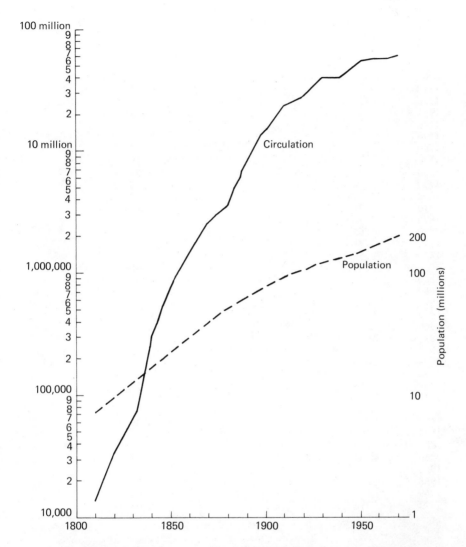

Figure 2A-2. Daily Newspaper Circulation and Population, 1810-1970
Source: Tables 2A-1 and 2A-5.

Tables 2A-3 and 2A-4 show changes in the size of individual daily newspapers. Average circulation per newspaper was about 550 in 1810, and grew to more than 13,000 by 1919. The largest daily newspapers grew from a circulation of about 900 in 1810 to one million by 1900. Press technology kept pace with the needs of the largest newspapers.

Daily circulation per 10,000 inhabitants grew from 19 in 1810 to 3,056 in 1970; in large cities like New York, circulation to population ratios have always

Table 2A-1. Number of Newspapers, 1704-1973

Year	Daily Series 1	Series 2	Series 3	Series 4	Weekly Series 1	Series 2	Series 3
1704					1		
1710					1		
1720					3		
1730					7		
1740					11		
1750					13		
1760					17		
1770					29		
1780					39		
1790	8 (6)				83		
1800	24 (16)				210		
1810	26 (24)				343		
1820	42 (37)				470		
1830	65				650		
1840	138				1,266		
1850	254				2,048		
1860	387				3,338		
1870	574				4,517		
1880	971	843	909		8,839	7,777	8,005
1889	1,610	1,494	1,522		11,042	12,474	12,911
1899	2,226	2,112	2,179		13,678	15,520	16,227
1909	2,600		2,427		14,611		16,796
1919	2,441		2,343		12,690		14,529
1923	2,271		2,310	1,977	6,389		13,817
1929	2,086		2,248		7,547		13,298
1933	1,903		2,199	1,745	4,492		12,516
1939	1,888				6,212		
1943	1,754			1,597			
1948	1,781			1,538			
1950	1,772				10,131		
1953	1,783			1,582			
1958				1,544			
1960	1,854				9,333		
1963				1,552			
1968	1,833			1,547	9,460		
1969	1,833				9,268		
1973	1,792			1,566	9,263		

Sources
Dailies

 Series 1: 1790-1820 from Brigham's bibliography; includes all firms in existence at some time during the year; numbers in parentheses are firms surviving through the year; 1830 estimated by Lee; 1840-1933 from census data which includes periodicals (daily) until 1921; all of preceding from Lee [44] Table VIII, p. 718. 1939-1953 from *Historical Statistics of the U.S.* series R-169 (from *Editor and Publisher*); 1960-1973 from *Statistical Abstract* (1973), table 820, p. 502 (from Ayer).

 Series 2: Rowell data; includes periodicals. From Lee [44], Table X, p. 721.

 Series 3: Ayer data; includes periodicals. From Lee [44], Table XI, p. 722-3.

 Series 4: Rosse et al. [79].

Weeklies

 Series 1-3 same as above. Includes semi- and tri- weeklies.

 Series 1 drops firms with sales under $5,000 per annum after 1921, and includes periodicals until 1909.

Table 2A-2. Circulation of Daily Newspapers (circulation in millions)

Year	Daily	Morning	Evening	Sunday
1850	.8			
1860	1.5			
1870	2.6			
1880	3.6			
1889	8.4			
1899	15.1			
1909	24.2	9.6	14.6	13.3
1920	27.8	–	–	17.1
1930	39.6	–	–	26.4
1940	41.1	–	–	32.4
1950	53.8	21.3	32.6	46.6
1960	58.9	24.0	34.9	47.7
1970	62.1	25.9	36.2	49.2

Source:
1850–1909 Lee [44], Table XIII, p. 725 (from census data).
1920–1940 *Historical Statistics of the U.S.* Series R170, p. 500.
1950–1970 *Statistical Abstract* (1973), Table 822, p. 503.

Table 2A-3. Average Circulation per Issue of Daily Newspapers, 1810–1973 (copies per day)

	Mean	% Change	Median
1810	550	–	
1820	800	45	
1830	1,200	50	
1840	2,200	83	
1850	2,986	36	
1860	3,820	28	
1870	4,532	19	
1880	3,673	-19	
1889	5,209	42	
1899	6,785	30	
1909	9,312	37	
1919	13,531	45	
1923	15,000	–	4,000
1933	21,000	40	5,000
1943	28,000	33	6,000
1953	34,000	21	8,000
1963	39,000	15	10,000
1973	39,000	0	12,000

Source:
1810–1919 Lee [44], Table XV, p. 728.
1923–1973 Rosse et al. [79].

Table 2A-4. Maximum Press Capacity and Maximum Daily Circulation, 1819-1973[a]

Year	Maximum Capacity[b]	Max. Daily Circulation[c]
1810	400	900
1814	1,100	
1820		4,000[d]
1824	2,000	
1830		4,000
1835	4,000	
1840		21,000
1845	20,000	
1850		35,000
1856		55,000
1860		77,000
1868	24,000	
1870		85,000
1874	36,000	
1876	60,000	
1880	60,000	147,000
1881	120,000	
1887	192,000	
1889	288,000	
1890		300,000
1895	384,000	
1900		1,000,000
1902	1,152,000	
1923		623,000
1933		1,411,000
1943		2,013,000
1953		2,180,000
1963		2,055,000
1973		2,103,000

[a]Source: Lee [44], Chapter V, *passim*, 1810-1902; Rosse data, 1923-73.

[b]For earlier presses, impressions per hour. For later presses, completed pages (printed both sides) per hour. To the extent that page sizes differ, the data are not strictly comparable.

[c]Largest daily circulation.

[d]Maximum circulation of a New York daily in 1816-1820 (Lee [44] p. 116).

been higher than for the country as a whole, in part because these cities have newspapers with large suburban and rural readerships. New York city was publishing 245 copies per 10,000 inhabitants per day in 1810; by 1929 it was publishing 10,528. (See Tables 2A-5 and 2A-6 and Figs. 2A-3 and 2A-4.) The striking feature of these statistics is the very small newspaper reading population in the first three-quarters of the nineteenth century. No direct estimate of newspaper readers can be made; the population data include, for instance, children, while some people surely bought more than one newspaper, and others read newspapers purchased by institutions or businesses. It can hardly be said that daily newspaper reading was a habit of the general population by 1850. The big

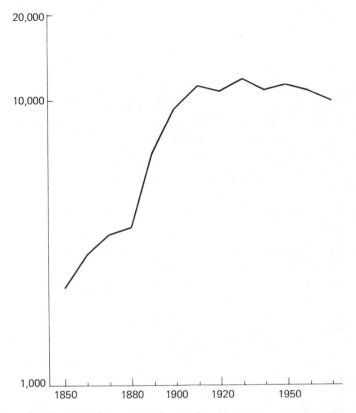

Figure 2A-3. Daily Newspaper Copies Per 10,000 Households, 1850-1970

explosion came in the period after 1880. A big surge in circulation per population came between 1850 and 1900; but it then leveled off and even declined as people turned to other media for news and entertainment. When this is corrected for households, as in Figure 2A-3, it becomes apparent that the period 1880-1910 was one of revolutionary change.

Table 2A-8 (below) and Figure 2A-5 tell an interesting story. The nineteenth century witnessed a steady growth in the number of newspapers published per inhabitant. There were 278,000 persons per newspaper issued in 1810, but only 34,000 in 1899. After the turn of the century the steady decline in newspaper firms, combined with growing population, increased this number, reaching 113,000 in 1970 (equivalent to the state of affairs in the decade 1840-1850). Large cities like New York, on the other hand, seem always to have had a declining number of newspapers per inhabitant, suggesting that the geographical growth of the industry in the nineteenth century merely offset this trend for the country as a whole—that is, the number of newspapers increased as more cities

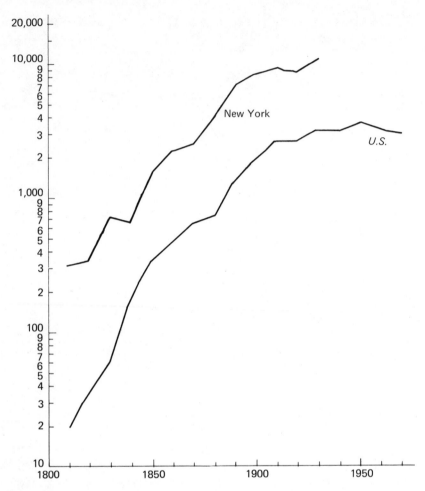

Figure 2A-4.   Daily Newspaper Copies per 10,000 Inhabitants, 1810–1970
Source: Table 2A-6.

became large enough to support them, but there was never a more than temporary growth in the number of papers per inhabitant in individual cities.

Table 2A-9 reviews the history of the foreign language press; as one might expect it was most important in the decades following the great waves of immigration. Foreign language daily newspaper circulation reached a maximum of 1,947 copies per 10,000 foreign born inhabitants in 1919–20. Newsprint prices (Table 2A-10 and Fig. 2A-6) demonstrate a dramatic decline over the whole period, 1800–1900. (These prices are in current dollars; prices in general fell during the last third of the nineteenth century, and have of course risen since.) The data on newsprint consumption, together with the circulation data, can be

Table 2A-5. Circulation and Population U.S. Daily Newspapers, 1810-1970

Year	Agg. Daily Circulation (000)	Copies per 10,000 Population per day	Copies per 10,000 Households per day	% Change in copies per Household
1810	14	19	–	–
1820	34	35	–	–
1830	78	61	–	–
1840	303	178	–	–
1850	800	344	2,222	–
1860	1,500	477	2,885	30
1870	2,600	653	3,421	19
1880	3,600	718	3,636	6
1890	8,400	1,334	6,614	82
1900	15,100	1,987	9,438	43
1910	24,200	2,631	12,100	28
1920	27,800	2,630	11,583	-4
1930	39,600	3,223	13,655	18
1940	41,100	3,121	11,743	-14
1950	53,800	3,570	12,512	7
1960	58,900	3,300	11,113	-11
1970	62,100	3,056	9,857	-11

Source: Estimates based on Tables 2A-1, 2A-2, 2A-3 and U.S. Census data.

used to form a rough estimate of the sizes of newspapers. If all newsprint consumed in 1828 had been used for daily newspaper production, newspapers would have been on average 7.7 modern standard pages; the same assumption shows growth to 12.2 pages in 1880, 17.5 pages in 1899, and 31.7 pages in 1919.

Postage was probably a significant expense for newspaper publishers, until home delivery became significant in the present century, although it is difficult to find historical statistics to support this view (Table 2A-11). Certainly newspaper publishers have always been important lobbiests before Congressional committees setting postal rates, and have succeeded in receiving subsidized rates for most of two centuries. It was almost universal in the eighteenth century for newspaper publishers to be postmasters, a practice that apparently continued into the nineteenth century under the spoils system (Kennedy [40], Rich [71]). Postmasters had the frank, and mailed their own papers free, while possibly harassing competing newspapers. Prepayment of postage for newspapers was not required until 1875, postmen collected from subscribers, and often fees were not collected at all. Moreover, postal rates for periodicals declined steadily throughout the nineteenth century. This presumably encouraged the spread of urban newspapers into suburban and rural areas, where they competed with local daily and weekly newspapers.

Table 2A-12 and Fig. 2A-7 summarize the data on subscription prices, discussed in the text. Table 2A-13 provides what seem to be the only data available

Table 2A-6. Number and Circulation of Daily Newspapers in Large Cities

	New York City				Five Other Cities[a]			
Year	Number (M + E)	Combined daily Circulation (000)	Population (000)	Copies per 10,000 Population	Number (M + E)	Combined daily Circulation (000)	Population (000)	Copies per 10,000 Population
1790	3	1.2	49	245				
1800	5	2.5	79	317				
1810	7	4.2	120	350				
1820	8	10.8	152	711				
1830	11	16.0	242	661				
1840	18	60.0	391	1,535				
1850	14	153.6	696	2,213				
1860	18	300	1,174	2,555				
1870	26	590	1,478	3,992				
1880	33	814	1,912	4,257	82	1,009	2,107	4,800
1889	55	1,781	2,448	7,275	97	2,335	3,155	7,400
1899	29	2,732	3,344	8,170	137	3,432	4,279	8,000
1909	85	4,091	4,423	9,249	116	5,481	5,383	10,200
1919	–	4,807	5,576	8,621	–	6,654	6,578	10,100
1929	55	6,385	6,065	10,528	84	7,783	7,642	10,200

[a]Chicago, Boston, Philadelphia, San Francisco, Cleveland.

Source: Based on Lee [44], Tables XVII and XVIII, pp. 730–732, plus census data.

Note: Compare Table 2A-7.

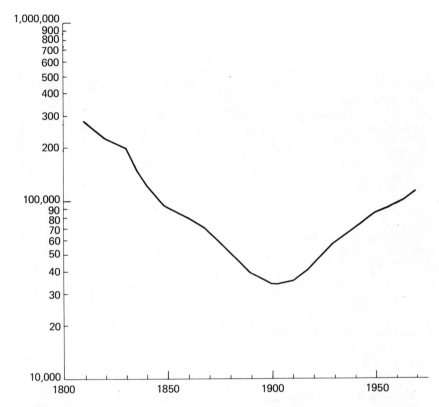

Figure 2A-5. Inhabitants per Daily Newspaper Issue [Firm], 1810–1970
Source: Table 2A-8.

on weekly newspaper circulation. It is, perhaps surprisingly, increasing over the past twenty years at a rather substantial rate.

Table 2A-14 shows (for newspapers and periodicals combined) the late nineteenth and early twentieth century trends in industry revenues. Advertising increased steadily in importance as a source of revenue, while subscription revenues and job printing declined in importance.

From 1880 onwards there has been a continuing increase in the number of cities able to support a daily newspaper, as Table 2A-15 and Figure 2A-8 demonstrate. But, since the decade of World War I, there has been a dramatic decline in the number of newspapers *within* a given city. Indeed, this decline has been so dramatic that the number of dailies *declined* by 30 percent between 1909-10 and 1970-71, while the number of cities with a daily increased 25 percent.

The preceding data has been taken from a variety of sources—the census, Ayer [1] series, and Lee [44], most prominently. The sources have numerous infirmities, as discussed above. Some notion of the problem can be gleaned from

Table 2A-7.   Changing Structure in Five Leading Cities[a] (English language general circulation dailies only)

	1881	1902	1923	1973
Population (000)	2,106	4,278	6,578	7,406
Number of Newspaper firms by publication schedule				
Evening	15	14	13	2
Evening and Sunday	0	2	1	1
Morning	9	6	4	2
Morning and Sunday	8	10	9	1
Morning and Evening	2	1	1	0
Morning, Evening and Sunday	4	5	3	5
Daily	0	0	0	0
Daily and Sunday	0	1	0	1
Total	38	40	31	12
Total with known circulation	31	35	30	12
Total circulation (000)	763	3,151	5,370	6,037
Largest circulation (000)	105	279	504	1,179
Mean circulation	25	90	179	503
Circulation per 10,000 population	3,623	7,366	8,171	8,151
Failures (or mergers) over period	–	12	17	20
Entries over period	–	14[b]	6	1

[a]Philadelphia, Boston, Chicago, Cleveland, San Francisco
[b]Nine in Chicago
Source: Compiled from Ayer [1] and *Editor & Publisher Yearbook.*

Table 2A-8.   Inhabitants per Daily Newspaper Issue (000)

Year	United States	New York City	Five other Cities
1790	–	16	
1810	278	16	
1820	229	17	
1830	198	19	
1840	124	22	
1850	91	49	
1860	81	65	
1870	69	57	
1880	52	58	26
1889	39	45	33
1899	34	115	31
1909	35	52	46
1919	43	–	–
1929	59	110	91
1939	70	–	
1950	85	–	
1960	96	–	
1970	113	–	

Source: Tables 2A-4 and 2A-6.

Table 2A-9. Foreign Language Publications in the United States

Year	All Regular Publications	Daily News papers	Daily Newspapers Circulation (000)	Foreign Born Population (000)	Copies per 10,000 Population
1810	20	1			
1820	17	2			
1839	45	–			
1850	158	30[a]		2,245	
1860	298	–		4,139	
1870	315	64		5,567	
1880	799	90	474	6,680	710
1890	1,028	116	–	9,250	–
1900	1,159	123	–	10,341	–
1909–10	–	137	1,786	13,516	1,321
1914	–	160	2,599	–	–
1919–20	1,040	154	2,710	13,921	1,947
1929–30	913	127	2,325	14,204	1,637

[a]1856

Source: Lee [44], Tables XIX, XXIV, pp. 733–741.

a comparison of Tables 2A-6 and 2A-7 above. The five major cities are the same in each table. Table 2A-6 is based on census data. Table 2A-7 for 1881 and 1902 is based on data in Ayer. The Ayer data, compiled by the author, includes only general circulation English language dailies, excluding for instance business and mercantile dailies. The difference in the number of firms is considerable. Even if the data from Ayer are expanded to include foreign language dailies, business publications, and if separate editions of the same paper are counted as separate papers, there is still a substantial difference between the two sources. Either Ayer is less inclusive than the census, or the census was counting publications that simply were not daily newspapers.

Fortunately, the circulation data are less difficult to reconcile, leading to the hypothesis that the census included firms of very low circulation. From 1923 onwards we do have consistent, well defined time series and cross-section data compiled undei the direction of J.N. Rosse [79] from *Editor and Publisher Yearbook* issues. These data are limited to general circulation English language dailies (excluding, for instance, business dailies and campus newspapers). The data are all oriented to newspaper firms publishing at least five days a week. Many of these firms publish morning and evening and Sunday editions, but these are not counted as independent newspapers. Tables 2A-16 to 2A-21 provide a summary of this body of data.

Table 2A-10. Newsprint Prices and Consumption, 1790-1970 (Prices in $/lb—consumption in tons of 2,000 lbs)

Year	Newsprint Consumption	Price	Standard Pages per Newspaper (Index)
1790		.150	
1800			
1810		.150	
1821		.170	
1828	1,300	.160	7.7
1832		.120	
1853		.100	
1860		.083	
1870		.123	
1875		.085	
1880	94,573	.069	12.2
1885		.052	
1890		.038	
1895		.031	
1899	569,000	.021	17.5
1905		.024	
1909	1,159,000	.021	22.3
1914	1,567,000	.023	
1919	1,895,000	.039	31.7
1923	2,778,000		
1929	3,775,800	.031	44.3
1933	2,680,600	.021	
1950	5,521,000[a]	.047	47.7 (36)
1960	6,800,000[a]	.064	53.6 (43)
1970	9,071,000[a]	.070	67.9 (47)

[a]Consumption by dailies only.

Source: Lee [44], Table XXVI, p. 742, for consumption and price data, 1790-1933; *Statistical Abstract* (1973), Table 576, p. 353, for prices, 1950-1970, and Table 823, p. 504 for consumption. Pages per copy calculated by formula: pages = (tons used X 2000 X 72) / (daily circulation X 310). There are nowadays approximately 72 standard size pages per pound of newsprint, and the formula assumes 310 days of publication per year. However, newsprint consumption includes weekly and Sunday papers; therefore this series should be regarded as a rough index only. (Data in parenthesis for 1950-70 are actual averages for daily papers only from *Statistical Abstract* (1973), Table 823, p. 504.)

Table 2A-11. Copies of Newspapers Mailed, by Circulation of Daily Newspaper, 1965

Circulation (daily)	Percent of Total Circulation Mailed
less than 5,000	29
5,000–10,000	19
10,000–25,000	12
25,000–50,000	9
50,000–100,000	8
more than 100,000	8

Source: *Mathematica* [50] p. 4-1083.

Table 2A-12. Daily Newspaper Subscription Prices, 1851-1970

Year	Newspaper Prices in Cents per Copy	Consumer Price Index (1860 = 100)	Real Newspaper Prices (1860 cents)
1851	1.9	92	2.1
1855	1.9	104	1.8
1860	2.1	100	2.1
1865	2.8	175	1.6
1870	2.9	141	2.1
1875	2.9	123	2.4
1880	3.1	110	2.8
1885	2.7	102	2.8
1889	2.3	104	2.2
1899	1.3	94	1.4
1909	1.4	103	1.4
1919/20	1.9	211	.9
1929/30	3.0	192	1.6
1970	9.2	436	2.1

Percentage Change Between selected years:

1880-1899	-58	-14	-50
1900-1919/20	+46	+124	-36
1880-1919/20	-39	+92	-68

Sources: These data are patched together from a number of sources. The earlier years are based on prices in a handful of sample cities, while the later years (1899 onwards) are based on industry wide census data which are polluted with weekly newspaper and periodical data. The 1970 data are based on a random sample from *Editor and Publisher Yearbook*. Several different price indexes have been linked together; in general this produces rather unreliable results. Accordingly the data should be regarded as indicative only of broad trends. The basic sources are: Ethel Hoover, "Retail Prices After 1850," in NBER Studies in Income and Wealth, volume 24; *Trends in the American Economy in the Nineteenth Century* (Princeton Univ. Press, 1960), pp. 142, 149, 162, 176; Clarence Long, *Wages and Prices in the United States 1860-1890*, (NBER and Princeton Univ. Press, 1960) p. 160; *Historical Statistics of the United States*, pp. 125-126; and Tables 2-3 and 2-11.

Table 2A-13. Weekly Newspaper Circulation, 1951-1970

Year	Aggregate Weekly Circulation (millions)
1951	17.3
1960	22.8
1970	29.4

Source: *Mathematica* [50], p. 4-1103.

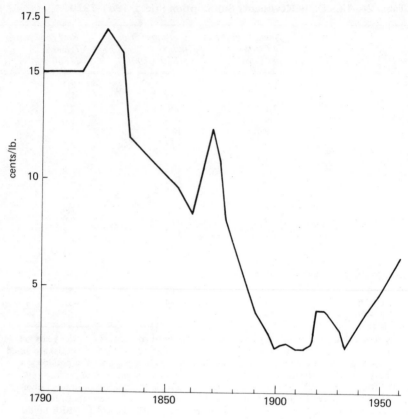

Figure 2A–6.   Price of Newsprint, 1790–1960 (current cents per pound)
Source: Table 2A–10.

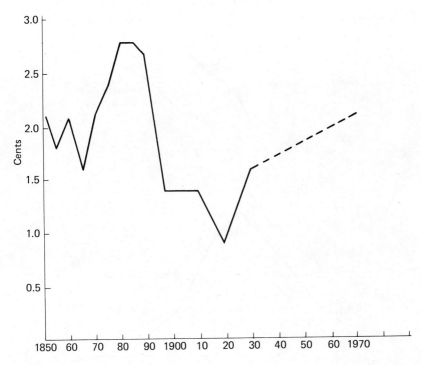

Figure 2A-7. Real Daily Newspaper Subscription Prices (in 1860 Dollars)

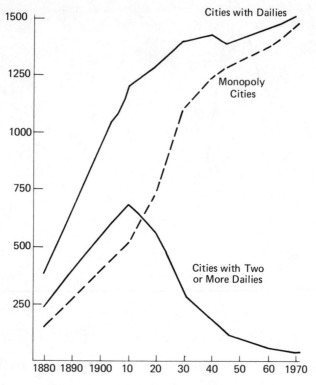

Figure 2A-8. Newspaper Cities, 1880-1970
Source: Table 2A-15.

Table 2A-14. Newspaper and Periodical Revenues, 1849-1929 (millions of dollars)

Year	Industry Revenues	Job Printing	Sub-scriptions	Advertising	Percent Industry Revenue from Newspapers
1849	9				
1859	21				
1869	25				
1879	89	–	50	–	39	
1889	180	36	73	71	
1899	223	47	80	96	
1909	406	68	135	203	69
1919	924	118	278	528	70
1929	1,738	158	460	1,120	68
			Percentages		
1879	100	–	56	–	44	
1889	100	20	41	39	
1899	100	21	36	43	
1909	100	17	33	50	
1919	100	13	30	57	
1929	100	9	26	64	

Source: Based on Lee [44], Tables XXX and XXIX, pp. 748-750.

Note: *Daily and Sunday Newspaper Revenues, 1958-1967*

	Total	Advertising	Subscriptions
1958	3,125	2,209 (71%)	916 (29%)
1963	3,792	2,728 (72%)	1,064 (28%)
1967	4,962	3,653 (74%)	1,039 (26%)

Source: Statistical Abstract (1973) p. 502.

Table 2A-15. Daily Newspaper Competition, 1880-1971 (General Interest English Language Dailies)

Year	Cities with Daily	Cities with 1 Daily Firm	Cities with 2+ Daily Firms
1880	389	150	239
1910	1,207	518	689
1920	1,295	743	552
1930	1,402	1,114	288
1940	1,426	1,245	181
1945	1,396	1,279	117
1961	1,461	1,400	61
1971	1,511	1,474	37

Source: *Editor and Publisher*, July 17, 1971, p. 1.

Table 2A–16.   Structure of Daily Newspapers, 1923–1973

	Year									Percent Change 1923–1973
	1923	1933	1943	1948	1953	1958	1963	1968	1973	
No. Firms	1,977	1,745	1,597	1,536	1,582	1,545	1,552	1,547	1,566	−21
Agg. Circulation (10^6)	30	37	44	51	54	57	60	61	61	103
Mean Circ. (000)	15	21	28	33	34	37	39	39	39	160
Median Circ. (000)	4	5	6	7	8	9	10	11	12	200
Max. Circ. (000)	623	1,411	2,013	2,402	2,180	2,079	2,055	2,112	2,103	238
Agg. Sunday Circ. (10^6)				44			47	48	50	
Mean Sunday Circ. (000)				91			87	85	84	
No. Sunday papers				486			539	562	594	
Agg. Morning Circ. (10^6)				20			23	24	24	
Mean Morning Circ. (000)				65			80	81	76	
No. Morning papers				310			288	296	314	
Agg. Evening Circ. (10^6)				30			34	36	36	
Mean Evening Circ. (000)				21			23	26	26	
No. Evening Papers				1,405			1,430	1,411	1,397	
No. Firms by Type										
Evening	1,339	1,141	1,024	972	964	938	930	901	875	−35
Morning	106	80	65	49	63	45	69	66	80	−24
Evening Sunday	204	222	225	249	301	309	309	332	359	76
Morning Sunday	282	133	96	77	59	60	55	56	71	−75
Morning, Evening, Sun.	26	139	151	154	165	166	170	165	155	496
Daily & Sunday	1	0	2	5	5	4	5	11	12	1,100
Morning & Evening	19	29	30	30	23	17	9	11	9	−53
Daily	0	1	3	1	2	6	5	5	5	—
Monopoly Cities	795	1,183	1,297	1,283	1,364	1,377	1,425	1,450	1,482	86
Cities with 2 Firms	404	205	118	93	74	57	42	38	33	−92
Cities with 3+ Firms	103	38	19	16	17	9	9	5	4	−96
Total Cities	1,302	1,426	1,434	1,392	1,455	1,443	1,476	1,493	1,519	17

Source: Based on Rosse et al. [79].

Table 2A-17. Competition in the Newspaper Industry

Year	No. of Firms in Multipaper Cities	Percent of Firms in Multipaper Cities	Percent of Daily Papers Sold by Firms in Multipaper Cities
1923	1,182	59.8	88.8
1933	562	32.2	73.9
1943	318	19.9	64.2
1948	253	16.5	62.0
1953	218	13.7	54.2
1958	168	10.9	51.7
1963	127	8.2	43.3
1968	97	6.3	36.1
1973	84	5.4	32.2

Source: Based on Rosse et al. [79].

Table 2A-18.   Daily Newspaper Size Distribution—Daily Circulation, End Points of Deciles, Smallest to Largest

Year Decile	1923	1933	1943	1948	1953	1958	1963	1968	1973
0%	211	385	480	500	840	910	1,100	1,215	600
10	1,286	1,659	2,372	2,725	3,082	3,273	3,681	3,844	4,000
20	1,829	2,439	3,225	3,775	3,929	4,291	4,609	5,027	5,378
30	2,460	3,060	3,984	4,639	4,944	5,397	5,813	6,223	6,937
40	3,050	3,815	4,835	5,851	6,284	6,837	7,410	8,085	8,619
50	3,871	4,731	6,072	7,322	8,217	9,104	9,805	10,521	11,643
60	5,276	6,626	8,571	10,293	11,116	12,191	13,374	14,504	15,591
70	8,424	10,102	13,187	15,540	17,106	18,325	19,723	21,429	22,674
80	14,246	18,439	24,974	27,848	29,321	31,057	31,049	34,509	35,461
90	32,240	42,012	60,598	74,173	76,431	81,020	76,549	75,318	76,015
100	622,749	1,410,901	2,013,200	2,402,368	2,179,693	2,079,423	2,055,266	2,112,244	2,103,363

Source: Based on Rosse et al. [79].

Table 2A-19. Percent of Total Daily Circulation, by Quartiles

Years	Smallest 25%	Second 25%	Third 25%	Largest 25%
1923	2.2	4.8	10.4	82.5
1933	2.2	4.4	9.2	84.2
1943	2.2	4.2	9.3	84.3
1948	2.2	4.2	9.1	84.5
1953	2.3	4.4	9.7	83.6
1958	2.3	4.5	9.7	83.5
1963	2.4	4.6	10.0	83.0
1968	2.5	4.9	10.7	81.9
1973	2.8	5.4	11.4	80.4

	Percent of Total Daily Circulation for Largest 10%, 5%, 1% Firms		
Years	10%	5%	1%
1923	64.9	50.3	22.6
1933	67.4	52.8	23.2
1943	66.6	51.3	22.4
1948	67.9	52.5	22.8
1953	66.6	50.8	21.0
1958	66.5	50.2	19.2
1963	65.7	52.3	22.1
1968	64.8	50.3	20.7
1973	66.3	49.3	20.6

Source: Based on Rosse et al. [79].

Table 2A–20. Circulation and Population, 1923–1973

	Year						Percent Change 1923–1973
	1923	1933	1943	1953	1963	1973	
Combined Daily Circ. (10^6)	30	37	44	54	60	61	103
Population (10^6)	112	126	137	160	189	210	88
Households (10^6)[a]	24	30	35	43	53	63	162
Circulation per population × 100	27	29	32	34	32	29	7
Circulation per household × 100[a]	125	123	126	126	113	97	–22

[a]Households are for preceding decade years (1920, 1930, etc.) from Census data.

Source: Based on Rosse et al. [79].

Table 2A-21. Daily Newspaper Firms and Circulation, by City Size

| Year | *City Size (000)* | | | | | |
	less than 10	*10-99*	*100-500*	*500-1,000*	*more than 1,000*	*Total*
	Circulation (000)					
1948	1,676	13,280	13,908	8,533	13,947	51,345
1958	1,753	15,594	16,594	10,255	13,013	57,209
1968	1,741	18,113	17,957	11,052	11,955	60,817
1973	1,758	19,728	17,460	10,950	11,389	61,285
Percent change, 1948-1973	+5%	+49%	+26%	+28%	-18%	+19%
	No. of Firms					
1948	451	881	137	337	30	1,536
1958	409	927	137	44	28	1,545
1968	365	975	151	34	22	1,547
1973	333	1,030	149	33	21	1,566
Percent change, 1948-1973	-26%	+17%	+9%	-11%	-30%	+2

Source: Rosse et al. [79].

Chapter Three

Radio and Television

The result [of a right of paid access to broadcast stations for editorial announcements] would be a further erosion of the journalistic discretion of broadcasters in the coverage of public issues, and a transfer of control from the licensees who are accountable for broadcast performance to private individuals who are not. The public interest would no longer be "paramount" but, rather, subordinate to private whim. . . .

—Opinion of the Chief Justice
(and the Court) in *CBS v. DNC*,
412 U.S. 94, 124 (1972)

Nor is it enough that he should hear the arguments from his own teachers, presented as they state them, and accompanied by what they offer as refutations. That is not the way to do justice to the arguments, or to bring them into real contact with his own mind. He must be able to hear them from persons who actually believe them; who defend them in earnest, and do their very utmost for them.

—J.S. Mill, *On Liberty*

Deep down most politicians feel that the broadcasters have too much power. They will make conversation about newspapers too, but they know they cannot expunge First Amendment history. They know from the polls and by the record that most of the voters are too preoccupied or too lazy to read newspapers or magazines in depth, but that they do look and listen.

—From an editorial in *Broadcasting*,
August 12, 1974

INTRODUCTION—EARLY HISTORY
OF BROADCASTING

Broadcasting is unique among the mass media in America, for it is the only medium subject to direct government regulation and licensing. Licensing of the press has always been contrary to the spirit of the First Amendment. It was initiated for broadcasting in an era when sober men did not regard broadcasting as a part of the "press," and it continues today for rather different reasons.

Aside from its peculiar status as a regulated medium, broadcasting seems to have enormous social import. The survey firms that supply ratings of programs claim that Americans spend an almost unbelievable number of hours each day watching television. Children especially view television a great deal, and there is considerable controversy concerning the effects of this on their development. Many (perhaps most) adults depend on television for news and entertainment to a greater degree than on newspapers and other print media.

In this chapter we are concerned with the economics of television, the theory and practice of regulation, and the ways that economic analysis can give insight into policies designed to increase freedom of expression in broadcasting, both radio and TV.

The early history of broadcasting has left an unfortunate legacy for freedom of expression. From the beginning, congressional committees and courts, with no real understanding of the technology of spectrum utilization, combined with happenstance to produce a framework of legal and policy attitudes favoring what now seem to be exactly the wrong institutional structures for the broadcast media.[1]

Four factors were influential from the beginning. The first was the obvious usefulness of radio to military units and to safety and rescue services. This invited early government control. The second was that broadcasting emerged first as an amateurish novelty, used, for example, by department stores for publicity stunts, and that these uses challenged use of the spectrum for safety purposes. The third factor was the absence of any serious attempt to establish by legislation a system of transferable property rights in the spectrum. Finally, early broadcast technology was characterized by the absence of any practical mechanism for enforcing payment by listeners for the service they received.

Speculation about historical events that take the "for want of a nail" line are seldom fruitful. Nevertheless, the consequences of the early history of broadcasting are sufficiently important that some insight may be gained from a few "what if" questions. For instance, if initial uses of the electromagnetic spectrum had not involved military and safety services, it is possible that the governments of the world would have been less ready to exercise control over the allocation of this resource. In that event, commercial users who faced the problems of interference and chaotic allocation conditions would presumably have exerted pressure on courts and Congress to establish a system of property rights in the spectrum. In any event, this trend was thwarted by the government's direct resort to fiat allocation. Similarly, broadcasting might have begun with wire transmissions rather than over-the-air transmissions, or it might have begun with sufficiently complex receivers that broadcasters could have exercised control of a rental market in receivers in order to collect from listeners for the broadcast service.[a] In either case, the dominant role of advertising in determining industry structure might not have developed.

The climate of opinion generated by early uses of the technology resulted, however, in fiat allocation and in free (zero price) radio service. These "accidental" beginnings were incorporated in the Radio Act of 1927 and later in the Communications Act of 1934. Fiat allocation of the spectrum in the public interest by a group of administrative agencies (chiefly the FCC and IRAC[2]) became imbedded in the law, and it was not long before a body of judicial philosophy evolved to defend this state of affairs (see *National Broadcasting Co. v. United States*, 319 U.S. 190 (1943)). Of course, no one in the early days of radio could foresee the enormous importance that television would come to have. Probably few people saw radio, in 1927, as an important source of news and opinion, or as a part of the "press" contemplated by the First Amendment.

The Federal Radio Commission and its successor, the FCC, embarked on a program of awarding radio broadcast licenses. Initial concern was centered on technical questions of interference: power levels, antenna locations, hours of operation, and the like. But at a zero price there was more demand for licenses than the amount of spectrum the government wished to make available for this particular use. Some criterion was needed for selecting among the applicants and for renewing existing licenses.

Congress's instructions on this point were far from clear: the Commission was to award licenses in a way that served the public interest. Since no reasonable application of this criterion by the Commission could avoid examination of the content of communications, that content became the subject of regulation. It is true that at first this regulation was quite general and benign. But as we shall see, the foundation was laid for increasingly detailed federal regulation of content in the electronic media.

The remaining major implication of early decisions was equally profound. The Commission allocated less spectrum to broadcasting than was demanded at the price of a license. The result was the creation of scarcity rents or excess profits associated with the license itself. This in turn established a class of firms with a vested economic interest in the status quo of regulation and technology—an interest group with both economic and political power—and this precedent was perpetuated and worsened when television frequencies were allocated.

The elementary economic and political error involved in this allocation decision might have been avoided either by providing more spectrum for broad-

---

[a] Actual receivers were too easy to build—or "pirate"—thus making them useless as exclusion devices.

casting (and therefore less for other services) or by changing technical standards so as to accommodate all the demand, or by charging a license fee that cleared the market at the supply level preferred by the Commission. These things might have been done at the onset with little political cost. The moment they were not done, the vested interests created a formidable block to reform which has continued to the present day. Perhaps worse, a myth was created that there was a limited supply of spectrum for broadcasting, and this myth provided the rationale for a long series of judicial decisions confirming the Commission's policies, and undermining freedom of expression in the electronic media.

The major point can be illustrated vividly by a hypothetical example. Suppose the government decided that because of its (considerable) effect on the environment, the papermaking industry should be nationalized as a public resource: "trees belong to the people." Moreover, the "Federal Paper Commission" would grant licenses to individuals allowing the consumption of paper produced by the government. The licenses would be awarded in a manner that served the public interest, and at a zero price. Obviously, at a zero price, demand would exceed supply at present production levels, and the government would either have to expand production or allocate licenses on some other basis. Since expansion of production would harm the environment, licenses would have to be awarded only to a limited number of individuals who used the paper in a manner that served the public interest. The Commission would have to inquire into the content of matter printed on the paper. Before long, government control of print media content would be full blown. This example seems silly only because no one is frightened by the technology of paper introduction. But the historical development of radio regulation has no greater justification, save only the absence of a preexisting set of rules governing property rights in the resource itself.

SPECTRUM ALLOCATION

The electromagnetic spectrum is a medium of communication as well as an input to various noncommunication production processes. Among the uses to which the spectrum can be put, besides radio and television broadcasting, are: radar, military communications, microwave relay systems, police radio systems, ham and amateur services, taxicabs and delivery vehicle dispatch, microwave ovens, and communication satellites. The signals involved in these uses can, in many cases, be sent over wires (or otherwise be "contained") as well as over the air.

The physical characteristics of the spectrum are such that a full specification of the signal requires a multidimensional enumeration of characteristics.[3] Among these are frequency or wavelength, modulation technique, polarization, geographic space, and time. A crucial characteristic of the signal for reception purposes is the signal to noise ratio, where "noise" is the presence of unwanted interference from various sources. Thus the "quality" of a signal is a function not merely of its own characteristics but also the character of interfering signals. In the absence of a property right, this phenomenon can be regarded as an externality. The nature of the externality is such that negotiation among users is difficult, so that the Coase Theorem cannot be applied.[4]

There are two solutions to the interference problem. The first is the use of private markets and private property rights.[5] These could evolve either through common law adjudication of infringement suits, or by legislation. Some parts of the spectrum have an international character, requiring that the problem be dealt with on that level. The second approach is government or monopoly allocation. This internalizes the interference externalities. In either case, the spectrum can be allocated more or less efficiently among users and uses by equating marginal social costs and benefits, to the extent that appropriate information is available. One way to generate this information in a centralized system of allocation is to auction off leasehold or rental rights. Any of these alternatives can in principle achieve economic efficiency in the use of the spectrum; if this were all that was at stake, the choice among them would be purely pragmatic.

But more is at stake. The use of part of the spectrum (not a large part) for broadcasting means that both the monopoly solution and the government allocation solution raise certain First Amendment issues. These difficulties are not insuperable. There is no necessary conflict between centralized spectrum allocation and freedom of expression, provided that the allocation rules are neutral with respect to the content of the signals. But even this is too strong a statement; since the content of signals has something to do with the economic value of the signal, the allocation system can take this into account without losing its neutrality. For instance, the government can allocate spectrum by auction, and adjust the rights definitions until the criteria for efficiency are met as nearly as possible.

The spectrum is not a limited resource in any sense beyond the sense in which other economic resources are limited. Indeed, physically, the spectrum is infinite, although only parts of it are usable for communication under current technology. The spectrum can thus be used more or less intensively. The best analogy is that as the price of paper goes up, one would expect people to use narrower margins. The "margins" in spectrum use are also variable: if more money is spent on equipment quality, less spectrum is needed for a given signal.[b] Similarly, spectrum has many substitutes, including wires, paper, and travel. The presence of substitutes, and the fact that spectrum can be used in variable proportions with equipment to produce signals, means that the allocation mechanism, whether centralized or private, must take account of the prices of substitutes and complementary inputs in order even to approximate efficiency.

[b]For example, communication equipment is seldom perfectly on the correct frequency. Accordingly, there are buffer zones to prevent interference between adjacent channels. As the accuracy and cost of the equipment (both transmitter and receiver) increases, these buffer zones can be decreased, thus allowing more channels.

The preceding analysis of spectrum allocation, when contrasted with the actual manner in which the allocation is presently carried out, leads directly to two serious indictments: (1) The present allocation scheme cannot be economically efficient; society would, from a purely economic point of view, be better off with some allocation other than the present one. (2) The present allocation scheme is quite unnecessarily in conflict with the First Amendment.

These two indictments are based on the fact that the allocation of spectrum is now based on what are, from an economic point of view, entirely arbitrary rules and traditions. The FCC allocates spectrum in the public interest. In practice, this means spectrum is allocated according to tradition and current political equilibria, equilibria in which the consumers' interest is not in fact well represented. Since license fees are minimal, no user has anything like the proper incentives to use inputs in the right proportion, or to substitute other media appropriately.[c] Moreover, in broadcasting, the allocation is far from independent of the content of messages. Allocation is not neutral from the First Amendment viewpoint; instead, the government decides what kinds of messages, and how many, shall be broadcast, purely from the point of view of its own ill-defined standard of public welfare. This is to be distinguished from an attempt to simulate the results of a private market, which is for some reason thought to be impractical. In the latter case there must be an explicit attempt to determine the parameters of consumer demand, while in the former there is reference only to what consumers "ought" to see and hear. The process by which the government determines what messages shall be broadcast includes both direct regulation of these messages and the selection of licensees on the basis of their representations as to what programs they will broadcast in the future.

CURRENT STATUS OF BROADCASTING

Broadcast stations sell audiences to advertisers. They attract the audiences, of course, by broadcasting "free" programs. In this respect also, broadcasting is a unique medium: other media combine advertiser and subscriber support, or depend on subscribers entirely. There are more than 900 TV broadcast stations in the United States, and upwards of 7,500 radio stations. Many of these (220 of the TV stations) are educational or public broadcasting stations (see Table 3-1). Tables 3-2 to 3-10 present a financial profile of the television industry in 1972 and 1973. Note the dominance of the networks in general, and of VHF network affiliated stations in the top 100 markets (cities) in particular.

Networks dominate TV broadcasting, which is a result of the economies of sharing program costs over large audiences. The overwhelming majority of viewer hours are spent watching shows produced or selected by the three net-

---

[c]This is aggravated by the fact that much of the spectrum is allocated for government use, where incentives for internal efficiency are slack to begin with. See Weitzman [94] for an explanation of spectrum users' resistance to fees and property rights.

Table 3-1. Broadcast Stations on the Air, October 31, 1974

Type of Station	Number on Air
Radio	
Commercial AM	4422
Commercial FM	2605
Educational FM	711
Television	
Commercial VHF	514
Commercial UHF	196
Educational VHF	95
Educational UHF	144

Source: FCC data.

Table 3-2. Broadcast Revenues, Expenses, and Income of Television Networks and Stations, 1973 (in millions of dollars)

	1973
Broadcast revenues[a]	
3 networks	$1,404.9
15 network owned-and-operated stations	353.1
All other stations	
474 VHF[b]	1,497.4
177 UHF[c]	209.4
Subtotal	1,706.8
Industry Total	3,464.8
Broadcast expenses	
3 networks	$1,220.0
15 network owned-and-operated stations	250.3
All other stations	
474 VHF[b]	1,124.3
177 UHF[c]	217.0
Subtotal	1,341.4
Industry Total	2,811.7
Broadcast income (before federal income tax)	
3 networks	$ 184.8
15 network owned-and-operated stations	102.8
All other stations	
474 VHF[b]	373.1
177 UHF[c]	(7.7)
Subtotal	365.4
Industry Total	653.1

[a]Net, after commissions to agencies, representatives and brokers, after cash discounts.

[b]The 474 VHF stations represent 496 operations including 22 satellite stations that filed a combined report with their parent stations. The 1972 data reflect 475 VHF stations representing 493 operations including 18 satellites that filed a combined report with their parent stations.

[c]The 177 UHF stations represent 181 operations including 4 satellites that filed a combined report with their parent stations. The 1972 data reflect 173 UHF stations representing 182 operations including nine satellites that filed a combined report with their parent stations.

Notes: Last digits may not add to totals because of rounding. ( ) denotes loss.

Source: FCC data.

Table 3-3.   Revenue and Expense Items for All TV Stations Reporting, 1973 (in thousands of dollars)

	Individual Items	Totals
Broadcast revenues		
A. Revenues from the Sale of Station Time:		
(1) Network		
Sale of station time to networks:		
Sale of station time to major networks, ABC, CBS, NBC (before line or service charges)	$ 227,310	
Sale of station time to other networks (before line or service charges)	5,699	
Total		$ 233,009
(2) Nonnetwork (after trade and special discounts but before cash discounts to advertisers and sponsors, and before commissions to agencies, representatives and brokers).		
Sale of station time to national and regional advertisers or sponsors	1,221,058	
Sale of station time to local advertisers or sponsors	895,663	
Total		2,116,721
Total sale of station time		2,349,730
B. Broadcast Revenues Other than from Sale of Station Time (after deduction for trade discounts but before cash discounts and before commissions):		
Program Expenses:		
Payroll for employes considered "talent"	251,115	
Payroll for all other program employes	218,601	
Rental and amortization of film and tape	1,451	
Records and transcriptions	16,269	
Cost of outside news services	11,799	
Payments to talent other than reported above	41,557	
Music-license fees	23,486	
Other performance and program rights	116,398	
All other program expenses		
Total program expenses		680,677
Selling Expenses:		
Selling payroll	99,317	
All other selling expenses	101,192	
Total selling expenses		200,510
General and Administrative Expenses:		
General and administrative payroll	91,300	
Depreciation and amortization	107,921	
Interest	37,964	
Allocated costs of management from home office or affiliate(s)	44,357	
Other general and administrative		

(1) Revenues from separate charges made for programs, materials, facilities and services supplied to advertisers or sponsors in connection with sale of station time:			
(a) to national and regional advertisers or sponsors	9,121		
(b) to local advertisers or sponsors	36,454		
(2) Other broadcast revenues	30,338		
Total broadcast revenues, other than from time sales		75,913	215,145
Total general and administrative expenses			496,688
Total Broadcast Expenses			1,591,044
C. Total Broadcast Revenues		2,425,644	
Broadcast income			$2,059,934[b]
Net broadcast revenues			1,591,718[b]
Broadcast expenses			468,216
Broadcast operating income			
(1) Less commissions to agencies, representatives, and brokers (but not to staff salesmen or employes) and less cash discounts	365,797		
Total of any amounts included in expenses (salaries, commissions, management fees, rents, etc.) for services or materials supplied by the owners or stockholders or any close relative of such persons or any affiliated company under common control			32,809
D. Net Broadcast Revenues[a]		2,059,847	
Broadcast expenses			
Technical expenses:			
Technical payroll	$ 146,993		
All other technical expenses	66,176		
Total technical expenses	$ 213,169		

[a]Includes $61,438,000 from barter and trade-out transactions.

[b]Stations reporting less than $25,000 in total revenues are not required to report items under revenues and expenses but are required to report total income. Therefore, totals under revenues and expenses are somewhat lower than totals under income.

Note: Last digits may not add to totals because of rounding.

Source: FCC data.

Table 3–4. Broadcast Financial Data of Three Television Networks and 692 Stations, 1973 (in millions of dollars)

Broadcast Revenues, Expenses and Income	Networks	15 Owned-and-Operated TV Stations	677 Other TV Stations[a]	Total Three Networks and 692 Stations[a]
Sales to advertisers for time, programs, talent, facilities, and services.				
Network sales	$1,835.3			
Deduct: Payments to owned-and-operated stations	35.3			
Deduct: Payments to other affiliated stations	193.3			
Retained from network sales	1,606.7	$ 35.4[b]	$ 197.6[b]	$1,839.7
Nonnetwork sales				
- To national and regional advertisers	—	$273.4	956.7	1,230.2
- To local advertisers	—	113.4	818.8	932.2
Total nonnetwork sales	—	386.8	1,775.6	2,162.4
Total sales to advertisers	1,606.7	422.3	1,973.1	4,002.1
Sales to other than advertisers	74.9	5.8	24.6	105.2
Total sales	1,681.6	428.1	1,997.7	4,107.3
Deduct: Commissions to agencies, representatives, etc.	276.7	74.9	290.9	642.5
Total Broadcast Revenues	1,404.9	353.1	1,706.8	3,464.8
Total Broadcast Expense	1,220.0	250.3	1,341.4	2,811.7
Total Income (before federal income tax)	184.8	102.8	365.4	653.1

[a]Includes 64 satellites, 26 of which filed combined reports with their parent stations.
[b]Includes payments from networks other than ABC, CBS or NBC.

Notes: Last digits may not add because of rounding. ( ) indicates decline.

Source: FCC data.

Table 3-5. Broadcast Expenses of Three Networks and TV Stations, 1973[a] (in thousands of dollars)

Item	Technical	Program	Technical plus Program	Selling	General and Administrative	Total Broadcast Expenses
3 Networks	b	b	$1,075,815	$ 40,836	$103,369	$1,220,020
15 Network owned-and-operated stations	$ 42,604	$128,702	171,306	30,751	48,267	250,324
410 Other VHF network-affiliated stations	117,081	372,687	489,768	116,054	326,722	932,544
110 UHF Network-affiliated stations	17,332	37,553	54,885	16,045	41,666	112,595
Total 535 network-affiliated stations	177,017	538,942	715,959	162,850	416,655	1,295,463
32 VHF independent stations	20,518	98,201	118,720	20,009	43,777	182,506
50 UHF independent stations	13,012	40,763	53,775	15,716	30,455	99,946
Total 82 independent stations	33,531	138,964	172,495	35,725	74,232	282,452
Total 617 stations	210,547	677,906	888,453	198,575	490,886	1,577,915
Total 3 networks and 617 stations	—	—	1,964,268	239,411	594,256	2,797,935

[a]Excludes part-year stations, satellite stations and those with less than $25,000 of time sales.

[b]Because methods of treating technical and program expenses differ among the networks, the two figures have been combined.

Note: Last digits may not add to totals because of rounding.

Source: FCC data.

Table 3-6. Revenue and Expense Items of Three National TV Networks, 1973 (in thousands of dollars)

	Amount
Net broadcast revenues	
I. Network Revenues:	
(a) Revenues from sale of time when program is supplied by advertiser	$ 44,134
(b) All other advertising revenues	1,791,167
(c) Revenues from stations for cooperative programs	4,226
(d) All other broadcast revenues	70,655
Total gross broadcast revenues	1,910,182
Value of trade-out and barter transactions included in "all other broadcast revenues"	11,004
II. Deduct:	
(a) Payments to stations	228,568
(b) Commissions to advertising agencies, representatives, brokers and others, and cash discounts	276,745
Total deductions	505,314
III. Net Broadcast Revenues	1,404,869
Network broadcast expenses	
General Categories of Expenses:	a
Technical expenses	
Program expenses	$1,075,815
Selling expenses	40,836
General and administrative expenses	103,369
Total Broadcast Expenses	1,220,020
Selected Expense Items	
Salaries, wages and bonuses of officers and employees engaged in following categories:	a
(a) Technical	
(b) Program	163,421
(c) Selling	14,559
(d) General and administrative	48,682
(e) Total (all officers and employes)	226,663
Depreciation of tangible property	18,390
Amortization expense on programs obtained from others (total)	624,430
(a) Feature film shown or expected to be shown in U.S. theaters	140,481
(b) All other feature film	17,391
(c) All other programs	466,558
Records and transcriptions	3,128
Music-license fees	6,248
Other performance or program rights	75,467
Cost of intercity and intracity program relay circuits	53,148
Total expense for news and public affairs[b]	139,836
Network broadcast income	
Broadcast revenues	$1,404,869
Broadcast expenses	1,220,020
Broadcast operating income	184,848

[a]Because methods of treating technical and program expense differ among the networks, the two figures have been combined.

[b]This figure contains costs already shown above. Costs of sports programs are not included.

Note: Last digits may not add to totals because of rounding.

Source: FCC data.

Table 3-7.   Share of Top 100 Markets in TV Revenues, 1972

	Top 100 Markets (369 stations)		All Others (294 stations)	
	($000)	*% total*	*($000)*	*% total*
Time sales:				
Network	179,900	80.1	44,344	19.9
Spot[a]	1,066,347	91.3	101,005	8.7
Local[b]	645,873	82.9	132,197	17.1
Total	1,892,165	87.2	277,746	12.8
Other revenues	61,487	81.8	13,598	18.2
Commissions paid[b]	307,032	91.1	29,889	8.9
Net revenues	1,646,619[c]	86.2	261,456[d]	13.8
Expenses				
Technical	163,420	82.2	35,242	17.8
Program	553,027	87.7	77,470	12.3
Selling	156,437	84.5	28,555	15.5
General & Adm.	354,333	78.4	97,943	21.6
Total	1,227,216	83.6	239,210	16.4
Operating income	419,347	95.0	21,932	5.0

[a]After trade and special discounts but before cash discounts to advertisers and sponsors and before commissions to agencies, representatives and brokers.
[b]Paid to agencies, representatives and brokers, but not to staff salesmen or employes. Figure also includes cash discounts.
[c]Includes $48,706,000 from barter and trade-outs.
[d]Includes $5,966,000 from barter and trade-outs.
Source: FCC data.

works, rather than by stations themselves. Stations can of course choose to produce or purchase their own shows, but it is nearly always less profitable to do so.[6] Independent stations are independent because there are not enough networks to go around in cities with more than three stations. Nevertheless, stations are responsible for program selection in the legal sense, since they and not the networks are licensed. In practice, stations have little power to select programs, especially if there are more than three stations in a city; the network whose programs are not "cleared" often enough will simply threaten to switch affiliations. A station that carries network programs is paid by the network for the audiences thus produced. Of the $1,835 million in gross network revenues in 1973, $229 million was paid to affiliated stations (see Table 3-4). The stations are also allowed to sell commercial time during station breaks in the programs. Stations are interconnected with their networks by microwave commucation channels supplied by the telephone company, for about $50 million per year. In the future these links may be supplied by domestic communication satellite systems.

Table 3-8. Number of Television Stations Reporting Profit or Loss by Amount of Profit or Loss, 1973

	Total		Network Affiliated		Independent	
	VHF	*UHF*	*VHF*	*UHF*	*VHF*	*UHF*
Total number of stations reporting	457	165	425	112	32	53
Number of stations reporting profits	395	77	374	61	21	16
Profitable stations as percent of total	86.4	46.7	88.0	54.5	65.6	30.2
Number of stations reporting profits of:						
$5,000,000 or over	18	–	18	–	–	–
3,000,000–5,000,000	26	–	25	–	1	–
1,500,000–3,000,000	56	1	51	–	5	1
1,000,000–1,500,000	37	–	33	–	4	–
600,000–1,000,000	44	6	41	4	3	2
400,000– 600,000	40	6	39	5	1	1
200,000– 400,000	66	16	60	13	6	3
100,000– 200,000	45	12	45	9	–	3
50,000– 100,000	27	16	26	15	1	1
25,000– 50,000	16	7	16	4	–	3
Less than 25,000	20	13	20	11	–	2
Number of stations reporting losses	62	88	51	51	11	37
Unprofitable stations as percent of total	13.6	53.3	12.0	45.5	34.4	69.8
Number of stations reporting losses of:						
Less than $10,000	4	2	4	1	–	1
10,000– 25,000	4	9	4	5	–	4
25,000– 50,000	6	9	6	7	–	2
50,000–100,000	18	18	17	13	1	5
100,000–200,000	12	15	7	9	5	6
200,000–400,000	12	18	10	14	2	4
400,000 and over	6	17	3	2	3	15

Note: Stations operating full year only excluding satellite stations. Profits are before federal income tax.
Source: FCC data.

For our purposes, the most important role played by local stations—both TV and radio—is in the production of local news stories. Local TV news is popular and profitable.[7] It is often the only source of local news other than a local monopoly newspaper. Unfortunately (perhaps by virtue of its very form), television news on the local level leaves much to be desired. Even leaving aside the recent trend toward "happy talk" local news, dripping with banality, the medium is not a good substitute for print when it comes to detailed coverage of complex events—there simply is not time. Moreover, for reasons to be discussed, local news stories avoid controversy, and avoid catering to minority tastes.

Table 3-9. Investment in Tangible Broadcast Property of TV Networks and 666 TV Stations as of Dec. 31, 1973 (in thousands of dollars)

	Number of Stations[a]	Original Cost[b]	Original Cost Minus Depreciation
Three National networks	–	$ 245,798	$103,395
Network owned-and-operated stations	15	93,954	33,194
Other TV stations			
VHF	474	1,161,795	491,153
UHF	177	229,110	121,362
Total	666	$1,730,658	$749,104

[a]Eight of these stations did not report investment in tangible property; some of these may be operating under lease arrangements. The count of 666 stations represent 692 operations including 26 satellites whose figures were reported in the parent stations' reports.

[b]In case of stations which have been sold, represents that portion of price assigned by licensee to property.

Note: Last digits may not add to totals because of rounding.

Source: FCC data.

Table 3-10. Revenues and Expenses of Stations, by Type, 1972

	452 VHF Affiliates ($000)	34 VHF Independents ($000)	116 UHF Affiliates ($000)	58 UHF Independents ($000)
Time sales:				
Network	206,782	1,631	15,800	276
Spot[a]	943,945	146,691	40,314	36,403
Local[b]	604,668	63,515	58,021	51,866
Total	1,755,396	211,836	114,136	88,544
Other revenues	45,948	18,881	3,729	6,526
Commissions paid[b]	272,202	37,183	13,362	14,172
Net revenues	1,529,141[c]	193,533[d]	104,503[e]	80,898[f]
Expenses				
Technical	149,084	19,935	16,548	13,095
Program	461,008	95,532	33,252	40,706
Selling	137,549	18,584	14,321	14,537
General & Adm.	343,157	40,405	38,688	30,027
Total	1,090,799	174,455	102,808	98,364
Operating income	438,130	19,078	1,628	(17,556)

[a]After trade and special discounts but before cash discounts to advertisers and sponsors and before commissions to agencies, representatives and brokers.

[b]Paid to agencies, representatives and brokers, but not to staff salesmen or employes. Figure also includes cash discounts.

[c]Includes $39,390,000 from barter and trade-outs.

[d]Includes $6,243,000 from barter and trade-outs.

[e]Includes $4,003,000 from barter and trade-outs.

[f]Includes $5,035,000 from barter and trade-outs.

Source: FCC data.

Table 3-11. Hours of Network TV Series Programs per Week Produced by Hollywood Studios, 1974-75 Season

Columbia	4.5
MGM	1.0
Paramount	3.5
20th Century Fox	1.5
Universal (MCA)	13.5
Warner	3.0
Independent Studios	19.5

Source: McAlpine [48].

Local stations are of course in competition with each other and with local newspapers for audiences and advertisers, but this competition is attenuated by the dominant role of network programming. The networks are a three-firm oligopoly with the usual features of oligopoly behavior. There is rivalry among the networks in those dimensions where implicit cooperative behavior is difficult or impossible, especially in program quality.[8]

It is difficult to characterize viewer behavior in general. The evidence is consistent with the view that viewers are rather passive, on average, in their choice of programs: it takes extreme provocation to switch channels. (Network executives apparently believe that a large part of the audience for a given program is determined by the popularity of the preceding program.) On the other hand, viewers may appear to act in this way simply because the programs available are all pretty much alike. In any event, TV viewers spend an enormous amount of time at it—upwards of six hours per adult per day, on average, it is claimed. A successful prime time network TV show reaches about 15,000,000 homes, giving it an audience larger by far than that of most other media messages.[d]

Entertainment programs are produced by program producers or series packagers in Hollywood. This industry is rather competitive. Although the major studios as a group dominate it, independent producers can and do succeed quite often in entering the market. The main market, of course, is for network sales (see Tables 3-11 and 3-12). The syndication market is dominated by shows that have previously run successfully on the networks, and is limited to independent stations and a few hours per day on affiliates of the networks[9] (see Table 3-13).

THEORY OF BROADCAST REGULATION

The legal theory of broadcast regulation rests on constitutional tests of the Communications Act of 1934 and individual Commission policies stemming from that Act. Such tests have not been very numerous: the "network case,"[10]

---

[d]Wire service stories may reach a larger audience, but it is difficult to measure their circulation.

Table 3-12. Program Production Revenues at Major Studios, 1973
(millions of dollars)

Studio	Revenue from Television
Columbia	81
MGM	53
Paramount	50
20th Century Fox	36
United Artists	48
Universal (MCA)	120
Warner	57
Total	444

Note: See Tables 3-3 and 3-5 for expenditures on programming by stations and networks.
These firms had revenues in 1973 from theatrical films of $887 million.
Source: McAlpine [48].

Red Lion (1968), *CBS v. DNC* (1972), and *Midwest Video* (1972).[11] The first and last deal with extentions of FCC authority to technologies or institutions not covered in the Act, under the doctrine of ancillary regulation. (This will be discussed in a later section.) *Red Lion* and *CBS v. DNC* deal with the constitutionality of content regulation, and the First Amendment rights of listeners, viewers, and broadcasters. All of these cases and others (e.g., *Carroll* 1958)[12] share a common theory of broadcast regulation. I will outline this theory and then criticize it.

The premises of the theory are straightforward. The electromagnetic spectrum, so the story goes, is a valuable public resource, and it is in scarce supply. In the absence of government regulation the resource would be unusable because interference among users would result in chaos. Therefore some regulation of private users is essential, and this implies that some persons who would like to use the airwaves must be excluded. To compensate for this, those who are allowed to use the airwaves must adopt a fiduciary relationship to the public, serving as proxies for those who cannot speak directly. Some say, going further,

Table 3-13. Sources of Programming on TV Stations, 1973 (Commercial stations; numbers are percent of total schedule)

Source	Network Affiliates	Independents
Networks	64	11
Syndicated	32	84
Local Production	4[a]	5

[a]This represents about 5½ hours per week.
Source: *Broadcasting Yearbook*, 1974, p. 70.

that licensees become in effect instrumentalities of the state.[e] In any event, the behavior of the licensees must be carefully regulated to ensure proper fiduciary behavior. In particular, they must be required to act "in the public interest." This regulation would not be required if it were not for the scarcity of licenses (or frequencies) and for the role of the licensees as public fiduciaries.

These premises, it is said, require a balancing between the First Amendment rights of the licensee and the public's "right to hear." This balancing permits certain kinds of regulation of the behavior of licensees that would not otherwise be tolerable from the First Amendment viewpoint.

From these premises a number of more specific conclusions are said to follow. Among these are:

1. The ability of a licensee to perform his public service responsibilities is not unrelated to his economic viability. Hence, the government is not free to ignore the effects of its allocation policies on the profits of existing licensees.
2. The FCC can require a licensee to behave in a certain specified way with respect to his carriage of opinions and views on controversial public issues.
3. There does not exist a right of access by the public to the facilities of licensees.
4. The Commission may extend its regulatory jurisdiction to institutions (networks) or technologies (cable television) if this is necessary in order to preserve the Commission's scheme of broadcast regulation.
5. The public interest in broadcast service precludes a general right on the part of the public to enter into contracts with broadcasters to pay for programs.[13]

The implementation of this theory of regulation requires that the government select licensees who promise to perform in the public interest. At certain times, as at license renewal or license challenge, the Commission must evaluate performance in terms of this criterion—that is, the public interest and the promises. This requires examination of program content. While the theory of broadcast regulation clearly and explicitly requires active responsibility by the licensee for program content, and is grounded on the notion that the editorial function is performed solely by licensees, the reality is far different. In practice, broadcasters relinquish control of program content to networks, because this is more profitable than local control.

Advertising time is, for most purposes, sold on a common carrier basis to a well defined subclass of customers. That is, the station or the network publishes

---

[e]The notion that broadcast licensees are instrumentalities of the state under the so-called state action doctrine has not been accepted by a majority of the Supreme Court (see *CBS v. DNC*, 412 U.S. at 171, (1973), Brennan, J., dissenting). It was, however, accepted by the court of appeals in that case. The state instrumentalities theory is not essential to the argument summarized here.

a rate card setting forth the prices at which it will accept advertising matter. Commercial advertisers who wish to buy time simply pay the rate; so long as they are advertising standard products or services there is no discrimination among them. This would not be true of someone who wished to advertise noncommercial ideas. The audience, far from being the object of service, is merely an intermediate product. Audiences are not served in the sense of the legal theory; they are instead attracted and then sold to advertisers. The broadcaster's concern for his audience is akin to the farmer's concern for his cattle.

Finally, the government does not live up to its own theory of regulation—that is, notions of the public interest that might generally be considered consistent with the paternalism of the overall theory are not in fact employed in the process of license award and renewal. Activities that from the paternalistic viewpoint could be regarded as rather atrocious violations of the fiduciary role are tolerated by the Commission until overwhelming external pressure is brought to bear. Examples include the quiz show scandals, cigarette advertising, and violence on children's programming.

What I have called the paternalistic view of media regulation has perfectly respectable roots in philosophical thought, going back to the Platonic notion that art should serve some social purpose. This is in contrast to the Aristotelian view of art as an emotional purgative. Thus Plato and the Puritans would endorse prohibitions on televised violence while Aristotle would defend such programming as a vicarious substitute for real action. Neither argument is concerned with notions of freedom, but the Aristotelian view is of course more consistent with freedom of expression. (One can, I think, make the case that political expression and news are "art.") One of the problems faced by modern day conservatives is that they are apt to believe in both freedom of expression and the Platonic view of art; libertarians seldom wish to be libertines.

The premises of broadcast regulation are largely false. The conclusions which have been asserted to follow from those premises are not, in fact, logical derivations, and are in any event not unique—that is, there are other conclusions that could be drawn which are more consistent with freedom of expression. Finally, the reality of broadcaster behavior and the practice of regulation do not accord with the theory. There are a number of levels on which the theory of broadcast regulation can be criticized. One can attack the premises, or the logical consistency of the conclusions, or the departure of reality and theory.

It is important to point out at once that one of the principal reasons why reality and theory diverge is that the legal theory contains no recognition of economic incentives. There is a pretense that licensees can be expected to act in a fiduciary role without regard for their own self-interest. Moreover, because the theory recognizes no divergence between the economic interests of the licensee and his fiduciary trust, it fails to provide any mechanism for balancing or channeling these conflicting incentives—much less a mechanism for actually harnessing the economic incentives to achieve the public interest objectives.

To the extent that such a mechanism exists, it lies in the threat of license revocation or nonrenewal, a brutal and awkward tool.

What lies beind this failure of law and policy? We have already examined the historical and technological "accidents" involved. There seem to be at least two factors at work. The first is simple ignorance on the part of courts, commissions, and congressional committees of the economics and technology of broadcasting. They are uninformed about the first and frightened by the second. The other factor is a certain psychological attitude toward the electronic media. Many people regard television, for instance, as being too powerful and influential to be allowed freedom from government control. This attitude is not at all limited to liberals; many people who would otherwise regard themselves as conservative have this feeling.[f]

Of course, a good deal of the "power and influence" of television is due to government policies limiting spectrum allocations to broadcasting and otherwise tending to produce concentration of control. This is somewhat Orwellian. The power of the networks, often cited as a rationale for government control, is the *result* of government control. But the feeling is deeper than this. Perhaps it has something to do with McLuhan effects—the nature of the medium conditioning and interacting with sociological phenomena. Hard as it may be to defend, this feeling plays an enormously important role in determining media policy. There may be something to it. If so, there exists a range of tools available to policy makers for dealing with it: tools which are less intrusive on First Amendment freedoms (and certainly more effective) than present regulatory policy and practice. If television is dangerous to society, maybe we would be better off without it. That is an acceptable proposition. What is not acceptable is the notion that a dangerous medium should or can safely be "controlled" by the government, in the sense of content regulation and licensing.

It may be that all of this is no deeper than the fear with which the medieval church and state viewed the technology of printing. (The *Index Liborum Prohibitorum* was first published in 1564.) That technology certainly did have "dangerous" sociological and cultural implications for the status quo, though these are easily exaggerated. If television is only dangerous in that sense, then we have a real conflict between the principle of free expression and the interest of the state in internal order. It would be unfortunate if the argument were put in these terms, since the Court has generally favored the latter interest in balancing these goals.

The analysis of the theory of broadcast regulation can, however, proceed in a less general plane. Let us turn to the premises:

1. The electromagnetic spectrum is a valuable public resource only because the

---

[f]"Liberal" and "conservative" distinctions break down on these issues. See, for instance, the opinions of the Justices in *CBS v. DNC.*

government has chosen to nationalize it; otherwise it is in no wise distinguishable from paper, ink, land, or other resources.

2. The spectrum is not in "scarce supply" to any greater extent than steel, plastic, or pencils.

3. A chaos of interference would accompany the end of government regulation only if private property rights could not be (and were not) defined. But such rights can be defined.[14]

4. Broadcasters need not be fiduciaries of the public. The law that makes them so is subordinate to the Constitution. There is no technological or economic necessity for this role.

5. If licenses are peculiarly scarce it is only because the FCC has chosen to make them so. Moreover, some licenses (e.g., UHF assignments) are not scarce; they go begging. In any event, the necessity for regulation of content does not follow from the premise of scarcity. A more reasonable proposition from this premise is the necessity for common carrier status. By this I mean that broadcasters be required to sell time to all comers at published rates. This may or may not be accompanied by profit regulation. The Communication Act's rejection of common carrier obligations must be subordinated to the Constitution.

6. There is no reasonable interpretation of the Constitution which endows the public with a "right to hear" (be informed by) a government conceived scheme of regulation; on the contrary, the Constitution appears to say that government is to have no direct control over the process by which people are informed.

In sum, broadcasting does not logically possess any peculiar characteristic that would enable one to distinguish it from the print media for First Amendment purposes. Moreover, even if it did—that is, if the spectrum could only be allocated by fiat or if the spectrum were peculiarly scarce—there would logically flow from this certain different propositions more consistent with freedom of expression, such as a public right of paid access to broadcast transmitters.[g]

Pragmatically, if one wanted to achieve the most obvious sorts of paternalistic goals, there are perfectly straightforward tools available by which broadcasters can be led, as if by an invisible hand, to provide such programs—e.g., subsidies, tax incentives, and the like, perhaps tied to spectrum use fees. These economic incentives are not employed, and the theoretical coercive powers of the FCC are (luckily) not in practice much used either. That is, licenses are seldom actually revoked. This does not mean that the threat of revocation does not significantly affect behavior. Nuclear deterence does not require actual explosions. Even on pragmatic grounds, the structure of broadcast regulation is bankrupt.

[g]The opinion of the Court in *CBS v. DNC*, rejecting this notion, is quite simply illogical, as several dissenting Justices point out.

Many of the people involved in producing network television news and documentaries believe that the present structure and regulation of broadcasting is essential to their survival and to the survival of their product. Whether or not one has sympathy for their essentially arrogant and elitist view that the public ought to see what they (the producers of these programs) regard as "good" programming, we can evaluate the strength of the claim itself.

The problem, of course, is that this material is now regarded by the networks as unprofitable by itself. Its costs exceed its advertising revenues. It is, however, profitable in the broader sense that it helps to retain FCC licenses and serves as a justification for government restriction on competition from new technologies. But the notion that the material is unprofitable in the direct sense is due to the dependence on advertising and the fewness of competing outlets. A program that produces an audience of "only" a million homes is unprofitable when only three networks split a potential audience of 65 million homes. It might look better if there were ten networks, and it would certainly look better if the one million were allowed to pay 10¢ each for the program.

Although the preceding considerations are of course irrelevant to the constitutional question, one suspects they underlie much judicial thinking on these issues. The ultimate point is that speakers, operating without constraints in the marketplace, must produce what people will see and hear; neither the government itself nor its licensees are appropriate or proper proxies for speakers. Moreover, it is not technically or economically necessary that there be proxies for speakers in broadcasting, as the courts and Congress seem always to have assumed—usually without further support than 40-year-old congressional committee reports.

THE *CARROLL* DOCTRINE AND
TAXATION BY REGULATION

The ability of regulators to require broadcasters to provide programming other than that programming which maximizes profit depends on the extent to which broadcasters are protected from competition. If broadcasters were subject to free entry of competitors, their profits would be reduced in equilibrium to normal levels. At these profit levels, any attempt by the government to alter program content would push broadcasters over the brink of bankruptcy. Accordingly, broadcasters must be allowed to earn more than normal profits in order to be able to provide public service programming.

For many years the FCC refused to accept this elementary economic fact, and tried to have things both ways. Finally, the court of appeals in the *Carroll* case educated the Commission. The specific issue in the case was the complaint of an existing licensee that the FCC's proposed grant of a competing license in his market would destroy his economic ability to perform his public service obligations. The Commission refused to accept this argument, and the court had to tell the Commission that it could not have its cake and eat it too. (However, in practice, no broadcast license application has ever been denied on *Carroll* grounds.)

Richard Posner [69] has aptly called this behavior "taxation by regulation." Certain services which the government decides ought to be provided are made over into obligations of regulated firms. These firms can perform the obligation only if protected from entry, and thus enabled to earn monopoly profits on their nonpublic service functions. The cost of this falls on the purchasers of the unsubsidized services, and on profits. There are many examples of this outside broadcasting, one case being the ICC's insistence that railroads provide passenger service.

Taxation by regulation is usually bad policy, and this is so for several reasons. First, there may exist a number of more efficient ways to produce the revenue required to support the public services in question, ways which do not produce the dead weight loss of monopoly pricing. In this respect taxation by regulation is in the same category as the old monarchical practice of granting chartered monopolies in order to raise revenues. Second, the consequence of this practice is the creation of a vested interest with claims on the scheme of regulation. These claims serve as a rationale for protecting the interests against institutional and technological change. In broadcasting the best current example of this is cable television. Broadcasters have more or less successfully argued that cable, with its multiplicity of channels, must not be allowed to compete freely with broadcasters because this would destroy the broadcasters' ability to perform their public service obligations.

The Commission, mesmerized by its own theory of regulation and the myth that public service programming really exists, has largely accepted the argument, as have the courts. Thus the Commission's interest in an objective (public service programming), which bears no obvious relationship to consumer wants, is allowed to dominate the valid consumer interest in greater choice. Finally, of course, from the First Amendment viewpoint, the *Carroll* doctrine creates an unfortunate alliance between the government and an artificially small group of media interests, an alliance which is in necessary conflict with forces promoting greater competition and hence freedom in the marketplace of ideas. In a word, the effect is to raise the price of access to the public through the media higher than it needs to be, and to create unnecessary monopoly of control over the channels of mass communication. This monopoly is reinforced by the notion that only the licensee can control content on his facilities.

Even if one accepts the public service thesis, there are better ways of proceeding. For instance, auctioning of property rights or leasehold rights in the spectrum would produce a great deal of revenue that could be used to subsidize public service programming. (See Table 3-14 for station sale prices; compare with Table 3-9 above.)

A natural corollary of the *Carroll* doctrine is that new technologies and in-

Table 3-14. Number and Value of Broadcast Stations Changing Hands, 1970–1972 (dollar figures in thousands)

	Number of Stations	Total Sale Prices	Average Price
Radio only	777	$326,220	$ 420
Combined radio & TV	4	1,788	447
TV only	83	511,656	6,165

Source: *Broadcasting Yearbook 1974*, p. 73.

stitutions cannot be allowed to disturb the monopoly profits of broadcasters; otherwise, the base of taxation would be destroyed.[h] Accordingly, the courts and Congress have upheld or extended the Commission's right to regulate these new technologies or institutions. The first instance of this was the extension of FCC power to networks, which do not themselves use the spectrum and accordingly are not subject to Commission licensing. (This is the "network" case.) The Commission now makes rules for the networks by forbidding station affiliation with a network which does not behave. Later, the FCC's authority was extended to certification and specification of equipment produced by electronics manufacturers, to communication satellites, and to cable television. In some of these cases Congress has acted; when Congress had not, the courts simply endorsed FCC extensions of power.[i] In each case, however, the theory by which the extension is justified is the protection of the FCC's regulatory schemes. In practice, the extensions are promoted by vested interests seeking to protect monopoly profits, and sometimes by unregulated firms seeking federal protection from local regulation or relief from "excessive" competition.

Certainly the effect of the extensions has been to remove or control threatened sources of competition or institutional arrangements that respond better to the incentives of the marketplace—that is, to consumer demand. Consumers did not want to purchase UHF converters for their TV sets, so Congress and the Commission required manufacturers to install them.[15] Consumers still did not use them, so the Commission required manufacturers to put "clicks" on the UHF turning dials.[16] Consumers showed that they were willing to pay for additional channels provided by cable systems. The Commission limited the number and kind of channels that could be thus supplied, and proceeded to impose a series of regulatory taxes on the cable systems.[17]

This behavior is consistent with the hypothesis that the Commission is simply a tool of rich and powerful broadcasters. There is some truth in the hy-

[h]See Levin [45], Greenberg [32] for measures of rents. A rough calculation shows that the average TV station has a market price about three times greater than the original cost of its initial investment in tangible property.
[i]The latest case involves cable. In *Midwest Video* the court began to seem uncomfortable in this role, and invited suitable legislation.

pothesis, but the reality is more subtle. In practice, the Commission responds to political pressures exercised through Congress and the executive branch, and these pressures reflect all of those interests to which the broader political process is responsive. Many of the failures of the Commission can be traced to fundamental imperfections in the democratic process itself, of which one is the well known underrepresentation of large groups, each of the members of which has a small stake in the issue at hand. Such groups are not readily organized, and their weight is small in political decisions, particularly obscure decisions involving apparently complex technological or institutional policies.

Probably the only way in which such groups can be protected—and by "such groups" I mean principally consumers—is by broad legislation affecting a wide range of administrative behavior. Thus it is probably best to argue for laws that proclaim that "no regulatory agency may . . ." do this or that, than to take individual cases seriatum. But the development of a general theory of regulatory behavior must precede such policy making, and that theory does not yet exist.

LOCALISM

A persistent theme in FCC regulation of broadcasting is the doctrine of localism. There are two levels at which this can be discussed. The first is the political and economic motivation for the doctrine, and the second is the economic viability of localism as a goal—that is, its economic costs.

Localism is a goal with deep roots in the American political experience. It is associated very closely with representative democracy and populist suspicions of large national corporations. In the context of broadcasting, localism means three things: local ownership of broadcast facilities, a preference for smaller as opposed to larger service areas for each station, and actual program control and selection being exercised at the station level. The source of this doctrine can be traced to early decisions about spectrum allocation. There was a trade-off to be made between the creation of stations that would cover large areas, so that every viewer could have access to many channels, and the creation of less powerful stations, each covering a single city, giving viewers fewer choices but, in return, a locally owned facility.[j] The latter course was taken.

From the point of view of freedom of expression, there are arguments on both sides of this question. The regional station approach provides greater direct competition among stations, and provides each viewer with a wider range of choice. The local station provides an opportunity for discussion of local issues,

[j]See discussion of the "DuMont plan" in Noll, Peck, and McGowan [58]. TV stations use a part of the spectrum where only line of sight communication is possible, thus limiting the coverage area which can be reached by a single antenna. But additional areas can be (and are) secured by using additional antennae; these are called repeater stations. Sometimes these auxiliary transmitters broadcast the same programs on a different frequency, in which case they are called translators. These are common in rural areas, where they compete with cable television systems.

and perhaps reduces the power of monopoly local newspapers. Politically, the right choice is not obvious. In practice, the FCC allowed 30 percent of the stations to be owned by local newspapers, and in any event the local stations do not in fact serve as a significant forum for the discussion of local issues—in part for economic reasons, and in part because the fairness doctrine inhibits controversy on television.

In practice localism is futile because it is much more profitable for stations to affiliate with a network than to produce or select their own programs. This is due to the "public good" nature of programs, or the economies of scale in program supply relative to audience size. This is not inevitable, of course; it simply turns out that local tastes in TV programming are not sufficiently strong or unique to offset the economies of national programming, given the number of outlets. As a result, local programming is limited to local news and a few programs whose audiences are small, put in to satisfy the FCC's penchant for localism.

Given the economic facts both on the demand and supply sides, it is doubtful that pursuit of localism is worth its cost. The cost can be measured by the consequences of the doctrine for the number of competing voices in the marketplace of ideas. One consequence of localism in spectrum allocation is that only three national networks are viable, because not enough cities have more than three VHF-TV assignments. A reformation of the allocation scheme could provide all viewers with more choices and insert greater competition in the marketplace of ideas, without in practice giving up any of the unobtainable benefits of localism except local news shows. The reader must judge for himself whether local TV news shows are worth the cost involved in maintaining them.

ECONOMIC BIASES IN PROGRAM SELECTION

Firms in a market environment must choose not merely the price or quantity of output they will produce (the variables emphasized in traditional economic theory) but also the character of their product. The problem of firm location in product space has not received the same attention as the traditional price-quantity relationships have. But partly because broadcasters do not charge consumers a price for their programs, there is a good deal of economic literature on the problem of program choice. The ultimate question, of course, is whether broadcasters under one or another structure of incentives will produce the "right mix" of programs.

There are two different notions of what constitutes the right mix of programs. The notion explicit in the traditional legal theory of broadcasting is that programs ought to serve the public interest. This is not very helpful. In practice, it means that entertainment programs ought to be leavened with news, public affairs, educational, and other program types that appeal to the paternalistic standards of regulatory theory. The economic standard of an optimal program mix is that mix which maximizes the sum of consumers' and producers' surplus, given whatever constraints are relevant on the production side.[k]

The traditional theory of program patterns in broadcasting put enormous emphasis on the distortionary role of advertising support.[18] Moreover, the traditional analysis did not utilize the surplus welfare measure, but instead emphasized audience sizes and the number of viewers receiving their first choice program. According to this analysis, since broadcasters sell audiences to advertisers rather than programs to viewers, consumers can exercise choice only on a one man, one vote basis, and are not free to express the intensity of their preferences for programs.

Depending on the structure of competition in broadcasting, the number of channels, and the nature of preferences, this could have varying results. If there are only a few channels, then noncollusive competition among broadcasters tends to produce duplication of programs—i.e., excessive sameness. This is a phenomenon recognized for many years in two party political systems and other contexts. Monopoly control of the few channels, on the other hand, elicits a tendency toward "common denominator" programs. These are programs that most people will prefer to turning off their sets, but which are not anyone's first choice. As taxonomic concepts, both duplication and common denominator programs have certain infirmities. The existence of either phenomenon depends critically on the nature of consumer preferences, about which little is known.

It had been thought that the underlying problem was advertiser rather than viewer payment to broadcasters. Given this constraint, a possible solution is to have competing broadcasters but lots of channels, or to have competition for audiences over time on the few channels. But for some combinations of tastes, costs, and channel capacity, monopoly control of all channels did produce the best economic result in these models, and this is a difficulty for First Amendment goals.

More recent works suggest that advertiser support per se is not the problem. Firms competing in product space always have a bias against certain kinds of products, provided there are any fixed costs of production.[l] In particular, there is a bias against products demanded by a relatively small group of consumers with rather intense preferences—that is, products for which demand is relatively insensitive to price. Broadcasting would have this problem even if consumers could pay directly for programs, because fixed costs are very important. But advertising support and limited channel capacity almost certainly make the problem worse.

---

[k]"Consumer surplus" is the difference between what the programs are worth to consumers and what is actually paid for them. Producer surplus is essentially profit. For a defense of this measure of economic welfare see Harberger [33] and Willig [99].

[l]See the Appendix to this chapter for an explicit welfare analysis of the relationship between broadcast structure and program patterns.

Given the present structure of broadcasting, this means that minority taste programs, opinions, and views are probably systematically discriminated against, strictly as a result of economic incentives facing broadcast firms. (Minority taste here means preferences for material that are held by relatively small groups, each member of which might be willing to pay quite a lot for them.) Even with direct viewer payment and lots of channels there would still be some tendency in this direction, although things probably would not be as bad.

The political implications of this are obvious, and they are worsened by the fairness doctrine's incentive to avoid controversy. (Controversy is in this context closely related to minority tastes—that is, tastes or views held by a minority of the population that are likely by virtue of their unpopularity to be controversial.) Given the existence of these effects, one has to ask what structure for the broadcasting industry would produce the best possible results in terms of consumer welfare. An "optimal" result is not obtainable unless centralized planners or discriminating monopolists know everything about individual consumer preferences. This is, of course, impossible, and even if it were not impossible it would be undesirable for First Amendment reasons.

The structure of the broadcast industry is, as we have seen, entirely the creation of government policy regarding spectrum allocation, pay TV, cable television, and the like. Hence this is the crucial policy variable. The present structure of broadcasting, with artificially limited channels and rules against pay TV, is very nearly the worst structure that can be imagined. The solutions are clear, and they follow both from the Steiner analysis and from the analysis of monopolistic competition in product space: remove the artificial barriers to channel expansion, and let people express the intensity of their preferences by paying directly for programs. These policies are not going to produce a perfect result, but they will almost certainly improve matters.

Fortunately, these policies are also consistent with greater freedom of expression, with this caveat: it is conceivable that FCC regulation does result in the airing of some programs of very limited appeal that would not be produced in a competitive, multichannel pay TV system. I regard this as a doubtful proposition, but it cannot be dismissed out of hand. The real import of these bias effects is that the current system of broadcasting is very far from being the best that is available, almost no matter what set of premises are made about spectrum allocation, channel capacity, or consumer preferences. This is a serious indictment. What the present structure of regulation and policy does do is to ensure excess profits for existing broadcasters, and provide a rationale for continued direct government intervention in program content.

PAYING FOR PROGRAMS

Because early technology made it difficult to charge listeners directly for the services provided by broadcast radio, revenues had to come from advertising.

Early stations were associated with, and promoted, department stores.[19] Later, independent stations sold time to advertisers, who supplied whole programs. This is in marked contrast to early newspapers where advertising was a relatively late development. Things might have been otherwise if radio had been delivered by wire, as it is sometimes today in carrier current systems, which use electrical power lines to carry the signal, and are common on college campuses. The British experimented with wire delivery, but eventually abandoned it, apparently because it threatened the BBC monopoly on broadcasting. The parallel with U.S. cable television policy is remarkable (see Coase [14] for a description of the British experience).

One result of the exclusive dependence on advertising was the aggravated program bias effects we have already explored. Another was occasionally serious advertiser influence on news and program content. This was particularly apparent in the McCarthy era, when no advertiser could afford to support programming with blacklisted talent. But the most serious implication of advertiser support was the creation of a myth—the myth that television was "free." Television is free only in the sense that viewers cannot pay directly for programs. They certainly pay for sets, and they pay indirectly for the advertising, which pays for the programs. It is an open question whether the price of consumer goods would fall in the absence of television advertising. Certainly most advertisers would substitute other media.

The notion that television is free is an example of Orwellian doublethink— like the notion that the "fairness doctrine" is fair. The rules and institutions surrounding television are in fact constraints on freedom, since they prohibit a whole range of possible contracts between viewers and programmers. Free television means that it is illegal for firms to offer most programs to the public for a price, and illegal for viewers to pay for them.[m] Unfortunately, unlike most such government attempts to intervene in the marketplace, technology does not permit a black market in this area. The prohibition on pay television ensures that the economic welfare of society is lower than it would otherwise be.

Why does government policy prohibit voluntary contracts between viewer and programmer? The answer really is not obvious. No doubt many people think that they would be worse off paying for something which is now "free." But this is incorrect, because that something would be different, and worth more. The most compelling argument *for* pay TV requires that channels not be artificially limited. Pay TV with continued artificial limitations on channel capacity might well only make consumers worse off, and broadcasters better off, depending on the structure of preferences and whether or not advertising was allowed (see the Appendix to this chapter).

---

[m]The FCC rules and regulations on pay TV prohibit pay TV broadcasts or cablecasts of most sports, many movies, and all "series" programs, and they prohibit any commercial advertising on pay TV programs (see note 13). The latest version of these rules asserts FCC jurisdiction over persons who lease channels on cable systems—another outrage.

Some interest groups would be harmed by pay television, among them theater owners. Some portions of the TV industry associate pay television with the increased channels—and therefore increased competition—of cable, and disapprove of it for that reason. And there are certainly some viewers who would be worse off with pay television; these would be viewers who place no value on any conceivable programming other than that now offered, and who do not mind commercials. Advertisers would not be harmed particularly by pay television unless there were a continued outright ban on advertising in pay programs, and even then it is not obvious that harm could result, so long as competing advertisers were affected equally.

Nevertheless, there are few safer predictions than the forecast that Congress (and therefore the FCC) will continue to prevent people from paying to see the programs they want. There is sufficient folk ignorance associated with the Orwellian "freedom" of television, and so strong a public preoccupation with the medium, that politicians would be foolish to seem to tamper with the electronic genie. Pay TV, if it is possible at all, can only be achieved as an indirect result of other policies, or new technologies such as cable.

The rules against pay TV have direct First Amendment consequences. Assuming for the moment that there were sufficient channel capacity (via UHF and cable), speech and press are directly inhibited. A great many messages that would otherwise be uttered on television are not, because the required market contracts are forbidden. It is as if Congress prohibited subscriber payment for newspapers and magazines. The effect would be to reduce the number of these media, and especially to reduce the number of those small journals catering to minority tastes, which receive little advertising revenue. Even if the channel constraint is still binding, the nature of communication is biased by the ban on subscriber support, away from minority taste messages.

RED LION AND THE FAIRNESS DOCTRINE

For all the reasons indicated in previous sections of this chapter, the government has decided to make sure that television is fair. And who could be against a fairness doctrine?

The fairness doctrine was invented by the FCC and only later enshrined in the organic statute of communications regulation.[20] It is to be distinguished from the equal time provision for political candidates. The fairness doctrine says that (1) licensees must, as part of their public service obligation, give appropriate coverage to controversial issues of public importance; (2) in doing so, the licensee must afford reasonable opportunity to all "sides" of opinion on such issues; and (3) the station itself is responsible for the airing of opposing views. There is no implied right of direct access by any group. The practice of regulation of program fairness by the government is certainly antithetical to the spirit of the First Amendment. Nevertheless, the constitutionality of the fairness doctrine was upheld by the Supreme Court in 1968 in the *Red Lion* decision, whose theory was outlined earlier. This decision gave the FCC not merely the right but the obligation to regulate broadcast content.

The *Red Lion* decision itself, it now appears, provides an instance of government/political manipulation. The original case stemmed from a fairness complaint by one Fred Cook against a radio station in Red Lion, Pennsylvania. Recent research by Fred Friendly [30] suggests that Mr. Cook was directly or indirectly in the pay of the Democratic National Committee, which was conducting a clandestine anti-right wing propaganda campaign. The Supreme Court was not aware of this in 1968, nor was it aware that its decision upholding the fairness doctrine would be utilized by the Nixon administration to manipulate broadcasters to its own ends (Whiteside [96]); nor would such awareness alter the legal issues. But there is a certain poetic justice in Professor Friendly's discovery of this original moral taint in the *Red Lion* case itself. The fairness doctrine, in its own context, is certainly not unreasonable. But it epitomizes that very context of assumptions about broadcast technology, regulation, and economics which is itself so outrageously unreasonable as to shake one's faith in the judicial system.

In practice, the fairness doctrine probably discourages controversial TV programming, particularly on small stations. The reason is that the airing of "all sides" of an issue can be very expensive, and the licensee leaves itself open for the resulting contingent costs of litigation before the FCC and the courts. Any group which thinks itself disadvantaged by a licensee's treatment of some issue files a complaint with the FCC, which must then review the actual content of the program in order to adjudicate the dispute. If the complainant is upheld, the licensee can be ordered to present the views of the complainant. This kind of detailed review of program content has become increasingly frequent over the years.[n]

There are other ways in which the FCC regulates program content. An important one is the license renewal process, in which the overall record of the station is reviewed through public interest glasses (see *Harvard Law Review* [34]). Another is through the operation of such rules as the prime time access decision, barring network or off-network programming from the 7:30–8:00 time period. The Commission entertains, and grants, waivers of this rule to certain programs, such as "National Geographic."[21] The effect is direct content regulation of programming.

The fairness doctrine and the related content regulating activities of the FCC are not only antithetical to freedom of expression, they are quite unnecessary as tools designed to achieve the appearance of freedom. Or, more to the point, no one has claimed that freedom necessarily results in fairness in programming. Freedom to say what one likes means, among other things, freedom to be unfair. Fairness comes in, if at all, through the notion that a system of freedom of expression will result in a tendency toward fairness in political and private actions.

[n]The FCC received 1,124 fairness doctrine complaints in fiscal 1971, and 2,406 in fiscal 1973. Of these received in FY 1973, 94 were referred to the network or licensee concerned, and of these six resulted in adverse decisions.

A corollary of this is that the FCC might somewhat ease its impingement on freedom by considering whether its licensees taken as a group in some area (geographical or intellectual) achieve balance, rather than enforcing such obligations on each licensee individually. As an example, a politically conservative radio station in Media, Pennsylvania, was recently forced off the air because its own programs were not "fair," without regard for its place in the spectrum of opinion available to the citizens of Media.

The rationale of these devices, it must be remembered, is a scarcity of licenses and the concomitant power in the hands of broadcasters. Never mind that this state of affairs is itself unnecessary and artificial; there are other ways than direct content regulation to deal with it. One way is through a direct right of paid access for editorial announcements, or even full-fledged common carrier access obligations. Another is to increase competition in broadcasting directly by removing the present barriers to entry. This would eliminate any rationale for a departure from the laissez faire interpretation of the First Amendment.

ACCESS AND DIVERSITY

The public interest in TV programming is often interpreted by the Commission to mean diversity in programming, and the presentation of a diversity of views on public issues. In practice, program diversity means that stations must air at least some regular programs in categories which the Commission likes but which are not profitable. In this context, "not profitable" means that there is a small or negligible audience for the programs. Examples include local public affairs and religious programs. At license renewal time, the amount of broadcast hours devoted to these programs in a composite week must be reported to the Commission.[22]

We discussed the poverty of the concept of program diversity in Chapter One above. There is no necessary relationship between diversity and either economic efficiency or freedom of expression. Moreover, the kind of diversity introduced in practice by these rules is limited to obscure times of the day and week. What does make some kind of sense is diversity of sources of programming; this is clearly tied to the freedom of access to the medium. Certainly this is more relevant to the First Amendment issue. From the economic point of view, what matters is the extent to which programming approximates that which would maximize consumer welfare—those programs that would result under pay television, for instance.

The issue of access is fundamental to the constitutional question.[o] Granted

---

[o]By access I mean the opportunity to employ the means of transmission (the airwaves), not the opportunity to insert one's message into the midst of an edited collection of messages prepared by someone else. The distinction is somewhat blurred when we consider marginal changes in the existing system as opposed to wholesale reform.

the (erroneous) theory of a frequency scarcity transcending that of other resources, the natural policy conclusion is the necessity of a right of access at nondiscriminatory prices. To be sure, these prices will reflect the artificial scarcity of outlets in television, but that is a subsidiary problem. The constitutional issue would be fully satisfied by a right of paid access to television transmitting stations, and an end to control of programming both by licensees and by the government.

Could such a system work? The answer depends on the extent to which there exist externalities over time among programs, and to a lesser extent on the degree to which the price of access systematically excludes a particular range of views. If the audience for a program on a channel is a function not only of the content of that program but of preceding and succeeding programs, then externalities do exist, and can lead to distortions of incentives in a system of paid access.

Certainly television executives now believe that these externalities are important. Whether they would also be important in a common carrier system is an open question. As to prices, it must be remembered that one of the important functions of prices is to exclude transactions that are uneconomic. In television, the artificial scarcity of VHF licenses will mean that prices will be higher than otherwise, and more people will be excluded who should not be; this is inefficient. Whether there will be a systematic content related bias to this exclusion is a more difficult question.

If the access is gained under current conditions, then only programs that will survive under advertising support will appear. These will be different from present ones only if the menu of programs necessary to maximize profits on a given number of channels under advertiser support is not "unique"—that is, if two or more programs are close substitutes economically even though they represent different intellectual interests or political slants. It is precisely under these conditions that a right of paid access is crucial to First Amendment freedoms, and where government regulation of private monopolists is most clearly unhealthy.

The immediate effect of a change to a system of paid access would be the creation of new firms to serve as brokers between stations or networks and program producers and advertisers. These firms would assemble a group of advertisers for a particular program or series of programs, buy air time, and purchase the program. It is not unlikely that these firms would be large advertising agencies. Depending on regulatory policies regarding the packaging of units of airtime, there would also be groups prepared to buy time for editorial announcements— the broadcast of opinion or propaganda. (It matters whether, for instance, access can be bought only in three-hour "chunks," or three-minute units. The continuity problem suggests something closer to the former.)

Wealthy organizations will be better able to do this than poor organizations, reflecting both the popularity of the organizations and the underlying distribution of wealth in society. If this is inequitable it is no less inequitable than the commercial opportunity to buy newspaper space or to have access to the mails and printing presses of the nation, and it reflects a broader social problem than can be dealt with in the context of television alone.

Is the television medium "too powerful" to allow freedom of access? Would society be less stable if anyone with the money could buy an hour of network time? Certainly there is a mystique surrounding the medium that suggests this. How much would it cost to have an impact? Currently, a one hour program of sufficient popularity to attract one-third of the TV audience (roughly 15,000,000 households) costs about $250,000 to produce. A group wishing to present its views to such an audience once a week would have to spend about $10,000,000 per year (39 weeks of the TV "season"). This is nearly enough to start up a major city daily newspaper, and it would represent only 1/84 of the prime time network channel hours per week available on television. It does not seem likely that this represents much of a threat to liberty. The real danger lies in the fact that today three organizations each controls one-third of these channel hours, and the government controls, more or less directly, 100 percent.

Just as in newspapers, scarcity of outlets in the means of transmission requires a system of unregulated access. But we do not need to grant the premise of scarcity in broadcasting. Newspaper printing and distribution contain a degree of "natural" monopoly. There is nothing in broadcast technology which is naturally monopolistic. The question of access to television station transmitters need not be addressed at all if we can eliminate the government created scarcity of such transmitters. Thus, a policy directly consonant with a literal interpretation of the First Amendment in broadcasting is the creation of a system of private property rights and a free market in the electromagnetic spectrum. Nearly everyone agrees that this is utopian (which is to say impossible), either because of the political power of the broadcast industry, or because politicians so enjoy having the benefits of power over the media. It is nevertheless a goal worth fighting for if we really believe in freedom of expression.

To a nonlawyer, it is simply incredible that the Supreme Court has not long since found the Communication Act of 1934 to be unconstitutional. Such a decision could have monumental social implications. Perhaps the courts are frightened at the implications. If so, the fear is misplaced. The notion that television is uniquely powerful and influential, and hence requires government regulation for "McLuhanesque" reasons, is almost certainly the result of the unnatural degree of economic concentration and advertiser dominance that flows from present regulatory policy.

NETWORK POWER

The FCC's decision to pursue localism in license allocation, rather than a system of regional or national control, has led quite ironically to a greater degree of centralized national concentration than would have existed if the FCC had eschewed localism. The reason is that the economics of broadcasting (given consumer preferences) dictate nationally shared programming, so that the "natural" equilibrium is national coverage. But localism requires a strict limit to the number of local outlets, and this in turn limits the number of possible parallel national services. (The strict limit results both from the frequency allocation problem and from the economic viability side, given only advertiser support.) In practice, there can only be three national networks because there are generally only three acceptable local outlets.[p] If localism had not been a goal, the regional system proposed in the Dumont Plan could have produced half a dozen or more national networks.

Affiliation with a network is the most profitable choice available to local stations. As a result, the decentralization of control that might have resulted from localism is utterly frustrated in practice, even though the FCC clings stubbornly to the old theory. Three organizations control what people shall see and hear on television, the "most powerful" of media. Whenever there are only three competitors in a market, there exists both the incentive and the opportunity for noncompetitive, collusive behavior. Such behavior is illegal under the antitrust laws, but is almost impossible to prevent in its subtler forms without structural changes in the industry. The result is that the networks compete and collude in various dimensions of their economic game. In this case, it seems likely that the networks end up spending too much money on programs, and producing too few individual episodes of these programs.[q]

But the implications of fewness in networking go far beyond economic consequences. The three networks are interbred; they are located physically close together, their standards of success, particularly in journalism, are virtually identical, and they are heavily influenced by the same external opinion leaders— the *New York Times* and the *Washington Post*. Journalistic decisions, and subjective policy decisions about program content, are as a result likely to be made on remarkably similar criteria and by men with nearly identical aspirations and environments. This is unhealthy from the First Amendment viewpoint, and it facilitates the exercise of government control. It would be far less dangerous to have such organizations be more numerous, and more geographically, intellectually, and culturally decentralized. It would be wrong to try to achieve this directly, but we can legitimately try to create the conditions under which it is at least possible.

The networks do not represent a cabal of evil men intent on dictating social and political attitudes. On the contrary, they regard themselves as responsible seekers of objectivity, and even slaves of the fickle audience. More important,

---

[p]See Park [65] for analysis of the viability of a fourth network.

[q]See Owen, Beebe, Manning [62], Chapter 4. This is not necessarily bad for viewers; presumably at least some people would prefer more expensive programs to more original programs, provided that the added expense is reflected in program quality values rather than higher rents to scarce talent.

their behavior is entirely consistent with the incentives produced by the structure of their industry and its regulators. The difficulty lies in the policies which produced that structure and regulation. These policies have created an unfortunate and dangerous nexus of power in society. This situation is all the more dangerous when it is exercised unself-consciously, because it is then less visible and more self-righteous.

Aside from wholesale revision of the system of television allocations, there are two levels of policy available to deal with this problem. The first is the encouragement of new technology, such as cable television, which affords an opportunity for decentralization and attenuation of network power—that is, to create more channels and therefore more competition in the marketplace of ideas. The other is to break up the networks by antitrust action.[r] Both of these approaches would of course be opposed by the networks. Ironically, the possibility of engendering such a policy change is small precisely because it can so easily be made to appear to be government retribution for network antagonism to administration policies.[s] Thus does the unhealthy symbiosis between media and government perpetuate itself.

RADIO TODAY

The *Red Lion* decision upholding the constitutionality of the fairness doctrine on the grounds of the scarcity of frequencies was a radio station case, not a television case. This is curious because it is in radio broadcasting that the FCC has chosen *not* to create a significant scarcity of licenses. There are more than 7,500 radio stations on the air in the United States, and most citizens can receive at least a dozen stations on home or car radios. With the possible exception of magazines, radio is the most competitive of the media. (For financial data on the industry, see Tables 3-15 to 3-20.)

The numbers of competing stations in radio provide an attractive opportunity for instructive contrasts with television. Some phenomena in radio seem to be closely associated with the increased fragmentation of the audience associated with greater numbers of competing stations. There seems, for instance, to be a somewhat wider range of program types in radio, while duplication still persists.

[r]Antitrust action against the networks is by far the most politically feasible approach. The present Justice Department suit is, however, untenable—it alleges monopsony power in the program markets and seeks to keep the networks out of prime time program production, an end already accomplished by the FCC's prime time access rule. The correct approach is structural. For instance, the networks might be forced to sell time on their systems to others, or individual stations might be forbidden to affiliate with any one network more than say one day per week. Remedies of this type preserve the scale economics of networking while allowing additional networks to appear.

[s]The first Justice Department antitrust suit against the networks was dismissed without prejudice precisely because it appeared to be tainted by political motivation. It was, however, immediately refiled.

Local advertising and locally oriented content is more important, and national networking somewhat less important in radio than in television.

There are both more controversy and more extreme points of view on radio. There is no equivalent on television of the Pacifica stations or the McIntyre stations (far left and right, respectively). Competition in radio is relatively robust, and aside from the threat of FCC intervention there is little difficulty in gaining access to the medium at reasonable prices.[23] To be sure, the distortions caused by advertising support and by FCC regulation persist, but both seem to be attenuated by the number of competitors, even leaving aside competition from other media.

These observations suggest two propositions. The first is that there is no rationale for continued government content regulation in radio. The second is that an increase in the number of competing TV channels—to the extent it resulted in a situation similar to that in radio—would be a desirable thing. One reason that radio appears less socially powerful than television is precisely because it is less concentrated. There is no scarcity, artificial or otherwise, of radio station voices, although there are local exceptions to this "rule." There is robust competition, and extensive access, for economic reasons, despite FCC regulation that is theoretically identical to television.

The degree of robustness of debate on controversial issues is inhibited only by the FCC, which seeks in a desultory manner to require balance within the programming of each station, rather than across the spectrum of stations. There is an active market in radio licenses, and most transfers receive pro forma FCC approval. Taking away the FCC's attempts to control radio content, one has what must be the closest approach to uninhibited freedom of expression possible in the absence of subscriber payment. The case for deregulation of radio is overwhelming. When this suggestion was made to the FCC several years ago,[24] the Commission responded by undertaking a program of reregulation which involved reductions in the more onerous technical and reporting regulations, but which left the content regulation and license renewal policies unchanged.[25] To be fair, there is a serious question whether, in view of *Red Lion,* the Commission or even the Congress could choose to deregulate radio in all respects.

Would we be better off with a television medium that resembled the radio industry in structure? From the point of view of freedom of expression we would certainly be better off. From the economic point of view, we would probably be better off, but not so well off as with pay television in addition.

PUBLIC BROADCASTING

The intellectual community has never been happy with commercial television in the United States. The number of academics claiming that they never watch television is exceeded only by the number of antennae on their homes. Because

Table 3-15. Revenue and Expense Items for all AM and AM-FMª Stations Reporting Financial Data, 1973 (in thousands of dollars)

Item	Individual Items	Totals^b	Item	Individual Items	Totals
Broadcast revenues			Broadcast expenses		
A. Revenues from the sale of station time:			Technical expenses:		
(1) Network			Technical payroll*	$ 65,579	
Sale of station time to networks:			All other technical expenses	40,199	
Sale of station time to major networks, ABC, CBS, MBS, NBC (before line or service charges)	$ 9,242		Total technical expenses		105,778
Sale of station time to other networks (before line or service charges)	2,250		Program expenses:		
Total		11,492	Payroll* for employees considered "talent"	—	
(2) Nonnetwork (after trade and special discounts but before cash discounts to advertisers and sponsors, and before commissions to agencies, representatives and brokers):			Payroll* for all other program employes	231,374	
			Rental and amortization of film and tape	1,183	
			Records and transcriptions	5,523	
			Cost of outside news services	22,953	
Sale of station time to national and regional advertisers or sponsors	345,096		Payments to talent other than reported above	8,654	
Sale of station time to local advertisers or sponsors	1,069,451		Music license fees	33,653	
Total		1,414,547	Other performance and program rights	13,526	
Total sale of station time		1,426,039	All other program expenses	42,289	
B. Broadcast revenues other than from sale of station time (after deduction for trade discounts but before cash discounts and before commission):			Total program expenses		395,156
			Selling expenses:		
			Selling payroll*	155,595	
			All other selling expenses	87,675	
			Total selling expenses		243,270

(1) Revenues from separate charges made for programs, materials, facilities and services supplied to advertisers or sponsors in connection with sale of station time:

- (a) to national and regional advertisers or sponsors — 2,644
- (b) to local advertisers or sponsors — 11,293

(2) Other broadcast revenues — 12,829

Total broadcast revenues, other than from time sales — 26,766

C. Total broadcast revenues — 1,452,805

(1) Less commissions to agencies, representatives and brokers (but not to staff salesmen or employes) and less cash discounts — 137,620

D. Net broadcast revenues — 1,315,185[c]

General and administrative expenses:

- General and administrative payroll* — 142,140
- Depreciation and amortization — 60,402
- Interest — 34,029
- Allocated costs of management from home office or affiliate(s) — 31,091
- Other general and administrative expenses — 212,238

Total general and administrative expenses — 479,901

Total broadcast expenses: — 1,188,104

Broadcast Income

- Broadcast revenues — $1,316,117[d]
- Broadcast expenses — 1,189,758[d]

Broadcast operating income or (loss) — 126,359

Total of any amounts included in expenses which represent payments (salaries, commissions, management fees, rents, etc.) for services or materials supplied by the owners or stockholders, or any close relative of such persons or any affiliated company under common control — 80,004

*Payroll includes salaries, wages, bonuses and commissions. Total Payroll: $594,689

[a]Includes: 2,854 AM and 1,413 AM-FM combination stations. Does not include 361 FM stations that are associated with AM's but which reported separately.

[b]Last digits may not add to totals because of rounding.

[c]Includes $45,346,000 from barter and trade-out transactions.

[d]Stations reporting less than $25,000 in total revenues are not required to report items in revenues and expenses but are required to report income. Therefore, totals in revenues and expenses are somewhat lower than totals in income.

Table 3-15.   Revenue and Expense Items for all FM Stations[a] Reporting Financial Data, 1973 (in thousands of dollars)

	Individual Items	Totals[b]
Broadcast revenues		
A. Revenues from the sale of station time:		
(1) Network		
Sale of station time to networks:		
Sale of station time to major networks, ABC, CBS, MBS, NBC (before line or service charges)	$ 264	
Sale of station time to other networks (before line or service charges)	58	
Total		$ 322
(2) Nonnetwork (after trade and special discounts but before cash discounts to advertisers and sponsors, and before commissions to agencies, representatives and brokers).		
Sale of station time to national and regional advertisers or sponsors	34,967	
Sale of station time to local advertisers or sponsors	129,543	
Total		164,510
Total sale of station time		164,831
B. Broadcast revenues other than from sale of station time (after deduction for trade discounts but before cash discounts and before commissions):		
(1) Revenues from separate charges made for programs, materials, facilities, and services supplied to advertisers		

	Individual Items	Totals[b]
Broadcast expenses		
Technical expenses:		
Technical payroll*	$ 7,478	
All other technical expenses	6,788	
Total technical expenses		$ 14,267
Program expenses:		
Payroll* for employes considered "talent"	—	
Payroll* for all other program employes	28,901	
Rental and amortization of film and tape	593	
Records and transcriptions	1,240	
Cost of outside news services	1,977	
Payments to talent other than reported above	701	
Music license fees	3,657	
Other performance and program rights	884	
All other program expenses	4,772	
Total program expenses		42,725
Selling expenses:		
Selling payroll*	21,237	
All other selling expenses	16,341	
Total selling expenses		37,578
General and administrative expenses:		
General and administrative payroll*	16,701	

or sponsors in connection with sale of station time:	
(a) to national and regional advertisers or sponsors	55
(b) to local advertisers or sponsors	610
(2) Other broadcast revenues	2,708
Total broadcast revenues, other than from time sales	3,373
C. Total broadcast revenues	168,205
(1) Less commissions to agencies, representatives and brokers (but not to staff salesmen or employes) and less cash discounts	16,208
D. Net broadcast revenues	151,996[c]
Depreciation and amortization	11,240
Interest	4,516
Allocated costs of management from home office or affiliate(s)	4,569
Other general and administrative expenses	29,220
Total general and administrative expenses	66,245
Total broadcast expenses	160,816
Broadcast income	
Broadcast revenues	$153,615
Broadcast expenses	164,464
Broadcast operating income or (loss)	(10,849)
Total of any amounts included in expenses which represent payments (salaries, commissions, management fees, rents, etc.) for services or materials supplied by the owners or stockholders, or any close relative of such persons or any affiliated company under common control	7,405

*Payroll includes salaries, wages, bonuses and commissions. Total payroll: $74,317.

[a] Includes 361 FM stations that are associated with AM stations but that reported separately and 616 independent FM stations.

[b] Last digits may not add because of rounding.

[c] Includes $7,583,000 from barter and trade-out transactions.

[d] Stations reporting less than $25,000 in revenue are not required to report items in revenues and expenses, but are required to report in income. Therefore, totals in expenses are somewhat higher than the totals reported in revenues and expenses.

( ) Denotes loss.

Source: FCC data.

Table 3-16. Commercial Radio Stations in Operation in 1973

	AM	AM-FM (filing a combined report)[a]	Total AM, AM-FM	FM Associated with AM-FM Combination but Filing a Separate Report[b]	FM Independent	Total Radio[a]	Grand Total[c]
Stations in operation on Dec. 31, 1973							
Full-year operation	2868	1429	4297	349	604	5250	6679
Part-year operation	43	11	54	13	41	108	119
Total	2911	1440	4351	362	645	5358	6798
Stations not reporting[d]	63	27	90	1	30	121	148
Total stations reporting	2854	1413	4267	361	616	5244	6657

[a] AM-FM stations filing a combined report are counted as one station.

[b] Although these stations are associated with an AM-FM combination they are counted as separate.

[c] Figures in this column count AM-FM combinations as two stations.

[d] Stations that are counted as not reporting include those stations that were licensed but silent for the entire year, those commercial stations that obtained most of their revenues from contributions rather than time sales, and those stations that filed too late to be included in this report.

Note that there are in addition about 800 educational radio stations, and a number of "carrier current" operations.

Source: FCC data.

Table 3-17. Broadcast Financial Data of Nationwide Networks and 4,267 AM and AM/FM Stations, 1973 (in thousands of dollars)

Broadcast Revenues, Expenses and Income	Nationwise Networks[a]	18 Owned-and-Operated AM Stations[b]	4,249 Other AM and AM/FM Stations[c]	Total Networks and Stations
Sales to advertisers for time, program talent, facilities, and services				
Network sales	$56,974			
Deduct: Payments to owned-and-operated stations	829			
Deduct: Payments to other affiliated stations	8,598			
Retained from network sales	47,546	$ 829	$ 10,662[d]	$ 59,038
Nonnetwork sales				
To national and regional advertisers	—	42,508	305,232	347,740
To local advertisers	—	30,324	1,051,351[e]	1,081,675
Total nonnetwork sales	—	72,832	1,356,584	1,429,416
Total sales to advertisers	47,546	73,662	1,367,246	1,488,454
Sales to other than advertisers	1,643	601	12,228	14,473
Total sales	49,190	74,263	1,379,474	1,502,927
Deduct: Commissions to agencies, representatives, etc.	8,458	12,651	124,969	146,078
Total broadcast revenues	40,732	61,612	1,254,505	1,356,849
Total broadcast expense	43,813	52,501	1,137,256	1,233,570
Total income (before federal income tax)	(3,081)	9,111	117,248	123,279

[a]CBS, MBS, NBC and ABC's three AM networks and one FM network.

[b]Includes 14 AM stations and four AM/FM combinations. Fourteen of the owned and operated FM stations are excluded from this table for 1973. The 1973 revenues of the 14 FM owned and operated stations totaled $9.5 million and their expenses totaled $12.4 million.

[c]Excludes 347 FM stations that are associated with AM's but reported separately. The 1973 revenues of these stations totaled $480.0 million; expenses totaled $45.9 million.

[d]Includes $2,250 thousand in compensation from regional networks. The balance differs from the amount reported by the networks on line 4 because of differences in accounting methods.

[e]Since stations with less than $25,000 in revenues do not report a detailed breakdown, the total revenue of those stations is included in this item. Therefore, a small amount of network and national non-network time and program sales may be included here.

( ) Denotes loss.

Note: Last digits of detailed dollar figures may not add to totals due to rounding.

Source: FCC data.

Table 3–18.   Radio Station Profitability, 1973 (number of stations reporting profit or loss, by revenues)

	Profit			Loss			
Revenues Profit (Loss)	Over 500,000	10,000 500,000	0 10,000	0 25,000	25,000 500,000	Over 500,000	Total
AM and AM/FM							
Over $1,000,000	71	116	3	2	16	6	214
$50,000–$1,000,000	0	1,780	853	744	404	10	3,791
Under $50,000	0	13	70	107	17	0	207
Total	71	1,909	926	853	437	16	4,213
FM							
Over $1,000,000	1	5	0	0	0	0	6
$50,000–$1,000,000	0	119	92	101	136	2	450
Under $50,000	0	1	17	71	31	0	120
Total	1	125	109	172	167	2	576

Note: FM stations "associated" with AM's but reporting separately are included with FM's.
Source: FCC data.

Table 3-19. 1972 Employment and Investment in Tangible Broadcast Property of Nationwide Networks, Their 18 Owned-and-Operated Stations[a] and Other AM and AM-FM Radio Stations (in thousands of dollars)

Employment	Nationwide Networks[c]	18 Network Owned-and-Operated Stations[b]	Other Stations	Total
Full time	851	1,398	49,420	51,669
Part time	18	92	15,578	15,688
Total	869	1,490	64,998[b]	67,357
Investment in tangible broadcast property				
Original cost (thousands of dollars)	10,653	17,282	857,786[d]	885,721
Depreciated cost (thousands of dollars)	4,187	6,932	437,664	448,783

[a]Includes 14 AM's and four AM-FM combinations.
[b]Includes 4,241 AM and AM-FM stations.
[c]CBS, MBS, NBC and ABC's three AM networks and one FM network.
[d]Includes 4,221 AM and AM-FM stations.
Source: FCC data.

Table 3-20. 1973 Broadcast Expenses of Nationwide Radio Networks, Their 18 Owned-and-Operated Stations and 4,194 Other AM and AM-FM Stations, Reporting Revenues of $25,000 or More (in thousands of dollars)

Type of Expense	Nationwide Networks[a]	18 Network Owned-and-Operated Stations[b]	Other Stations[c]	Total
Technical	$ 3,405	$ 8,012	$ 98,765	$ 109,182
Program	28,428	18,864	340,292	387,584
Selling	7,607	14,130	229,140	250,877
General and administrative	4,373	11,494	468,406	484,273
Total broadcast expenses	43,813	52,501	1,135,603	1,231,917

[a]CBS, MBS, NBC and ABC's three AM networks and one FM network.
[b]Includes 14 AM stations and four AM-FM stations filing a combined report.
[c]Includes 2,790 AM stations and 1,404 AM-FM stations filing a combined report. Does not include 361 FM stations that are associated with AM's but reported separately.
Note: Last digits may not sum to totals because of rounding.
Source: FCC data.

of advertiser support and limited channels, television caters to mass tastes. Intellectuals, by definition, do not share these tastes.

This dissatisfaction was for many years reflected only in the theory of broadcast regulation and efforts to get the FCC to require the broadcasters to do better. This was the essence of Newton Minow's vast wasteland speech.[26] Finally, in 1967, the Carnegie Commission proposed and Congress accepted the idea of a system of public broadcast stations.[27] The idea was to create local stations that were not forced by the profit motive of commercial broadcasting to produce the programs of the wasteland. Public broadcasting was to produce quality programming, to be a medium of excellence. The instructional programming of the preexisting educational stations that served as a starting point for public broadcasting was deemphasized. (For an outline of the financial structure of the system, see Tables 3-21 to 3-23.)

The concept of localism was almost immediately abandoned, and a network (PBS) created. The economic reasons for this mirror the rationale of networks in commercial broadcasting: given limited funds, sharing of programs is strongly indicated. But in this case localism has an additional dimension—it provides a safety mechanism to insulate the system from political intervention that would naturally accompany the expenditure of federal funds. Federal funding means that Congress and the President have a tool and a responsibility for examining the performance of public broadcasting. The centralization of program decisions in Washington by a national network makes it easier to wield this power of intervention. There is considerable danger that the public broadcasting system can then be an instrument of the state, and this is surely contrary to the principles of freedom of expression.

The public broadcasting system was essentially a liberal concept, and it came into inevitable and immediate conflict with the Nixon administration, nicely illustrating the relationship between public broadcast content and political forces at their most dangerous level. The upshot, when the dust had settled, was a plan to partially decentralize control of program decisions (localism) along with long term funding by Congress.[28]

Table 3-21.   Income of Public TV Stations, Fiscal 1971

Source	Amount (000)	Percent of Total
Federal government	$ 8,935	6
Public broadcasting agencies	14,766	11
Institutions of higher education	9,554	7
State and local governments	66,613	47
Foundations	15,881	11
Auctions, individuals, and all other	25,067	18
Total:	$140,816	100

Source: CPB

Table 3-22. Corporation for Public Broadcasting Funds (Fiscal 1973)

	Thousands of Dollars
Income	
Federal Appropriations	35,000
Federal Grants & Contracts	21
Nonfederal income	3,535
Carryover from prior year	3,634
Total	42,190
Expenses (Budget)	
Programs for public TV	15,892
Distribution of TV programs (PBS)	9,250
Production & distribution of radio programs	3,500
Research	602
Grants for community service	6,626
Other grants	1,941
Administration	2,619
Total	40,430

Source: CPB

Is public broadcasting necessary? There are certainly deficiencies in the present system which a public corporation might, if it wished, help to remedy. This would require production of programs against which the commercial system is biased, despite their economic desirability. But these are not necessarily the same programs that will satisfy the social and intellectual elite who patronize public broadcasting and dominate its decision making. More to the point, public broadcasting is a singularly inefficient way to remedy the defects in the commercial system: it occupies valuable spectrum allocations with programs which have miniscule audiences;[t] it is (deliberately) nonresponsive to consumer tastes; and it is structured in a way that invites dangerous First Amendment confrontations. The principal merit of the system is that it is one of the few reforms that are politically feasible, and this is so precisely because it does not threaten the audiences and profits of commercial broadcasters. Effective reform requires heavy threats to both.

Public broadcasting as presently structured is neither a safe nor an effective remedy for the defects of commercial television. This does not necessarily mean that there is not a justification for federal subsidization of certain kinds of "merit good" programming. But one can imagine more efficient and less dangerous ways to accomplish this objective. For instance, federally funded local public committees might buy time on commercial stations for public service programs, or the National Endowment for the Arts might subsidize "high quality" entertainment programming on commercial stations. This would of course

[t]If the VHF educational allocations were available for commercial use, a fourth commercial network might well be viable (see Crandall [20]).

Table 3-23. Federal Funding for Public Broadcasting (in millions of dollars)

Fiscal Year	Corporation for Public Broadcasting		Educational Broadcasting Facilities Act	
	Authorization	*Appropriation*	*Authorization*	*Appropriation*
1963–1967 (total)	–	–	32	32
1968	–	–	11	0
1969	9	5	13	4
1970	20	15	15	5
1971[a]	35	23	15	11
1972[a]	35	35	15	13
1973[b]	65	65	25	13
1974[b]	90	45		
1973[a]	45	35[c]		

[a]Two-year authorization
[b]Two-year authorization; vetoed
[c]Continuing resolution
Source: CPB.

require changes in the communications regulations requiring commercial stations or networks to accept such programs at standard rates, which would be a good precedent for more open access generally. But any remedy for the inefficiencies and inequities of the commercial system would almost certainly have to hurt to be effective, and public broadcasting does not hurt commercial broadcasters.

Program choice in public broadcasting ought to be decentralized for political reasons. But the decentralized decision makers must, for economic reasons, be given the option of purchasing national programming. This requires both that federal appropriations flow through directly to local stations, and that there be a market in which the stations can purchase rather than produce programs. On a more fundamental level, program choice might usefully be made more responsive to viewer welfare, and less responsive to the notions put forward by philanthropic institutions of what people "ought" to see. Careful study of data from cable television and pay TV experiments, for instance, could produce reasonable estimates of what programs, or program types, are most needed to offset the distortions of advertiser supported commercial television. These programs may not be operas, ballets, and Shakespeare, but even if they are, public support of a separate network of stations may very well be the wrong way to produce them.

CABLE TELEVISION

Cable television uses a coaxial cable. The capacity of such a system depends on the amplifiers used, but new systems typically can carry about twenty TV channels. Theoretical capacity is much higher. Telephone wires cannot be used to transmit commercial TV quality signals; picturephone service has a lower resolution than commercial television, and requires four wires.

The idea of delivering television by wire is not particularly startling. It is, for a few channels, more expensive than over-the-air signals. The cost of a cable system varies widely depending on subscriber density and local construction conditions. An initial investment cost of about $200 per subscriber is perhaps typical. If such a system has twenty channels and serves a community of 100,000 households, the cost is about $1,000,000 per channel, which is not greatly different from the cost of a TV tower and transmitter. Typical cable fees are $6 per month, plus an installation charge. There are now (1975) about ten million cable subscribers, or 15 percent of all TV households.

Because it is more expensive cable developed mainly as a supplement to the broadcast system, helping to satisfy the consumer demand for television choked off by the restriction of broadcast frequencies. It does this in two ways. The original function of cable was to supply TV signals to viewers who could not receive existing stations very clearly, say in remote or mountainous areas. However, cable operators quickly realized that their wires could carry lots of TV channels, not just the few allowed by the Commission in any area. So they began to import TV signals from distant cities. Subscribers were willing to pay for this service, and a major controversy was born.

The essence of the controversy is that cable, with its unlimited channel capacity, threatens the profits of broadcasters whose markets had heretofore been protected from entry. More competition means smaller audiences and lower advertising revenues. The knife was turned in the wound by two Supreme Court decisions[29] interpreting the 1909 Copyright Act to allow use of local and distant signals without copyright liability. This brought the program producers down on the side of the broadcasters, an otherwise unnatural alliance. (Program producers generally favor cable TV and pay TV because of the implied increased demand for programs.)

The FCC's behavior with regard to cable has been reprehensible. As cable began to threaten broadcasters' profits, the FCC unilaterally asserted its jurisdiction over the industry, under the "ancillary services" doctrine discussed above. (The Supreme Court upheld the Commission in *United States v. Southwestern Cable Co.* 392 U.S. 157 (1968).) The Commission then proceeded to freeze cable growth for several years by barring any distant signal importation. In 1972, it issued a massive set of rules for cable, allowing some distant signals, and imposing heavy public service obligations on each system.[30] From the public's point of view, cable presents an opportunity for expanded choice and increased programming supply.

There is no efficiency justification for the FCC's action, and only a tenuous equity argument supporting the Commission. The equity argument is that some consumers may be hurt by cable—those who now receive "free" over-the-air signals, which would disappear because of cable competition. The argument is that local stations will lose so much audience to imported signals that advertising revenues would be insufficient to support them. But some stations must receive increased revenues from being imported, so there is no necessary reduction in the number of signals available to consumers, and the reverse is much more likely. This is, however, consistent with a reduction in the number of stations. It is not clear that such consumers exist, or if they do, that their loss is commensurate with the gain to others from cable growth.

The remaining point to make about cable technology is that pay television is much more practical with cable than with over-the-air signals, because the wire that carries the signal can also monitor program choices and provide for automatic billing, as with telephone calls.[31]

What is proper public policy with respect to cable? Some excellent suggestions are contained in the *Report* [10] of the Cabinet Committee on Cable Communications, headed by former OTP Director Clay T. Whitehead. The *Report* recognizes the vertical stages of mass media message production (creation, editing, transmission) and points out that cable technology is likely to result in local natural monopolies at the transmission stage. (There are strong economies of scale in several dimensions of cable television construction and operation.) Accordingly, freedom of expression and economic competition will both be served by giving cable operators common carrier obligations—making them in effect institutions like the post office or the telephone company, though not necessarily subject to rate of return regulation. We have no good evidence that consumers are better off when monopolies are subject to such regulation, and there are plausible reasons to suppose that the reverse is true.

Then there can be competition among message sources, any of whom can rent channel hours from the cable operators. Given the potentially large number of channels, there exists no rationale for regulation of the program sources or of program content. The *Report* also recommends the end of some present restrictions on pay television by cable.

Unfortunately, the *Report* recommends that they be implemented only at the time national cable diffusion reaches fifty percent of the population, and that the FCC meanwhile continue more or less on its present course. Given that course, it may be several decades, if ever, before cable does achieve fifty percent saturation of the population. Not surprisingly, good policy has difficulty engaging political reality. Worse still, if cable ever does reach fifty percent saturation, it will then likely possess sufficient political power to avert those parts of the Whitehead recommendations that will reduce its own profits, including the provision that cable operators themselves not control any programming. This in turn will provide the traditional rationale for continued federal regulation of content.

Cable technology is a first class opportunity for reform of our system of broadcast regulation. It provides the opportunity to insert competition into the industry, to increase freedom of expression, and to reduce or eliminate government regulation of message content. But it is only an opportunity. The same ends can be achieved within the context of present technology, and perhaps more cheaply. Cable is not necessarily the least expensive way to increase channel capacity and choice. Cable does provide a new political force, one that may eventually force an effective increase in competition. The great danger is that the political route to economic security for cable owners lies down the path of regulation, and there is no automatic mechanism providing for the withering of regulation when it is no longer required even by the theories criticized above.

With respect to such issues as cable, the FCC can be regarded as behaving very much like an automaton. The rules are these: Every regulated industry which encounters competition from an unregulated source can count on getting the threat under control by extending regulation to cover it. Thereafter, both entities will be protected by the regulators against each other so that catastrophic damage is impossible. The balance of rewards to each of the competing forces will reflect the political strength of the parties in Congress and the executive branch, taking due account of the role of public opinion in influencing each.

Cable used to be at a considerable disadvantage vis à vis broadcasters in this balance, but it has now begun to acquire some political power. Still, it will be a long time befor the local cable operator is as important to a Congressman as the local broadcasters and newspapers are. Whatever the long run outcome, the effect is certainly to dampen significantly the rate at which cable can serve as a remedy to the problems of television. This is the way public policy is made in such cases, and there is very little that can be done about it.[32]

SOCIAL AND CULTURAL EFFECTS: THE END OF HISTORY

Print journalism provides a permanent record of events, and to some degree reflects for posterity the tastes and conditions of culture and society. Indeed, journalism itself *is* history, albeit recent history. The broadcast media are the antithesis of history. Television is preoccupied with participation in events. The goal of television news, not always realized, is live "real time" coverage of events. In this it pretends to neutrality. But there is no record of events, no memory except the memory of the audience. All action is ephemeral. Moreover, the presence of media coverage profoundly affects the event. No event is the same with the cameras, lights, and technicians present. The coverage is obtrusive, and worse, easily manipulated. A media event is not a "real" event, in the preelectronic sense.[33]

The technology and institution of television do not lend themselves to thought, but to action. Investigative journalism, for instance—the activity that seems to play such an important role in theories of the First Amendment—is nearly impossible on television. The medium is not an efficient conveyor of actionless facts. On the other hand, few print media can match the impact of TV coverage of police dogs attacking civil rights demonstrators, of a riot, or pictures of a starving child, or a wartime fire fight. The McLuhan doctrine is certainly relevant.

But the medium without a memory has no pertinacity—nor does it, as its pundits claim, merely "mirror" reality. In fact, it changes reality, it sometimes creates reality, and it often ignores or submerges reality.

Now there is little doubt that the print media also affect reality, and that distortions, albeit of a different kind, are introduced by the traditional reporting techniques. But we have to ask whether the peculiar biases of television, given the public's remarkable preoccupation with it, are consistent with theories of the First Amendment. Leaving journalism aside, are the social and cultural impacts of TV programming sufficiently dangerous and important to justify departures from the principles of freedom of expression?

It must first be said that no one understands what these impacts are, or whether they really are dangerous. Despite volumes of research there is little agreement on the relatively narrow question, for instance, of the effect of televised violence on children.[34] Even if we did know that television has untoward social and cultural effects, it is far from clear that the correct policy is to give over into the hands of an increasingly powerful central government the right to regulate those effects. If television is powerful and influential that is all the more reason to wish that government had no hand in it.

On the contrary, one would wish that effective control were highly decentralized, both privately and publically. If television is an important social force, or a harmful one, it is too important to be left in the control either of bureaucrats or monopolists or both together. On the contrary, the medium must be democratized, its power dispersed over many decision makers, especially consumers themselves. It becomes all the more important to ensure that the only programming that survives is that programming (with or without advertising) which people are willing, individually, to pay for, and to ensure that they have the widest possible range of choice of sources.

It is possible, though far from obvious, that there may be a social, collective interest in eliminating or modifying actual or potential pathological behavior in the television medium, behavior that might exist in the context of economic and political freedom. A noncontroversial example is the need for copyright laws. A more controversial set of examples includes obscenity, libel, pornography, violence, and the like. It is not inconsistent for a democratic society to wish to deal with such phenomena; but it is critically important to choose carefully the manner in which this is accomplished. It can be done through structural reform,[u] and it can be done if necessary by laws that are quite specific and that are enforced in the courts. But it cannot be safely done by direct bureaucratic regulation, especially by bureaucrats with broad and ill-defined powers.

---

[u]"Structural reform" means removing the institutional incentives that produce the pathological behavior, as through antitrust action; or the introduction of economic counterincentives, such as taxes or subsidies. Such measures are to be distinguished from regulations requiring judgmental enforcement by an administrative body, and which constrain actions or behavior that is economically rewarding.

One must suspect that the peculiar place of television in our society, its unique power and influence, are due in very large part to the fact that lots of people watch the same programs (because they have so little choice) rather than because television per se is uniquely influential. If everyone had access to 20 to 40 competing channels, with or without pay TV, we would not all be watching the same news and entertainment programs, and the power of the medium as a whole to affect political decisions would surely be greatly attenuated.

CROSS-OWNERSHIP AND THE ROLE
OF ANTITRUST

If television were not a regulated industry it would be a very obvious target of antitrust activity under the doctrine of the *Associated Press* case. The network oligopoly is only one of the institutions that might be subject to attack. Another is pervasive newspaper–television station cross-ownership. The Justice Department has pressed the FCC to deal with this problem since 1968, but with little success. The situation neatly illustrates the problems of antitrust policy in the regulated industries.

About 30 percent of all TV stations are owned by newspapers in the same city.[35] Given the prevalent monopoly positions of newspapers, and the much vaunted "scarcity" of TV licenses, cross-ownership is an obvious affront both to economic competition and to freedom of expression, the latter being in this case far more important. There is evidence that joint ownership results, as common sense would suggest, in higher advertising prices charged by TV stations and newspapers than the prices charged in otherwise similar situations. This is a standard economic effect of a reduction in competition. The First Amendment effects are obvious, especially since many of these combinations are in small cities where the only local newspaper owns the only local TV or radio station.

Not surprisingly, the FCC has been reluctant to do anything about it. Former FCC Chairman Dean Burch, even in an otherwise unnatural alliance with Commissioner Nicholas Johnson, was never able to muster a Commission majority in favor of proposed divestiture rules. The political power of the A.N.P.A.[v] and the broadcasters is simply too great on an issue that does not seem to touch the public in a sensitive area. The Justice Department's antitrust division is hamstrung by the doctrine of primary jurisdiction. This legal precept requires a complainant to seek relief in a regulatory agency before approaching the courts. Accordingly, the antitrust division first petitioned the FCC for a divestiture rule making and then, after five years of inactivity by the FCC, began challenging licenses of newspaper owned stations. Congress immediately began hearings on

---

[v]American Newspaper Publishers' Association. In 1975 the FCC finally resolved the issue by ordering a few divestitures in the most outrageous cases, and banning future acquisitions that would result in cross-ownership. (See FCC Second Report and Order in Docket 18110, released January 31, 1975, FCC 75-104.)

legislation to prohibit Commission consideration of newspaper ownership in its license renewal process. Until the Commission acts one way or another in each case—which could take years—the division cannot resort to the possibly more congenial courts.

The debilitating effects of newspaper-TV cross-ownership are obvious. The defense offered by cross-ownership apologists, aside from simple denial of the obvious, is that TV stations help to keep financially shaky newspapers afloat. It has never been clear why TV stations are uniquely suited to this public spirited objective. Why is it only TV stations and not, say, steel manufacturers who can do this? The argument is disingenuous. Newspapers own TV stations because to do so reduces competition, increases advertising prices, and increases profits. (Cost savings from joint ownership are negligible or nil.)

The experience with cross-ownership suggests that measures might usefully be taken to strike the fetters from antitrust activity in broadcasting. This must be done with care, of course, since the antitrust division sometimes displays a monomaniacal preoccupation with competition for its own sake, rather than seeking that structure of industry which best serves the consumer interest. But a minimum reform would be legislation allowing the division immediate recourse to the courts in cases involving regulated industries, with the Commission itself as codefendant in relevant cases. This would at least reduce the ability of the administrative agencies to use endless delay as a tactic in fighting reform.

POLICIES TO PROMOTE FREEDOM OF EXPRESSION IN BROADCASTING

In reviewing the history of broadcasting, one is struck by two opposing phenomena. The first is the continuing effort of the FCC to promote policies that deter economic competition and freedom of expression. One could hardly improve on these policies if one started out to achieve such goals directly. But the other phenomena is the persistent tendency of economic forces, often taking advantage of new technology, to undo the mischief created by the Commission. Cable is an important example of this. Over the long term the Commission and its clients, the industry, are continually put on the defensive by the efforts of the market to break free from unnatural constraints.

Unfortunately, the result is a continuous state of disequilibrium which encourages those unhealthy private interest relationships with government policy makers that make for scandal and corruption. One or another of the mass media is always in a position of needing some favor of the government, either to protect its interests or to become part of the protected group. Most of these issues are obscure to the public. The process is no different from that in other regulated industries (that is, most industries) but in this case there is an entirely obnoxious actual and potential interaction with the First Amendment function of the media.

Examples abound. The National Association of Broadcasters and other lobby groups contribute heavily to political campaigns. Newspaper and TV coverage of these campaigns is critical to political success. When the *Washington Post* and the TV networks opened up their guns on Watergate, there were attempts at reprisal through the regulatory process. That these were unsuccessful is probably due more to their lack of subtlety than to the checks in the system itself.

If television is an important medium of expression with enormous social influence, then it is far too important to leave under the control of politicians and bureaucrats in alliance with private monopoly interests. Freedom of expression and economic competition require decentralization, deregulation, and disintegration: decentralization of decision making in the private sector; deregulation at least of message content; and vertical disintegration of "naturally" monopolistic transmission media from the processes of creation and editing. Finally, consumers must be free to express their preferences with dollars.

Appendix to Chapter Three

Television Programming, Monopolistic Competition and Welfare

by

Michael Spence and Bruce Owen

INTRODUCTION

Advertiser supported televison (and radio) has always posed a challenge to economic analysis. Various economists have examined distortions in program selection that result from advertiser support. These analyses have generally resembled models of spatial competition, and much of their flavor can be traced to Hotelling's [38] famous paper on location. But none of the papers has employed a defensible measure of welfare.[a] In most, the intensity of people's preferences are not fully taken into account.

There are several phenomena that make broadcasting a peculiar market. First, consumers are given a free product (the program) in order to generate audiences, which are then sold to advertisers. The program is free to the consumer not only because the transactions costs of collecting for programs are high, but also because the Federal Communications Commission (FCC) forbids per program charges for most programs. Second, TV programs have some of the attributes of public goods; the marginal cost of an additional viewer is almost literally zero. (Of course it may be necessary to spend more on program production to induce a larger audience to view the program.) Third, there is alleged to be an artificial scarcity of channels, due to FCC regulatory decisions.

The scarcity argument is ambiguous. There are too few VHF stations in the larger cities, given the FCC policies with respect to geographical distribution of stations. On the other hand, a fourth network might not be viable (see Park [65]), and some UHF licenses go begging. Thus, given advertiser support and

---

[a]The major papers are those of Steiner [88], Rothenberg [73], and Wiles [98]. For a critical survey of this literature, see Chapter 3 of Owen, Beebe, and Manning [62]. The traditional approach is to measure welfare by seeing which policy produces the largest audience, or the most "first choices" in viewers' rank orderings of the programs. This ignores intensity of preferences.

other FCC policies, the number of channels in some cities may not be far from its free entry equilibrium. None of the foregoing should be confused with the (erroneous) argument that the electromagnetic spectrum as a whole is "intrinsically" characterized by a scarcity transcending that of other resources. (See Greenberg [32], Levin [45].)

These three conditions have been used to explain deficiencies in television performance, particularly with respect to the number and types of programs that are offered. Most economists would probably agree with the argument that FCC rules limiting the number of channels are inefficient. A few might also agree that rules barring pay TV (that is, TV that charges on a per program basis) might also be a cause of inefficiency. There is a policy debate on these matters. The issues are these: (1) should cable television[b] systems be allowed to charge on a per program basis? (2) Should control over channels on cable television be in the hands of one firm (the operator) or leased out to competitive programmers on a common carrier basis? It is the purpose of this Appendix to try to shed some light on these and other policy issues from the point of view of welfare economics by considering the forces that influence program selection under different supply conditions.

There are four pure cases of interest: advertiser support, or direct viewer payment (pay TV), with either limited or unlimited channels. For our purposes, cable television is identical to over-the-air television, except that channel capacity on cable is not limited. We wish to compare economic welfare in each of these four cases with each other and with the optimum. In addition, we examine the welfare implications of the choice between monopoly and competition, because some authors have argued that, at least under advertising support, monopoly may perform more efficiently than competition—e.g., Steiner [88].

In most of what follows we are comparing second best outcomes. This requires a measure of welfare. We use the total surplus: the gross dollar benefits of a collection of programs, minus the cost of supplying the programs. It is the multimarket sum of consumer and producers' surpluses. It is unambiguously defined only when income effects are negligible, and for the present analysis, income effects are assumed away. (Willig [99] has shown that even when income effects are present, the percentage errors involved in taking areas under Marshallian demand curves may not be too large.)

The choice between pay TV and advertiser supported TV is a choice between second-best outcomes. Under any system, the marginal cost of supplying the program to an additional viewer is virtually zero. An efficient per program charge is therefore zero. Under advertiser support, the per program charge to the viewer is zero: pricing is efficient. However, the program is not supplied

---

[b]Cable television is simply television by wire. The wire makes it easier to exclude and bill people who consume the product. Also, the wire's capacity is not constrained (yet) by FCC policies: it has "unlimited" channels.

unless revenues cover the cost of producing the program, a cost that is independent of the number of viewers. The revenue under advertiser support comes from advertisers who pay a price of roughly two cents per viewer per hour in prime time. The issue with respect to program selection, then, is whether two cents is a reasonable estimate of the average value of the program to the viewers of it. If it is not, then revenues may understate the social value of the program, and some programs with a potential positive surplus may not be profitable.

Under pay TV, producers of programs can appropriate a larger fraction of the surplus generated by a program by pricing it above marginal cost. Provided programs are not perfect substitutes for each other, pay TV will have the character of monopolistic competition. There will be an efficiency loss due to nonmarginal cost pricing. However, by appropriating part of the surplus, the producers of some programs may be able to make positive profits when they could not with advertising support. Therefore, the attraction of pay TV is its potential for generating programs that cater to the tastes of groups of viewers whose size is sufficiently small that the program would be unprofitable under advertiser support. Pay TV has the ability partially to take into account the intensity of preferences. Thus the basic trade-off is between inefficient pricing on the one hand, and the failure of advertiser supported TV to respond to intensities of preference on the other.

Even under pay TV (and in monopolistic competition more generally), there are potential problems with program selection. These result from the fact that revenues are only a fraction of the benefits generated by a program. Thus programs that yield a positive contribution to total surplus may still be unprofitable because the revenues fail to cover fixed costs. But more important, the relationship between revenues and contributions to surplus will vary over programs, according to their demand characteristics. And therefore the market will be biased against certain kinds of programs in ways that are discussed below.

The analysis to follow deals with two related questions. The first is what biases in program selection arise under pay TV and under advertiser supported TV. Biases are to be interpreted as departures from the optimum. The biases are stated in terms of the demand and cost characteristics of programs. We argue that pay TV is biased against programs with low price elasticities of demand, and against high cost programs, and that advertiser supported TV is also so biased, but more strongly. The second issue concerns the number of programs and the sizes of their audiences. Leaving aside biases and focusing on collections of similar programs, one can ask whether either regime supplies too many or too few programs.

The study of program selection under pay TV is formally indistinguishable from the analysis of product selection under monopolistic competition.[c] Some

---

[c]Spence [87] contains a fuller treatment of this problem.

of the following models could be stated in more general ways at great cost in terms of notational complexity. We feel they illustrate the important forces better than would a more abstract analysis. Policy choices in this market are dependent on the structure of demand—an empirical matter. Our aim here is not to dispose of the policy issues (and we certainly have not). It is rather, in the context of an explicit welfare criterion, to focus attention upon important parameters that determine the welfare implications of regulatory policies. These parameters are objects about which one can have intuitions as well as evidence, and upon which the policy debate can be based.

SOURCES OF BIAS IN PROGRAM SELECTION

The Model

We begin by supposing that there are n different types of programs. The list can be rather long and is intended to be exhaustive. The number of viewers of the i-th program (the audience size) is x_i, $i = 1, \ldots, n$. The vector x is $(x_1, \ldots, x_n)$. Given a set of program offerings, each viewer will select his preferred program. Each viewer has a reservation price for the program he selects, a number that gives the dollar value of that program to him. We add up these dollar benefits for all viewers to arrive at a measure of the gross benefits for all viewers. These are denoted $B(x)$, the benefit function.

To illustrate biases in program selection, we shall use a benefit function with the following form:

$$B(x) = \sum_i \phi_i(x_i) - \sum_{i,j} A_{ij} x_i x_j. \tag{1}$$

Each $\phi_i(x_i)$ is concave. (That is equivalent to assuming demand curves are downward sloping. See below.) Without loss of generality, $A_{ii} = 0$ for all i. The coefficients A_{ij} are nonnegative so that $B_{ij} = -2A_{ij} < 0$ and all programs are substitutes.

This functional form gives us considerable flexibility in specifying the demand interactions among products. A pair of products i and j can be demand independent ($A_{ij} = 0$) or very close substitutes (A_{ij} large). We can characterize groups of close substitutes or what have been referred to as lowest common denominator programs within this framework. In addition, the functions $\phi_i(x_i)$ determine the shapes of the individual demand functions (see below) and these can be selected in any desired fashion. The form (1) is not perfectly flexible. But it can be generalized without affecting the qualitative conclusions set out here.

The results we derive using this functional form hold in a more general setting. The general forces at work in product selection under monopolistic competition are discussed in Spence [87]. Here competition under pay TV will correspond to monopolistic competition. The benefit function, $B(x)$, is the multimarket surplus gross of costs. It can be written (in terms of inverse demand functions):

$$B(x) = \sum_{i=1}^{n} \int_0^{x_i} p_i(x_1, \ldots, x_{i-1}, s_i, 0, \ldots, 0)ds_i ,$$

the form that most economists are used to.

We assume that viewers choose programs in a one period context (i.e., one hour), so that each viewer consumes only one program. No two programs are perfect substitutes though they can be very close substitutes.

When confronted with prices, $p_1, \ldots, p_n$, for the n programs, viewers will react by allocating themselves to programs so as to maximize the net benefits to them:

$$B(x) - \sum_i p_i x_i. \tag{2}$$

Therefore, maximizing (2) with respect to x, we have

$$\frac{\partial B_i}{\partial x_i} = B_i = p_i, \quad \text{for} \quad i = 1, \ldots, n. \tag{3}$$

The conditions (3) can be interpreted in another way. Since they hold for any set of prices $p_1, \ldots, p_n$, they define the inverse demand functions for the programs. *The inverse demand functions are the partial derivatives of the benefit function.*

Let us turn briefly to advertising and to program costs. Let z be the price per viewer paid by advertisers, and let F_i be the cost of producing a program of type i. For prime time network television, $F_i \approx 250,000$ dollars per hour and $z \approx 2$ cents per household for the six minutes of commercials permitted. In practice, z is a declining function of x_i, and there is some relationship between i and z. For example, viewers care about the amount of advertising. We could handle that by making the same programs with different numbers of minutes of advertising, different programs (because demands would be different). But then z_i would depend on the program. In what follows, we ignore these complications, though no important conclusion is affected by the simplification.

Since we are not interested in the advertising market per se, but only in its impact on programming, we shall assume that advertisers pay exactly what advertising is worth to them. (This amounts to assuming that the demand for advertising is highly elastic above the market price.) Thus the surplus in the advertising market is equal to the revenues it provides the suppliers of programs.

The surplus generated by both markets is the sum of benefits to consumers,

$B(x)$, and the advertising revenues, $z\Sigma_i x_i$, minus costs of programs, $\Sigma_i F_i$. Letting $T(x)$ be the total surplus, we have:

$$T(x) = B(x) + \sum_i (zx_i - F_i). \tag{4}$$

PROGRAM SELECTION UNDER PAY TV

We begin by considering program selection under pay TV with unlimited channels. The price per viewer for the i-th program is $p_i(x) = B_i(x)$. Therefore the profits of the supplier of the i-th program are:

$$\pi_i = p_i x_i + zx_i - F_i = B_i x_i + zx_i - F_i. \tag{5}$$

Note that advertising is permitted as well as per program fees.

The market is monopolistically competitive. Each firm maximizes profits by setting x_i, and entry occurs until all profitable programs are supplied. Thus we assume the game is played in quantities and the equilibrium is the Nash equilibrium. Price competition would generate somewhat different equilibria, but the qualitative properties would be the same. If the conjectural variation is to hold quantity constant, then firms anticipate price cuts in response to their own price cuts. This does not seem an entirely unreasonable assumption.

We want to characterize the market equilibrium in a way that facilitates comparison with the optimum. We do this by showing that the process of competitive interaction (including entry and exit) results in the implicit maximization of some function which is neither the total surplus, nor industry profits.

When $B(x)$ has the form (1), then the total surplus is:

$$T(x) = \sum_i (\phi_i + zx_i - F_i) - \sum_{i,j} A_{ij} x_i x_j. \tag{6}$$

The profits of the i-th firm are:

$$\pi_i = x_i \phi_i' + zx_i - F_i - 2\sum_j A_{ij} x_i x_j. \tag{7}$$

Industry profits are:

$$\pi = \sum_i \pi_i = \sum_i (x_i \phi_i' + zx_i - F_i) - 2\sum_{i,j} A_{ij} x_i x_j. \tag{8}$$

We shall show that the monopolistically competitive market implicitly maximizes the function:

$$R(x) = \sum_i (x_i \phi_i' + zx_i - F_i) - \sum_{i,j} A_{ij} x_i x_j. \tag{9}$$

The argument is straightforward; we give it and then comment. The argument is that:

$$R(x) - R(x_1, \ldots, x_{i-1}, 0, x_{i+1}, \ldots, x_n) = (x_i \phi_i' + zx_i - F_i) \tag{10}$$

$$- 2 \sum_j A_{ij} x_i x_j \qquad \text{(from (9))}$$

$$= \pi_i. \qquad \text{(from (7))}$$

Thus $\pi_i(x) = R(x)$ minus something that does not depend on x_i. Therefore, in maximizing π_i with respect to x_i, the i-th program producer is maximizing $R(x)$ with respect to x_i. Thus all producers together act so as to maximize $R(x)$. By comparing $R(x)$, $T(x)$ and $\pi(x)$, we can determine the ways in which competitive pay TV and monopoly under pay TV will deviate from the optimum both in terms of pricing and program selection. We turn therefore to these differences.

The difference between $T(x)$ and $R(x)$ is that the $\phi_i(x_i)$ in $T(x)$ are replaced by $x_i \phi_i'$ in $R(x)$. These small differences have large consequences. Since ϕ_i is concave (it must be for demand, $\partial p_i / \partial x_i = \phi_i'' < 0$, to be downward sloping), $\phi_i > x_i \phi_i'$. Thus revenues are less than the program's contribution to surplus. For reference, the contribution of program i to the surplus is:

$$\Delta T_i = \phi_i + zx_i - F_i - 2 \sum_j A_{ij} x_j x_i. \tag{11}$$

This means that ΔT_i can be positive when $\pi_i < 0$, in which case the program will be lost. To simplify notation, let the linear coefficient of x_i in T and R be:

$$c_i = 2 \sum_j A_{ij} x_j - z. \tag{12}$$

The pattern of pricing is also affected by the difference between ϕ_i and $x_i \phi_i'$. From (11) and (7) we have:

$$\frac{\partial \Delta T_i}{\partial x_i} = \phi_i' - c_i, \tag{13}$$

while:

$$\frac{\partial R}{\partial x_i} = \frac{\partial \pi_i}{\partial x_i} = \phi_i' + x_i \phi_i'' - c_i. \tag{14}$$

Therefore when $\partial \pi_i/\partial x_i = 0$, $\partial \Delta T_i/\partial x_i > \partial \pi_i/\partial x_i = 0$. This is the familiar tendency of monopolistic competition to price above marginal cost.

We can use this apparatus to analyze the biases in program selection which characterize monopolistic competition and pay TV. To facilitate the exposition, we consider the case in which $\phi_i(x_i) = a_i x_i^{\beta i}$, where a_i and β_i are parameters and $0 < \beta_i < 1$, so that ϕ_i is concave. Let:

$$\Delta T_i^* = \max_{x_i} \Delta T_i , \tag{15}$$

and let:

$$\pi_i^* = \max_{x_i} \pi_i . \tag{16}$$

A somewhat tedious calculation yields the conclusion that since $\pi_i = a_i \beta_i x_i^{\beta i}$ $- c_i x_i - F_i$, it is maximized with respect to x_i when $\partial \pi_i/\partial x_i = a_i \beta_i^2 x_i^{\beta i-1} - c_i = 0$, or $x_i = (a_i \beta_i^2/c_i)^{1/1-\beta i}$. At that point, $\pi_i^* = c_i((1/\beta_i) - 1) (a_i \beta_i^2/c_i)^{1/1-\beta i} - F_i$. Similarly $\Delta T_i = a_i x_i^{\beta i} - c_i x_i - F_i$ is maximized with respect to x_i when $x_i = (a_i \beta_i/c_i)^{1/1-\beta i}$. At that point $\Delta T_i^* = c_i((1/\beta_i) - 1) (a_i \beta_i/c_i)^{1/1-\beta i} - F_i$. Thus comparing π_i^* and ΔT_i^*, we have

$$\pi_i^* + F_i = \beta_i^{\frac{1}{1-\beta i}} (\Delta T_i^* + F_i) \tag{17}$$

as asserted.

In words, (17) says the maximized revenues for a program are a fraction $(\beta_i^{1/(1-\beta_i)})$ of the maximized gross benefits of that program. Equation (17) is the crucial relationship for examining biases in product selection.

It is easily verified that the function:

$$n(\beta) = \beta^{\frac{1}{1-\beta}} \tag{18}$$

increases monotonically from 0 to $1/e$ on the interval $[0,1]$.[d] Therefore, the smaller β_i is, the smaller will be the ratio of revenues to incremental benefits. It is now not difficult to see that the bias is against products with small β_i's. Specifically, assume two products i and j have the same program costs, $F_i = F_j$

---

[d]Let $n(\beta) = \beta^{1/1-\beta}$. When $\beta = 0$, $n(\beta) = 0$, and when $\beta = 1$, $n(\beta) = 1$. Moreover, $\log n(\beta)$ $= (1 - \beta)\log \beta \leqslant 0$, so that $0 \leqslant n(\beta) \leqslant 1$ for all β. Taking logs and differentiating we have $n'(\beta)/n(\beta) = (1/\beta) - 1 - \log \beta > 0$, so that $n(\beta)$ is monotonically increasing on the interval $[0,1]$.

$= F$, and suppose they contribute equally to the surplus, $\Delta T_i^* = \Delta T_j^*$. Then from (17) we have:

$$\frac{\pi_i^* + F}{\pi_j^* + F} = \frac{n(\beta_i)}{n(\beta_j)}. \tag{19}$$

Thus, if $\beta_i < \beta_j$, $\pi_j^* < \pi^*$. If $\pi^* = 0$ so that programming is just profitable, program i, which contributes equally to the surplus, will be unprofitable and will not be produced, though its contribution to the surplus is positive. In the present parameterization of the problem, the bias is against products with small β_i's. What is β_i? Since:

$$p_i = a_i \beta_i x_i^{\beta_i - 1} - c_i, \tag{20}$$

it is fairly clear that β_i determines the steepness of the inverse demand function. This is akin to but not the same as the own price elasticity of demand. Therefore the bias is against programs with steep inverse demand functions. These are precisely programs with small groups of high value viewers after which reservation prices fall off rapidly.

Stepping back from the present parameterization, *the general bias is against programs that have demands such that revenues capture a small fraction of the gross benefits.* This comes as no surprise. When the entry condition is profitability, revenues are the signal of benefits. They will be a more or less misleading signal depending upon the fraction of the benefits they actually capture. Programs for which revenues are a small fraction of the surplus are special interest programs.

It is important to note that not all programs with small β_i's are eliminated. Some may simply have huge audiences (i.e., a_i is large). That is why the bias is stated in terms of constant or equal contributions to the surplus.

There is another bias—one against costly programs. It is also derivable from equation (17). Suppose that for two programs, i and j, $\Delta T_i^* = \Delta T_j^*$, and $\beta_i = \beta_j = \beta$. It follows from (17) that:

$$(\pi_i^* - \pi_j^*) = (1 - \beta^{\frac{1}{1-\beta}})(F_j - F_i). \tag{21}$$

Therefore, if $F_j > F_i$ then $\pi_j^* < \pi_i^*$. If $\pi_j^* = 0$ then program j will be unprofitable and will not be produced even though its contribution to surplus is the same as that at program i. Thus there is a bias against costly programs, other things being equal. There seems no obvious relationship between program costs and the usual program categories. Some minority taste programs are expensive, others are not, and the same is true of mass appeal programming, leaving aside the effects of competition for scarce factors.

A word about monopoly is perhaps in order. $\pi(x)$ differs from $T(x)$ in two respects: the $\phi_i(x_i)$ are replaced by $x_i\phi_i'$ and the cross effects term is multiplied by two. Two conclusions follow. First, monopoly will exhibit biases similar to those just described for competition. And second, it will tend to hold prices up more and supply fewer programs than either the optimum or competition. The latter follows from the factor of two multiplying the cross-effects term. Thus monopoly tends to produce less "diversity" and to result in higher prices than monopolistic competition.

Monopoly, in addition to having the biases just described for competitive advertiser support, also tends to restrict the number of programs. It does this because the profits of a new program are greater than its contribution to industry profits, due to the substitution effect. An extreme special case of this tendency is referred to as common denominator programs in the literature (see Rothenberg [73]). There is a collection of programs among which there are no substitution effects. Then there is a program that interacts with each of the others. In terms of the matrix of cross-partials, the pattern is the following:

$$A = \begin{pmatrix} & & & \vline & A_{1n} \\ & 0 & & \vline & A_{2n} \\ & & & \vline & \vdots \\ & & & \vline & A_{n-1,\,n} \\ \hline A_{n1}, & \cdots, & A_{n,\,n-1} & \vline & 0 \end{pmatrix}$$

The n-th program is a common denominator (LCD). Suppose the common denominator is supplied and that the remaining programs are profitable even so. Competition would introduce the remaining programs and possibly drive the LCD out. The monopolist, however, may not introduce the non-LCD's because the net effect on profits is negative. This is usually thought to be bad for welfare. But the conclusion is unwarranted without further assumptions (see the section on numbers of programs).

It is, however, true that monopoly under advertiser support is more sparing in its supply of programs. And if there are too few programs under competition, monopoly will be less desirable. The evidence cited later seems to us to indicate that competition with advertiser support generates too few programs. In any case, LCD's are simply a special case of the monopoly tendency to restrict programs relative to competition with advertiser support.

PROGRAM SELECTION UNDER A COMPETITIVE, ADVERTISER SUPPORTED SYSTEM

We have examined certain biases in product selection associated with pay TV. Now we want to compare these problems with those that arise with an advertiser supported system like the present one. When advertising revenues are the sole source of support, all that matters is what the demand for a program is at a zero price. The products whose demands are depicted in Figure 3A-1 will generate equal revenues with advertiser support, even though both the surplus and profits under pay TV will be larger for product A. Therefore one might expect that advertiser supported TV is even harsher on low elasticity products than pay TV. And with suitable ceteris paribus assumptions, this can be shown to be true.

The point is most easily illustrated with linear demand functions, though the principle applies generally. Assume therefore that $\phi_i(x_i) = a_i x_i - A_{ii} x_i^2$. With this assumption, the demand for the i-th product is:

$$p_i = \phi_i' = (a_i - c_i) - 2A_{ii} x_i , \tag{22}$$

where c_i is as defined in (12). Under advertiser support, prices to viewers are zero so that audience size is:

$$x_i = \frac{a_i - c_i}{2A_{ii}} . \tag{23}$$

The profits of the i-th program produced under advertiser support are:

$$\hat{\pi}_i = z \left(\frac{a_i - c_i}{2A_{ii}} \right) - F_i . \tag{24}$$

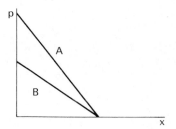

Figure 3A-1. Demand for Two Products

Under pay TV, the profits of program i maximized with respect to x_i are:

$$\pi_i^* = \frac{(a_i - c_i)^2}{8A_{ii}} - F_i. \tag{25}$$

For the linear case, $p_i = a_i - 2A_{ii}x_i - c_i$. At the optimum, $p_i = 0$, or $x_i = (a_i - c_i)/2A_{ii}$. The contribution to surplus is $\Delta T_i = (a_i - c_i)x_i - A_{ii}x_i^2$. At the optimum, $p_i = 0$, and

$$\Delta T_i^* = \frac{1}{4}\frac{(a_i - c_i)^2}{A_{ii}}.$$

Profits are $p_i x_i - F_i = (a_i - c_i)x_i - 2A_{ii}x_i^2 - F_i$. They are maximized when $x_i = (a_i - c_i)/4A_{ii}$. At that point

$$\pi_i^* = \frac{1}{8}\frac{(a_i - c_i)^2}{A_{ii}}.$$

The maximized contribution to the total surplus is:

$$\Delta T_i^* = \frac{(a_i - c_i)^2}{4A_{ii}} - F_i. \tag{26}$$

Notice that $(\pi_i^* + F_i)/(\Delta T^* + F_i) = \frac{1}{2}$. With linear demand curves, there are no biases *of the elasticity type,* under pay TV. However, from (24) and (25), we have:

$$(\pi_i^* + F_i) = \frac{1}{2}A_{ii}\left(\frac{\hat{\pi}_i + F_i}{z}\right)^2. \tag{27}$$

It is now easy to establish the biases from advertiser support. Suppose that for two products, i, and j, $F_i = F_j = F$ and $\pi_i^* = \pi_j^*$. From (27) it follows that:

$$\frac{\hat{\pi}_i + F}{\hat{\pi}_j + F} = \sqrt{\frac{A_{jj}}{A_{ii}}}. \tag{28}$$

Therefore, if $A_{ii} > A_{jj}$, then $\hat{\pi}_j < \hat{\pi}_i$. If two programs have the same costs and are equally profitable under pay TV, the program with the steeper demand curve is less profitable under advertiser support. Moreover, the same statement holds for products that contribute equally to the total surplus in the linear case, since with the same costs, the ratio of profits to surplus is always 1:2.

In general, advertiser support, by giving all viewers equal weight serves special interests poorly, and less well than pay TV. Under pay TV, those with strong preferences can, to some extent, vote with dollars. Advertisers, on the other hand, only count heads.

The price system can be thought of as a voting system of the following type. A program is accepted if a group can be found that will vote for it (provided every member of the group pays the same fee) and such that the fee times the size of the group covers the costs. What one wants, of course, is to allow members of the group to pay different amounts. This amounts to price discrimination, which is the requirement for any voting scheme to generate the efficient amount of a public good. (See Demsetz [21], Oakland [60], and Thompson [92] on public good aspects of TV.)

The program types (or, more generally, commodities) against which monopolistic competition is biased can often be provided by organizations outside the formal market system. There are clubs, societies, and other not-for-profit institutions formed for the purpose, among others, of publishing a newsletter or magazine or academic journal. We have, then, an explanation of the existence of such organizations in the failure of the market system to provide certain goods. However, there is a difficulty. The bias against such goods is greatest in precisely that case where individual valuations of the good vary widely, and thus where clubs may also have considerable difficulty in setting fees. If a uniform price would capture enough of the surplus to cover costs and normal profits, a club would not be needed. Perhaps this explains the proliferation of rates and membership categories which are often found in clubs. Also, it may be easier for potential members to identify each other than for outsiders to do this. Of course, FCC policies prevent this sort of response in television at present, although public broadcasting has some of the attributes of a club.

From the point of view of biases in product selection, pay TV is not ideal, because prices exceed marginal costs, but it appears to be preferable to advertiser support. The choice may be between not having a program at all, and having it available at an inefficient price. Half a loaf may be better than none.

NUMBERS OF PROGRAMS AND AUDIENCE SIZES IN EQUILIBRIUM

Our concern up to this point has been to show that there are biases against programs with certain comparative demand characteristics under both pay TV and advertiser supported television. Roughly speaking, the biases are against special interest and expensive programs, both being more pronounced under advertiser support.

Apart form these biases, there is the question of which system provides the better second-best solution. In this section, we consider this and related questions. Having discussed biases, it is convenient to set that issue aside and to conduct the present analysis by considering similar (but not necessarily highly substitutable) products. In part, this is a device for making the analysis of equilibrium tractable. Specifically, let us assume in the previous model that $\phi_i = \phi, F_i = F$ and $A_{ij} = A$ for all i and j. Since the demand parameters and costs of programs are similar in all respects, the audience sizes will be the same in equilibrium: $x_i = x$ for all i. The equilibrium and the optimum can therefore be characterized by n, the number of programs and by x, the audience size. (Note that programs are *not* assumed to be perfect substitutes for each other.)

With these assumptions, the total surplus in equation (4) becomes:

$$T(x,n) = n\phi(x) - Ax^2(n^2 - n) - nF + nzx . \tag{29}$$

The function implicitly maximized by monopolistic competition is:

$$R(x,n) = nx\phi' - Ax^2(n^2 - n) - nF + nzx. \tag{30}$$

Industry profits, the objective function of the monopolist, are:

$$\pi(x,n) = nx\phi' - 2Ax^2(n^2 - n) - nF + nzx. \tag{31}$$

At this point it is most useful to illustrate the optimum and various equilibria diagrammatically. This is done in Figure 3A-2, for a typical case.[e] In general, the pay TV equilibrium (E) is below and to the left of the optimum (O). Monopoly under pay TV (M) is below and to the left of E. There can be exceptions but they are not of great interest. The points S and T are second-best optima of a slightly different kind. T, for example, is the point of tangency of an iso-surplus line with the zero profit line ($R_n = 0$). Thus if entry cannot be controlled but prices can (via taxes or direct regulation), T is the highest attainable point. Similarly, S is the second best with monopolistically competitive pricing taken as given. It is achieved by subsidies to producers of programs. It is possible that E could correspond to either S or T, but not to both.[f]

Under a competitive, advertiser supported system, pricing is optimal so that ($T_x = 0$. Entry occurs until profits per program, $zx - F$ are zero. Thus

---

[e]The optimum in fact occurs when for each i, $\partial T/\partial x_i = \phi_i' - 2\sum_j A_{ij}x_j + z = p_i + z = 0$. Thus at the optimum $p_i = -z$, for all i. However, even if TV were subsidized, negative prices might be infeasible because people could leave their television sets on (without watching) to earn money. Thus, in what follows, the optimum is approximated by $p_i = 0, i = 1, \ldots, n$, which is the pattern of pricing under advertiser supported TV.

[f]The reason is that at S, an isototal surplus line is tangent to the line $R_x = 0$. At T, an isototal surplus line is tangent to $R_n = 0$. If S and T coincided at E, the isosurplus line through E would be tangent to two lines that cross, which is impossible.

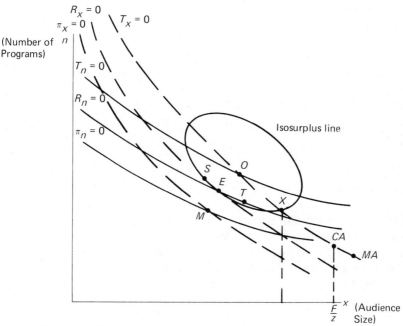

Summary of Points:

O　optimum
E　competitive pay TV equilibrium
M　monopoly pay TV
S　second best optimum given $\pi \geqslant O$ constraint
T　second best optimum given monopolistically competitive pricing
CA　competitive advertiser support equilibrium (with unlimited channels)
MA　monopoly advertiser support
X　If advertiser TV were subsidized to permit more programs, the
　point at which the total surplus is the same as at *E*.

Figure 3A-2. Welfare Comparisons

$x = F/z$, as shown (point *CA*). With monopoly and advertiser support, pricing is the same but the introduction of new programs stops before profits are zero, at a point like *MA*.

The point *X* is of some interest. At *X*, pricing is optimal and the total surplus is the same as at *E*. Thus *X* gives the number of programs that are required under advertiser support to equal the performance of pay TV.

THE RELATIVE POSITIONS OF THE EQUILIBRIA

The relative positions of the various equilibria in Figure 3A-2 obviously depend upon some assumptions about the magnitudes of the parameters in the model. And since these positions determine the attractiveness of the equilibria from a welfare point of view, it is important to discuss how the equilibria move about when the parameters change.

The relationship between E and O is determined largely by the own price elasticity of demand for the representative product. This is most easily seen by observing that the demand for a representative program is:

$$p = \phi' - 2A\bar{x}(n-1),\tag{32}$$

so that:

$$\frac{dp}{dx} = \phi''(x).\tag{33}$$

Thus if ϕ'' is small, the inverse demand curve is flat. But ϕ is also more nearly linear so that ϕ and $x\phi'$ do not differ greatly. The surplus, T, and the function implicitly maximized under monopolistic competition, R, differ in that ϕ is replaced by $x\phi'$. When this difference is small, the optima, E and O are close together. Conversely, it is when price elasticities are low that E and O are far apart.

In contrast, the relative positions of CA, the advertiser supported equilibrium, and O, the optimum, are determined by the cross elasticities of demand, and by the size of z relative to the average valuation of a program by viewers. Cross-elasticities or degrees of substitutability are determined by the parameter A. As A increases (programs become closer substitutes), the optimum can be shown to move downward and to the right as depicted in Figure 3A-3. (This is argued in the addendum.) Similarly, the equilibrium under pay TV, E, also moves down and to the right. The number of programs declines and the audience size increases. On the other hand, the advertiser supported equilibrium simply moves down. The number of programs is reduced but audience size remains the same.

Two conclusions follow immediately: If cross-elasticities are high, then

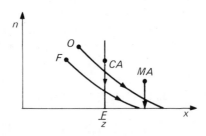

Figure 3A-3. Effect of Increasing Program Substitutability

competitive advertiser support may be preferable to pay TV; and if cross-elasticities are even higher, so that the optimum is to the right of the competitive advertiser supported equilibrium, CA, then monopoly under pay TV (MA) may be preferred to competitive advertiser support and pay TV. With very close substitutes, the tendency of monopoly to restrict programs becomes an advantage. This conclusion for the case of perfect substitutes appears in the literature, where it is argued that monopoly avoids duplication of perfect substitutes (see Steiner [88]).

Monopoly has another potential advantage. If the number of channels is limited, competitive advertiser support may use up scarce channels with close substitutes. Monopoly may limit the number of close substitutes, and use the remaining channels for programs that are less perfrect substitutes. Such programs may be less profitable individually but do not cut into the audiences generated by the other programs as much.

The importance of cross elasticities in determining the relative positions of the optimum (O) and the equilibrium (CA) is sufficient to justify a brief analytic treatment. The gross dollar benefits from n programs of audience size x are:

$$B = n\phi(x) - Ax^2(n^2 - n) \tag{34}$$

The rate of increase of these benefits with the number of programs is:

$$\frac{\partial B}{\partial n} = \phi - Ax^2(2n - 1). \tag{35}$$

Thus the rate of increase of benefits per viewer is:

$$\frac{1}{x}\frac{\partial B}{\partial n} = \frac{\phi(x)}{x} - Ax(2n - 1). \tag{36}$$

The rate of increase of costs (nF) per viewer, is clearly $(1/x) (\partial(nF) / \partial n) = F/x$.

Now let us examine those quantities at the competitive advertiser supported equilibrium. At that equilibrium, the audience size is F/z. In addition, prices are zero so that:

$$\phi'(y) = 2Ay(n - 1) \tag{37}$$

where $y = F/z$. This expression defines the equilibrium number of programs, n. Using (37), and substituting in (36), we find that the rate of increase of average benefits per viewer with the number of programs is:

$$g = \frac{1}{y} \frac{\partial B}{\partial n} = \left[\frac{\phi(y)}{y} - \phi'(y) \right] - Ay. \tag{38}$$

The rate of increase of costs is $F/y = z$.

One can now see precisely what determines the relationship between the optimum and the equilibrium. If g, the average benefits per viewer of the marginal program, exceeds z, the average cost, the number of programs should be increased from the equilibrium and conversely. From (38) one observes that increasing the cross effect, A, makes average benefits smaller. If A is large enough, g may be less than z—that is, the optimum has fewer programs than the equilibrium. The other factor that determines average benefits at the equilibrium is the term in square brackets in (38). It is positive because ϕ is concave. Moreover, speaking somewhat imprecisely, the more concave ϕ is, the steeper the inverse demand and the larger the average benefits of an *additional* program.

This can be stated more precisely. Suppose that $\phi(x) = dx^\beta$. It follows that average benefits are $a = d(1 - \beta)y^{\beta - 1} - Ay$. This function increases with d, decreases with A, and decreases with y. The derivative with respect to β is

$$\frac{da}{d\beta} = y^{\beta - 1} \left[d(1 - \beta)\log(y) - 1 \right].$$

It has an ambiguous sign. However, if β is near 1 it is negative and if β is small, it is positive.

To assess the performance of the present system, one wants to compare g and z, or equivalently gy and $zy = F$. This can be done for networks rather than programs with the available data. Table 3A-1 presents some rough and ready empirical data on the issue at hand. Using demand estimates for cable TV, Noll, Peck, and McGowan [58] estimated consumer surplus from (free) network TV channels. (These are presented in the table in 1970 dollars.) 1970 costs for the

Table 3A-1. **Benefits, Costs, and Profits from TV Channels (in millions of dollars per year)**

Number of Channels	Consumer Surplus	Marginal Consumer Surplus	Marginal Cost	Marginal Profit with Advertising Support
1	16000	16000	800	100
2	25100	9100	800	75
3	31300	6200	800	25
4	36000	4700	800	≈ 0
5	39800	3800	800	< 0

Source: Consumer surplus based on estimates in Noll, Peck, and McGowan [58], (p. 288); other data based on rough estimates by the authors—see text.

operation of the three networks and their affiliated stations averaged $800 million per channel. Various authors, including Park [65], have estimated that the profitability of a fourth advertiser supported network is approximately nil. The figures in the profit column are simply the authors' guess as to normal network profits averaged over the business cycle.

The point of all this is that while the addition of more networks clearly adds to surplus up to some point far beyond the present number (three), these new networks would not be profitable under advertising support. While the estimates are rough, the orders of magnitude are almost certainly correct. Thus, advertising prices fail by a wide margin to reflect viewers' valuations of programs. This suggests that the competitive, advertiser supported equilibrium (*CA* in Figure 3A-2) is not in fact very close to the optimum in absolute terms, and increases the likelihood that *E* is superior to *CA*.

CONSUMER SURPLUS

It might be arued that the total surplus is not what one ought to focus on, but rather consumer surplus (the benefits to the public). It is true that some of the benefits of pay TV accrue to the producers of programs. But that does not imply that consumers are hurt, on average. It is of course almost inevitable that a change from advertiser support to cable will redistribute benefits among consumers. The consumer surplus in the symmetric case is simply:

$$S = T(x,n) - \pi(x,n) = n(\phi - x\phi') + Ax^2(n^2 - n). \tag{39}$$

Isoconsumer surplus lines are tangent both to isototal surplus lines and to isoprofit lines. The isoconsumer surplus line through *E* is depicted in Figure 3A-4. It intersects the marginal cost pricing line at *R*. It is below and to the

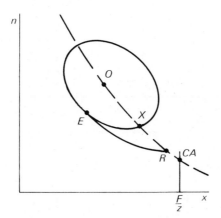

Figure 3A-4. Consumer Surplus

right of X, where the *total* surplus is the same as at E. It is possible for CA to lie between X and R. In that case pay TV would increase the total surplus but hurt consumers qua consumers—*someone* gets the revenues or profits. The position of CA relative to R is an empirical question. For the reasons cited above, we think CA is likely to be considerably to the right of X and R.

LIMITED CHANNELS

The FCC is alleged to artificially limit available channels, at least on the VHF band in the larger cities, with the result that broadcasters earn scarcity rents and program variety is reduced.

The effect of limiting the number of available channels can be examined with the aid of Figure 3A-5. If the number of channels is restricted to $\bar{n}_1$, competitive pay TV will generate the outcome C. It is worse than the equilibrium E. The constraint $n \leqslant \bar{n}_1$ has no effect on a monopolist. If n is constrained to be equal or less than $\bar{n}_2$, the monopolist under pay TV will be at D, and competition under pay TV is at S. And since $\bar{n}_2$ is the number of channels in an advertiser supported equilibrium, S is inferior to CA. In order that pay TV produce a preferred outcome, the channel constraint must be lifted to $\bar{n}_3$. The outcome then becomes N (N and CA are on the same isototal surplus line).

The two conclusions that follow are: first, if channel capacity is naturally limited, pay TV may not be desirable; and second, pay TV has few virtues if entry into the programming industry is effectively restricted by holding the number of channels down. Under pay TV, restrictions on entry serve no purpose

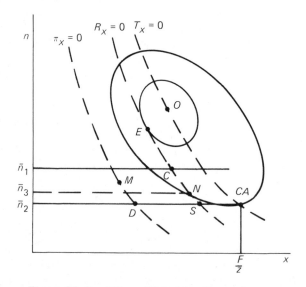

Figure 3A-5. Effect of Limiting Channels

beneficial to consumers. It is conceivable that the equilibrium, E, under pay TV, has more programs than the optimum constrained to nonnegative profits. That would provide a rationale for restricting channels under pay TV. But the information required to determine that such a restriction would be desirable is unlikely to be available. In fact, the number of channels is not "naturally" limited, especially in cable. But these results suggest that it may be a mistake for the FCC to allow pay TV in the existing artificially limited over-the-air channels unless steps are taken to allow expansion of channel capacity.

FIRST BEST OUTCOMES AND
INFORMATIONAL REQUIREMENTS

If one supposes, for the sake of argument, that suppliers of programs were perfect price discriminators, then it is not difficult to see that the program selection problem would disappear. For if each supplier of a program could perfectly price discriminate, he could appropriate exactly the marginal contribution of his product to the total benefits. Thus with price discrimination, the producer of the i-th program has profits of:

$$\bar{\pi}_i = \Delta T_i(x) - F_i \tag{40}$$

$$= B(x) - B(x_1, \ldots, x_{i-1}, 0, x_{i+1}, \ldots, x_n) - F_i$$

$$= [B(x) - \sum_j F_j] - [B(x_1, \ldots, 0, \ldots, x_n) - \sum_{j \neq i} F_j]$$

$$= \Delta T_i$$

$$= T(x) - T(x_1, \ldots, x_{i-1}, 0, x_{i+1}, \ldots, x_n).$$

When the i-th producer maximizes profits, he is maximizing the total surplus, $T(x)$ with respect to x_i. The equilibrium is optimal, and price discrimination would eliminate the problem. It is a general theorem that perfect price discrimination under monopolistic competition eliminates the product choice problem (see Spence [87]). A special case is monopoly: there, profits and the total surplus are the same.

The optimal policy would be to forbid any marginal fees (such as per program charges) and to supplement the resulting programs with direct subsidies to programs which, while contributing to surplus, did not appear in the private market. This is in fact almost exactly the present policy, in a superficial sense: per program charges are in practice forbidden and there are direct subsidies to public broadcasting stations. In fact, however, no attempt is made to subsidize those programs that would make the greatest contribution to surplus. One reason this is not done is that the costs of acquiring the information requisite to the task are enormous. (The government would require the same information needed by the price discriminator—in effect, the reservation price of each individual for each program, and all the substitution effects.) Even if the information were somehow available, there would be serious First Amendment questions involved in the subsidization policy, since presumably some programs would be controversial. It is for these reasons that we enquire into the probable effects of second-best institutional alternatives, despite the superficial suitability of present policies.

SUMMARY OF RESULTS

We have focused here on the welfare implications of alternative market structures and policies in the broadcasting industry. Welfare is measured by the sum of producers' and consumers' surplus. It has been demonstrated that any of the private market systems considered contain biases against certain kinds of programs. These biases result in the absence from the market of programs which "ought" to be produced, in the sense that their marginal benefits exceed their marginal costs. The programs that are likely to be omitted are those with low own price elasticity of demand ("minority taste programs") and those that are expensive to produce. The cause of this bias is the failure of prices, as marginal signals, to fully reflect the average intensity of preferences for certain programs. In the presence of fixed costs, this leads to the nonviability of such programs, since benefits but not revenues exceed costs.

The bias is present with pay TV, but it is *worse* under a competitive, advertiser supported structure such as we now have. This is so because pay TV prices reflect intensity of preferences better than the flat capitation rate paid by advertisers. In the pay TV case, monopoly does worse than competition, unless there is perfect price discrimination. An advertiser supported monopolist produces fewer programs—and has the same biases—as a competitive advertiser supported system.

Leaving aside the question of bias among program types, we can examine the positions of the various market structure equilibria with respect to each other and the optimum in terms of the number of programs produced and their audience sizes. This is done by taking the symmetric case in which all programs have identical demand and cost parameters. The relative positions of the equilibria depend on empirical issues, and in particular on the degree to which programs are close substitutes for each other. As the cross-elasticity of substitution among programs increase, advertising support becomes more (and pay TV less) likely to approximate a feasible second-best structure for the medium. Some sketchy empirical evidence suggests that the advertiser supported equilibrium is in fact not very close to the optimum. Another possible reason for preferring advertiser support is in the case where channels are either naturally or artificially limited. Here, pay TV may well make things worse. Thus the argument for pay TV does depend on channels being unlimited, or equivalently, on a policy of open entry.

Finally, a first-best solution requires a set of subsidies and rules that are remarkably similar on the surface to those that presently exist. Unfortunately, the information required to operate successfully in this mode is not available. Determination of the second-best policy requires empirical analysis. Casual empiricism suggests that a system of open entry and pay TV is probably the second-best market structure.

Addendum: Analysis of the Symmetric Case

The total surplus can be written as follows:

$$T(x,n) = n\phi(x) - Ax^2(n^2 - n) - nF \tag{43}$$

from (4) with $\phi_i \equiv \phi$, $F_i = F$ and $A_{ij} = A$ for all i and j. The two optimizing conditions are $T_x = 0$ or:

$$\phi' = 2Ax(n-1), \tag{44}$$

and $T_n = 0$ or:

$$n = \frac{1}{2} + \frac{\phi - F}{2Ax^2}. \tag{45}$$

Figure 3A-6 shows a picture of these two conditions. Note that when $n = 1$, $\phi'(x) = 0$. Let that occur at $x = \bar{x}$. Note also that the pick of the curve $T_n = 0$ occurs when $(\phi - F)/x^2$ is at a maximum. Let that quantity be $\bar{\bar{x}}$. The optimum is at O_1. Now suppose we raise A. Both curves crop downward (see (44) and (45)). However, the line $T_x = 0$ pivots around $(\bar{x},1)$, because, for every A, $\phi'(x) = 0$ when $n = 1$. Therefore, as A rises, the optimum must eventually approach the point $(\bar{x},1)$, because, eventually the line $T_n = 0$ will hit the x-axis to the left of $\bar{x}$. This means that as the cross-elasticities become high, the optimal number of programs falls and the optimal audience size rises toward $\bar{x}$.

To analyze the equilibrium with pay TV, we simply replace ϕ by $\mu(x) = x\phi' < \phi$ in the preceding equations. The equivalent of $\bar{x}$ occurs when $\phi' + x\phi'' = 0$. Let that point by $\hat{x}$. Clearly $\hat{x} < \bar{x}$. Similarly the analogue of $\bar{\bar{x}}$ occurs at the maximum of $x\phi'/x^2$. Call that point $\hat{\bar{x}}$. Again $\hat{\bar{x}} < \bar{\bar{x}}$.

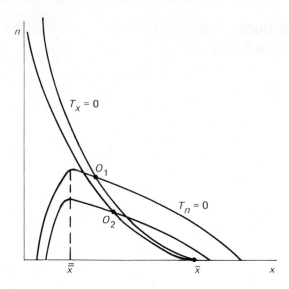

Figure 3A–6. Two Conditions

The fact that $\hat{x} < \bar{x}$ is of special importance. It says that as cross elasticities become large, and the programs become more perfect substitutes, the equilibrium and the optimum *do not* approach each other. The reason is that high cross elasticities keep the number of profitable programs down. It is for this reason that advertiser supported TV may be preferable for a group of close substitutes. It is also why forbidding advertising on pay TV is a risky strategy.

The difference between the equilibrium and the optimum is determined by the difference between ϕ and $x\phi'$. If ϕ is close to being linear, own price elasticity is high and ϕ and $x\phi'$ are close in value. The optimum and the equilibrium would not then be far apart. If ϕ is sharply concave, own price elasticity is low; ϕ and $x\phi'$ differ considerably and the equilibrium is further from the optimum.

Chapter Four

Magazines and Motion Pictures

INTRODUCTION

This chapter treats the magazine and motion picture industries in a very cursory fashion. There are two reasons for this. The first is that there has been very little serious economic research published about these industries. The second is that there are not in either case significant First Amendment issues raised by the economic structure of the industry. Thus, my principal purpose in including any comment on these media is to illustrate two practical ideals. Magazines are enormously encouraging examples of robust competition in the marketplace of ideas. The history of the motion picture industry provides a lesson in what can be achieved through structural reform. The granduer of the vision to which we should aspire in television and in newspapers is foreshadowed by magazines and movies.

MAGAZINES

The magazine industry in the United States provides perhaps the closest approximation possible to ideal competition and freedom. It is virtually impossible to count the number of periodicals published, primarily because it is so difficult to define a periodical. Still, by any reasonable definition it is clear that there are several tens of thousands of periodicals available to the American public, most of them very highly specialized in their content.[a]

Why are there so many periodicals? Why is this mass medium so unlike television and newspapers in the degree of competition and concentration within an industry? It seems clear that there are at least two factors at work. First, the

[a]One estimate puts the number of *scientific* journals at 40,000 with an average subscription rate of $15 and an average circulation of 800. See "Primary Journal Publication" UNESCO (October 2, 1967).

stages of production of a magazine are almost never vertically integrated. Creative, editorial and transmission functions are all separately owned. There is as usual a significant degree of concentration and economies of scale at the transmission level (physical delivery of periodicals from printer to reader or newsstand) but this concentration has not been extended backwards into the editorial process.

Second, the editorial and creative processes themselves are not characterized by economies of scale or significant fixed costs. This, combined with the apparent specialization of taste among consumers, allows the coexistence of thousands of editorial products, most of them poor substitutes for the others. The model developed in the Appendix to Chapter Three is directly relevant to this industry. Since periodicals are supported both by subscribers and by advertisers, and since fixed costs of production for the editorial product seem to be quite low, the monopolistic competition equilibrium is likely to be quite near the optimum level of output and audience size. (It cannot, of course, be *at* the optimum.)

It is tempting to think of the magazine industry in terms of the mass general interest publications with which we are all familiar (see Table 4-1). But these magazines do not comprise more than a few dozen of the thousands published. The "typical" magazine is small in circulation and highly specialized in its subject matter. Academic journals with a few thousand subscribers and news-

Table 4-1.   Large Circulation Magazines, 1971

Magazine	Circulation Per Issue (thousands)	Per Cent Newsstand Sales
Readers' Digest	17,995	10.2
TV Guide	16,351	65.0
Better Homes and Gardens	7,952	8.1
Women's Day	7,855	100.0
Family Circle	7,862	100.0
McCall's	7,516	9.0
National Geographic	7,235	0.0
Ladies Home Journal	7,035	13.5
Life	7,110	3.1
Playboy	6,154	77.0
Good Housekeeping	5,758	23.9
Redbook	4,731	21.4
Time	4,275	5.2
American Home	3,574	7.9
Newsweek	2,624	8.0
Farm Journal	2,279	0.0
Boy's Life	2,238	0.1
Sports Illustrated	2,162	3.7
Parent's	2,016	0.5

Source: Association of National Advertisers

letters with a few hundred subscribers are at the other end of the spectrum from *Readers' Digest* and *TV Guide*, the largest circulation periodicals.

The umbrella model of newspaper structure, discussed in Chapter two, can be applied to the magazine industry. The newspaper umbrella model was oriented toward content and advertising demand, specialized geographically in various communities. But we can omit the geography and imagine a similar structure of tastes among consumers. Then we will expect to find in layer 1 a set of fairly general and common interests, likely to support such publications as *Newsweek*, *Time*, and *Readers' Digest*, overlapping a series of less general but still quite large second layer interests—*Playboy*, *Cosmopolitan*, *Boys' Life*, *Journal of the American Medical Association*, and the like. Under this second layer is a third, made up of what may be regarded as specialty interests—gardening, literary, philatetic, academic disciplines, and so on. Finally, there is the most numerous bottom layer, comprised of very highly specialized, very small circulation editorial products.

It seems to be a fair, but not universally true, generalization that advertising revenue becomes progressively less important relative to subscription revenue as one moves down from layer 1 publications. In terms of the model put forward in the Appendix to Chapter Three, this suggests increasing inelasticity of demand among the lower circulation periodicals, or a negative correlation between the inelasticity of demand and the vertical intercept of the demand curve.

The magazine industry provides an extremely useful example of what might be achieved in television, and possibly in newspapers, with public policies designed to increase competition and freedom. The concentrated transmission stage of periodical publishing is simply the post office, which is in effect a common carrier. For layer 1 and layer 2 periodicals, newsstand sales are often very important, but here also there is, or has been, significant concentration at the wholesale distribution level.[b]

People who are presented with the magazine analogy as an ideal structure for mass communication often point out that the industry is "obviously" dying. Nothing could be further from the truth. To be sure, there has been a considerable attrition of very general interest (layer 1) periodicals, such as *Look* and the *Saturday Evening Post*, but this is due to competition from television, which has harmed these publications in the same way and for the same reasons it has harmed major city newspapers: television provided more competition for these periodicals in advertising markets. But the same period that witnessed the attack on layer 1 periodicals also saw a significant growth in the more specialized magazines.

[b]See Tables 4-1 and 4-7 below for newsstand sales. There have been a couple of antitrust cases against magazine wholesalers, who intermediate between publishers and newsstands. See *United States v. American News Co.*, 1955 Trade Cases 70,663 (S.D.N.Y. 1955); *American News Co. v. F.T.C.* 300 F. 2d 104 (2d Circuit, 1962).

Table 4-2.   Periodical Industry Statistics (Census data)

Year	Number of Periodicals	Total Circulation per Issue (000)	Revenues (millions)	
			Total	Advertising
1919	4796	N.A.	–	–
1929	5157	202,022	–	–
1939	4985	239,683	–	–
1947	4610	384,628	–	–
1955	7648	–	–	–
1958	–	408,364	1639	1018
1960	8422	–	–	–
1963	–	–	2036	1242
1965	8990	–	–	–
1967	–	–	2668	1547
1970	9573	–	–	–
1973	9630	–	–	–

Source: *Historical Statistics of the United States*, p. 500, Series R183-184; *Statistical Abstract* (1973), p. 502, Tables 820–821.

History of the Industry

According to Peterson [67] the mass magazine was born during the same period, 1880-1910, that saw the rise of mass circulation newspapers. Publishers of magazines in this period were the beneficiaries of the growing demand for advertising by manufacturers seeking a national market for their wares. They saw that a reduction in subscription prices could increase circulation sufficiently to attract mass market advertisers. In this same period, advertising agencies became common intermediaries in the market. Of course, editorial content had to change too, and it became more general and more "popular" in nature. Advertising moved from the back of the magazine to be spread between the editorial matter, and achieved for the first time an aura of "respectability."[c] Favorable postal rates helped considerably in reaching the mass audience (see Kennedy [40]).

Tables 4-2 to 4-9 present some of the available statistics on the periodical industry. There appear to be no comprehensive and reliable data encompassing the entire industry. Much of the data that are available refer to periodicals with important advertising revenues, as opposed to those which depend almost entirely on subscriptions.

Tables 4-2 and 4-3 summarize the Census Bureau data. These data indicate

[c]Between 1888 and 1928, the average number of pages in magazines increased by 71 percent in monthlies and 756 percent in weeklies. During the same period, the proportion of pages devoted to advertising increased from 42 to 63 percent in monthlies and from 16 to 58 percent in weeklies.

Average Number of Advertising Pages

	1888	1928	Percent Change
Monthlies	60	185	208
Weeklies	3	79	2,533

See *Printers' Ink* 225 (October 29, 1948): 108.

Table 4-3.   Periodical Census Data, 1958–1967 (all data in millions)

Categories	Circulation per Issue			Total Revenue			Advertising Revenue		
	1958	1963	1967	1958	1963	1967	1958	1963	1967
Farm	19	14	12	$ 67	$ 54	$ 57	$ 55	$ 46	$ 46
Specialized	52	–	–	380	535	675	294	413	525
General: (Total)	242	–	–	887	1,167	1,473	544	711	880
Comics	63	28	15	22	11	9	1	1	–
Women's	71	73	75	207	316	362	133	204	245
General interest	98	103	137	530	659	847	319	380	457
General news	8	7	10	101	141	204	73	106	146
Business news	2	–	1	26	28	40	18	15	25
Other	96	142	127	265	230	284	123	73	97
Total	408	–	–	1,639	2,036	2,668	1,018	1,242	1,547

Source: *Statistical Abstract*, p. 502, Table 821.

a 100 percent increase in the number of periodicals between 1919 and 1973, but show a high level of volatility among categories of magazines. The decline in comics, probably due to television, is particularly noteworthy. Table 4-4 reports registration of magazine *issues* for copyright. It is doubtful that a very large proportion of magazine issues are copyrighted, but those that are probably account for the bulk of circulation. The number of issues copyrighted increased 625 percent between 1880 and 1920, and 121 percent between 1920 and 1960. Although many magazines are sold on newsstands, second class mail volume gives a rough indication of the growth in aggregate circulation (probably overstated because of the declining importance of newsstand sales). Table 4-5 summarizes the mail volume data, indicating a 106 percent increase in aggregate circulation between 1926 and 1972. (Figure 4-1 depicts these trends graphically.)

The post office has informal estimates of magazine mail volume by type of magazine. These are reported in Table 4-6 for 1949-1970. Total circulation between 1955 and 1970 increased 78 percent, with the least increase in religion, education, and welfare periodicals (14 percent), and the greatest in the controlled circulation (business advertising, free distribution) category, which increased 561 percent. If we add to these data the 1.8 billion single copy newsstand sales reported by SRDS and ABC publications in 1970 (Table 4-7), total annual periodical circulation (total copies) in 1970 totals 10.15 billion, or 50 copies per person per year, or 161 copies per household per year.

Table 4-4. Registration of Copyright Data (thousands)

Year	Periodicals (issues)	Motion Pictures	Books (including pamphlets)
1880	4	–	–
1885	6	–	–
1890	8	–	–
1895	12	–	–
1905	23	–	30
1910	22	–	25
1915	24	3.0	32
1920	29	1.7	39
1925	41	1.8	66
1930	44	2.2	62
1935	36	1.7	51
1940	40	1.6	64
1945	46	1.7	41
1950	55	1.9	50
1955	59	2.7	54
1960	64	3.5	60
1965	78	3.8	76
1970	84	2.5	88
1972	85	3.2	103

Source: *Historical Statistics of the United States*, p. 606, Series W53, W57, W62; *Statistical Abstract* (1973), p. 504, Table 824.

Table 4-5. Second Class Mail, Pieces Delivered, 1926-1972

Year	Pieces (billions)
1926	4.6
1930	5.0
1935	4.1
1940	4.6
1945	5.5
1950	6.3
1955	6.7
1960	7.5
1965	8.6
1970	9.4
1972	9.5

Note: There is apparently a distinction between "pieces" and "copies." Compare Table 4-6.
Source: *Historical Statistics of the United States*, p. 498, Series R-151; *Statistical Abstract* (1973), p. 493, Table 800.

Table 4-8 presents a view of the financial operations of 42 large circulation magazines. It is noteworthy that these data are not greatly different than those for daily newspapers. The typical large magazine in 1970 received 44¢ in revenue per copy, 66 percent from advertising. It spent 5¢ on editorial costs, and an equal sum soliciting subscriptions. Rather surprisingly, only 4 cents was spent on postage of all kinds, half of this for mailing the magazine. On the other hand, profit was only 2¢ per copy, down considerably from earlier years.

This raises the postage subsidy issue. For at least a century the post office has subsidized periodicals and newspapers by charging postage rates below cost. The new guidelines for the postal service suggest that this policy is to end.[d] Even though postage costs account for only 9 percent of the revenues of a magazine, they are large compared to profit rates, and a significant increase will clearly drive some periodicals out of business despite the apparent inelasticity of subscription demand. (Postal costs are probably a larger fraction of costs for small circulation periodicals.) In light of the analysis of the Appendix to Chapter Three, it is likely that the postal subsidy was good policy—any lowering of marginal cost will increase the number of firms (products) in monopolistic competition. Without the subsidy there will be too few. One does not know how much the subsidy helps, but it probably helps somewhat. Thus, there is an economic rationale as well as a "political" rationale for the subsidy.

Finally, for what it is worth, the official data on concentration are reported in Table 4-9.

Magazines provide an excellent structural benchmark for policies designed to improve the performance of other media. If the data were available they also

[d] See Postal Reorganization Act of 1970, 39 U.S.C. 101-5605 (1970 ed.)

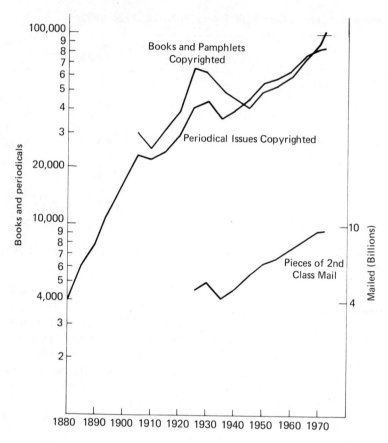

Figure 4-1.   Magazines Mailed and Copyrighted, 1880–1972

Table 4-6.   Post Office Estimates of Magazine Circulation by Categories, 1949–1970

Categories	Millions of Copies				
	1949	*1955*	*1960*	*1965*	*1970*
General Interest	1,111	1,660	2,409	2,732	2,923
Nonprofit	1,888	1,648	1,953	2,562	2,913
Agriculture, business, and professional	435	753	825	892	1,056
Classroom	–	482	861	1,257	844
Controlled circulation	17	85	125	281	562
Religion, education, and welfare	117	72	76	75	82
Total	5,542[a]	4,700	6,249	7,799	8,380

[a]Includes 1974 unclassified periodicals.

Source: *Mathematica* [50], p. 4–989.

Table 4-7. ABC and SRDS Magazine Circulation, 1950–1970 (millions of copies)

Year	Total Annual Circulation	Single Copy Sales	Percent Newsstand Sales
1950	3462	1459	42
1955	3856	1533	40
1960	4287	1371	32
1965	4847	1540	32
1970	5524	1768	32

Note: The post office in 1970 reported delivering 8,380 million copies of publisher's second class matter (Table 4-6). The data in this table account for 3,756 million copies, but refer only to a few hundred ABC and SRDS magazines–those with significant advertising aspirations. Thus, 4,624 million copies of periodicals eligible for second class rates were mailed in 1970, produced by publishers seeking, presumably, mainly subscription revenues.
Source: Foster Associates [29], p. 4–909. (ABC is Audit Bureau of Circulation; SRDS is Standard Rate and Data Service.)

Table 4-8. Financial Profile of Major Magazines, 1970

	$ Million	Percent Revenue	Per Copy Cents
Revenues			
Advertising (net)	670	66	29
Subscriptions (1961 millions copies)	260	26	13
Single copies (361 million copies)	86	8	23
Total (2,322 million copies)	1016	100	44
Expenses			
Advertising costs	111	11	5
Subscription selling	110	11	5
Newsstand selling	14	1	1
Fulfillment	42	4	2
Editorial	106	10	5
Paper	201	20	9
Printing	227	22	10
First class postage	21	2	1
Second class postage	49	5	2
Third class postage	25	2	1
Other distribution cost	27	3	1
Other costs	53	5	2
Total costs	985	97	42

Note: These data are aggregates for a sample of 42 leading magazines which together account for more than 40 percent of total ABC and SRDS circulation, and about 28 percent of total copies mailed.
Source: Foster Associates [29], 4–938, 939.

Table 4-9.   "Concentration" in the Magazine Industry, 1947-1967

Year	Number of Companies	Percent of Total Revenue Accounted For By			
		4 Largest Companies	8 Largest Companies	20 Largest Companies	50 Largest Companies
1947	2,106	34	43	58	–
1958	2,245	31	41	55	69
1967	2,430	24	37	56	72

Note: The data refer to companies, not individual magazines.
Source: U.S. Census Bureau, *Concentration Ratios in Manufacturing* (1967).

would provide a fruitful area for research aimed at testing the hypotheses put forward in the monopolistic competition model of Chapter Three. The important point in thinking about this industry is that it is wrong to focus on the handful of large, general interest, mass circulation periodicals as in any way representative of the industry as a whole. No doubt in this respect the size distribution of periodicals very much resembles that of daily newspapers. When mass circulation periodicals are considered, it is apparent that television is a fairly close substitute, both for readers and advertisers. Television, at least with its limited channels, cannot provide alternatives to the much more numerous specialized periodicals.

MOTION PICTURES

One does not readily think of motion pictures as a part of the media accorded First Amendment protection, and indeed such protection *is* less equal for this industry. Still, if the frequency with which various countries exercise political (and moral) film censorship is any indication, the political role of this medium is not inconsiderable. Our own courts have tolerated a greater degree of moral censorship of films than of most other media. Sober judges, as with television, did not treat novelty seriously.

In fact, the motion picture industry is rather highly regulated. It is regulated indirectly by the FCC, because much of Hollywood's output finds its way onto television. Some FCC rules, such as the prime time access rule, are designed specifically to affect the film industry. The industry is also regulated by the antitrust division of the Justice Department as a result of *United States v. Paramount Pictures, Inc.*[e] This regulation concerns only the relationship between exhibitors and distributors.

The film industry, like the other media, can be separated into the three vertical stages of production. In motion pictures, however, the critical "bottleneck" stage is distribution, for this is the place where economies of scale and

[e]334 U.S. 131 (1948), hereafter *Paramount*.

natural concentration are found. The creative production process seems to be at least potentially quite competitive, and of course exhibition is competitive, or monopolistically competitive with spatial differentiation.

Before 1948 the major studios were vertically integrated into all three of these stages. The government antitrust suit against the majors, called the *Paramount* case, resulted in a decree forcing the studios to divest their theater chains. The court retained jurisdiction over the terms of exhibition contracts, and so the Justice Department continues a permanent survvellience of this part of the industry, acting in effect as a regulator.

Soon after the *Paramount* decision, television began to dominate family entertainment. For this and other reasons, postwar motion picture admissions and revenues declined drastically. After about 1960, however, the invention of the telecine chain made it possible to show films on television, and since that time an increasing part of industry revenues have come from television, either by direct production of TV programs or by release of theatrical motion pictures to television. (In 1973 the seven major studios earned $440 million from television and $890 million from theatrical film revenue.[f])

The studios form a very loose oligopoly in the movie field. Entry into distribution is difficult, but in the TV market the networks perform the distribution function themselves. The product is not one that lends itself to tacit collusion. There is some rather weak evidence of tacit collusion on film output (releases), but since it is impossible to police film quality (popularity or expenditure), it is unlikely that this is successful. Independent producers can be barred by the major distributors from access to exhibition markets and, perhaps more important, financial backing, but it is difficult to imagine much successful collusion on this. The product is extremely risky, and the relationship between expenditure on production and success is highly stochastic. Indeed, this market presents problems that challenge even abstract economic modelling. The product (a film or a TV program) is a durable asset which is "rented" in the market to TV networks, TV stations, domestic theater circuits, and foreign buyers. The product depreciates not merely with time, but with audience exposure, but it can be rested between runs and between releases to restore some of its vitality.

There are apparently patterns of spatial and temporal price discrimination. Moreover, on the production side, the major factors of production are unique: there is a stochastic relationship not only between inputs and profitability, but even between the direction of input effects and profitability changes. Much of the concentration that does occur in the distribution stage may be due to these factors, especially risk spreading. This may also help to explain the recent trend toward conglomerate ownership of studios.

The Hollywood motion picture and TV programming industry is one with quite specialized factors of production available in a highly organized rental market. Talent, stages, and other factors come together for the production of a

[f]See McAlpine [48].

movie or a TV series, then break up and are reformed around another product. Thus, competition in the production or creation stages is enhanced by the ready availability of factors for rent; entry does not require large scale permanent investment.

The motion picture product, shown in theaters, is at the other end of the spectrum from television in the sense that it is supported almost entirely by viewer payments. Television, of course, is supported entirely by advertising, and most other media are supported by both. It is the program packagers and studios that stand to gain from pay television or pay cable television. The demand for their products by advertiser supported television has not made up for the losses in theatrical revenues caused by television. Some of the studios have begun to demonstrate the viability of pay TV by installing systems in hotels and motels that distribute movies to the television sets of guests for a fee. These are in effect cable systems. The experiments to date seem to have been successful.

The *Paramount* antitrust decree is a very useful model for structural policy affecting the other media. In fact, it involved the sort of vertical disintegration recommended for newspapers and television in previous chapters. The principal difference—and the principal complaint about the industry since the *Paramount* decree—has been the absence of a mechanism for nondiscriminatory access to the concentrated distribution stage. Arguably, this is unnecessary in the motion picture industry because of the relatively large number of distributors. (The other difference is that the studios were not barred from backwards vertical integration—that is, into production.) Nevertheless, the principle that an individual medium can be subject to vertical disintegration through the antitrust process without arousing First Amendment immunities makes this case an important precedent.

Whitney [97] provides an excellent economic history of the industry through the mid fifties. Table 4-10 displays some rough estimates of broad industry trends over the 1925-1970 period. These data are mostly from industry sources, and are generally even less reliable than the magazine industry data. The postwar decline in theater attendance and box office receipts is, however, very dramatic in these statistics, as is the considerable increase in admission prices since about 1950. It is nowadays impossible to regard the theatrical motion picture market and the television program production market as independent industries, and the history of the industry since 1960 is therefore inseparable from the history of television itself.

Most theatrical motion pictures are made with a view toward eventual television exhibition, and the same firms and factors produce both movies and programs. The distributors who deal with the theater circuits have stocks of films which are rented to the networks, usually in blocks. Also, two of the networks have recently attempted (not very successfully) to integrate backwards into movie production, and one (ABC) owns a very large chain of theaters.

Table 4-10. Motion Picture Industry Statistics

Year	(1) *Average Weekly Attendance (millions)*	(2) *Box Office Receipts ($000)*	(3) *Features Released*	(4) *Theaters*	(5) *Box Office Receipts as Percent U.S. Personal Consumption Expenditure*
1925	46	–	579	–	–
1930	90	732	595	23,000	1.05
1935	80	556	766	15,272	1.00
1940	80	735	673	19,036	1.04
1945	85	1450	377	20,457	1.21
1950	60	1376	622	19,106	0.72
1955	46	1326	392	19,200	0.52
1960	25 (est.)	951	387	16,901	0.29
1965	20 (est.)	927	452	14,000	0.23
1970	18 (est.)	1175	–	13,500	0.19

Sources:
(1) *Historical Statistics of the United States*, Series H-522, p. 225. (Figures for 1960 onwards are estimates by the author.)
(2) For 1930–1965, *Motion Picture Almanac* (1970), from July 1969 *Survey of Current Business*; 1970 from *U.S. Industrial Outlook* (1971).
(3) and (4) All years from *Film Daily Yearbook*.
(5) *Motion Picture Almanac* (1970).

Chapter Five

Conclusions and a Policy Shopping List

What should ye do then, should ye suppress all this flowery crop of knowledge and new light sprung up and yet springing daily in this city, should ye set an oligarchy of twenty ingrossers over it, to bring a famine upon our minds again, when we shall know nothing but what is measured to us by their bushel?

—Milton, *Areopagitica*

INTRODUCTION

A reading of the Long Parliament's June 14, 1643 *Order for the Regulation of Printing*, and of certain passages in Milton's *Areopagitica*, leaves one with the impression that government officials may have had more in mind than simply ensuring that no dangerous books were printed. One cannot, in fact, escape the conclusion that the "Company of Stationers and Printers" was being assisted in the maintenance of a monopoly of printing services in London. If this was so, it marked the beginnings of a situation which is with us today.

Both in broadcasting and in newspaper publishing, economic interests have been generally successful in directing the course of government policy toward the protection of profits and the prevention of competition. There are those who would ascribe the entire corpus of communications law and regulation to a conspiracy of the vested interests, although their influence and power is hardly a secret. Whatever the truth of this—and it is doubtless an extreme view—the regulations and policies must be cloaked in public interest rhetoric. There is little to be done about the vested interests, but much to be done about laying bare the fallacies of the rhetoric.

THE NEED FOR STRUCTURAL REFORM

In reviewing judicial, legislative, administrative, and public policy decisions in the mass media field, an economist cannot help but be dismayed. The natural tendency of policy makers and jurists, even of legal scholars, seems to be to engage in direct or indirect regulation of conduct or behavior, despite the obvious conflict with the First Amendment. This has resulted, at least in broadcasting, in tortured and procrustean interpretations of the Amendment in order to justify the desired level and kind of intervention. And on those occasions when policy makers have ventured into issues of structure, the results have often been equally unhappy, especially in television spectrum allocation decisions.

Still, it is structure that is crucial. The First Amendment bars regulation of conduct; and even if it did not, structure would be in nearly every case a preferable avenue to valid policy objectives. It is not possible or desirable to regulate fairness. It is both possible and desirable to structure an industry which is workably competitive and which therefore is conducive to freedom of expression. The best precedent for this may be the *Paramount* case.

Knowing that structure is the key policy variable is only part of the answer, however. One must still decide which of the many possible structures is best; seldom will there be any ideal solution. Our public decision making processes are biased against structural solutions to economic problems precisely because they are so difficult to conceptualize. It is much easier to pass a law making bad behavior illegal than it is to remove the incentive for that behavior.

The legislation of structures for which there is only analogous precedent simply appears too risky to decision makers; moreover, it inevitably requires a reshuffling of benefits in directions having no effective constituency. The benefits of structural reform accrue to someone, but that someone often has in the status quo no interest to protect, and no base of organization.

These considerations suggest that we need a new way of making industrial structure decisions, and that the decision making process should more effectively include the expertise of economists, industrial engineers, and other specialists who are not frightened by the notion of structural change. Further exploration of these issues would take us far afield, but it is an important problem nonetheless.

A POLICY SHOPPING LIST

It seems useful here to provide a summary of the major policy conclusions of the preceding chapters. This will be done by setting out a shopping list of desirable policies or policy changes. I have not felt constrained in constructing this list by notions of political feasibility, although these are obviously important. A list that took political feasibility into account would be a good deal more modest.

Newspapers

1. Antitrust activity seeking to preserve head-on, same city newspaper competition as traditionally conceived should be abandoned.
2. Antitrust and legislative action should be undertaken to divest newspaper printing and delivery systems from editorial and newsgathering services. Daily newspaper printing and delivery businesses if necessary should have a quasi-public utility status; at least they should be barred from entering into exclusive contracts with producers of editorial and advertising content.
3. The courts should continue, as in *Tornillo*, to reject the notion that there is any right of access to the editorial function of a newspaper. But they should recognize the constitutionality of a right of paid access to the means of transmission generally, including newspaper printing, if such a right is legislated. (Arguably, the courts might recognize such a right in the absence of legislation, but this is more tenuous.)
4. Newspaper-television cross-ownership in the same city should be prohibited.
5. The editorial and newsgathering processes should not be regulated by government.

Broadcasting

1. The Congress should establish private property rights in the electromagnetic spectrum, and sell it off at auction to the highest bidders. At a minimum, this should be done for that part of the spectrum presently occupied by VHF and UHF television and all radio stations.
2. The licensing and other regulatory authority over broadcasting content exercised by the FCC should be abolished.
3. The antitrust division should be free to seek structural remedies for network power, including such possibilities as limiting any one network to 24 continuous hours of operation per week.
4. The FCC rules against pay television should be eliminated, and Congress should not enact laws to replace them.
5. All public television stations should be turned over to commercial operators. Congress should subsidize cultural and educational programming, if at all, through grants allowing paid use of commercial stations.
6. Congress should make cable television systems into (at least quasi-) common carriers, to which there is a right of nondiscriminatory paid access, and in which there is no control of program content by the system owner or any regulatory authority.

Motion Pictures

1. There should be continued strict enforcement of the *Paramount* decision and the policy that underlies it.

Periodicals

1. Congress (but not necessarily other postal patrons) should subsidize at least small circulation periodicals by lowering the marginal cost of transmission through the postal system.

FREEDOM OF EXPRESSION IN THE TWENTIETH CENTURY

While it cannot be argued with any assurance that the diversity of sources of political news and ideas in general has decreased over the past 75 years, it is tempting to try to make this case with respect to specific categories of opinion. We know for sure that the number of daily and weekly newspapers has declined significantly in this century, and that the number of independent newspapers (not owned by chains or other media conglomerates) has declined still further. On the other hand, radio and television have risen to take the place of newspapers.

On the national scale, we have to ask whether the number of independent "gatekeepers"—persons with discretionary editorial power—has declined. To the extent that local newspapers obtain their national news from the wire services, AP and UPI, not much has changed, except that there has probably been an increase in the degree to which these wire services have exercised editorial control over the content of their stories—that is, an increase in the number of reporters working directly for the services rather than for cooperating newspapers whose editors decide what gets on the wire. On the other hand, it is not clear that the number of newspapers with independent national news bureaus (particularly in Washington) has decreased; certainly the White House press corps has increased in size.

Television and radio stations are not independent sources of national news and opinion, since nearly all of their material comes from the three networks and the two wire services. There has also been, probably, a significant increase in semiprivate publications of the newsletter type, particularly those oriented to members of various organizations. It is hard to evaluate the importance of this trend.

Meanwhile, there has been an enormous change in the pattern of information seeking by consumers, such that the political and social importance of the television networks is far out of proportion to their relative numbers. Almost certainly the concentration of influence with respect to certain issues has increased because of this. The networks in turn are influenced by a very few newspapers (mainly the *New York Times* and the *Washington Post*). If the three networks decide not to carry a story, there exists a cadre of informed people who may have read the story in one of these few newspapers, and who may call the networks to account. But this accounting will take place, say, in the pages of the

Columbia Journalism Review, and not before the public at large. It is difficult to make the case that any concentration of power equivalent to this existed at the turn of the century or earlier.

The important point is that one must weight the gatekeepers by audience size in order to discern their influence. When this is done, it is reasonably clear that the twentieth century has probably witnessed a decline in the effective number of independent general mass sources of national political news and ideas. At the same time it can be argued that there has been an increase in the number of "organizational" house organs (union and company newspapers, newsletters), and publications of interest to members of various special interest organizations. This no doubt reflects a number of changes in social and cultural patterns, including increasing population size, increasing mobility, and possibly increasing homogeneity of tastes within society, as well as those factors on the production side of the media that favor increasing concentration. The net effect may well be to make members of special interest groups rather better and more easily informed than they used to be, and even to make the public at large better informed, even though concentration of control over mass dissemination may have increased.

The picture is much clearer when it comes to local media. The local newspaper is, with respect to local political events, almost universally a monopolist, with only the most distant and tangential competition from other newspapers, and little more from the electronic media. There is not and there cannot be under present institutional arrangements anything like freedom of access for local speakers to local audiences through the media. Coverage of local events is controlled by monopoly gatekeepers.

ECONOMICS AND FREEDOM OF EXPRESSION

Freedom of expression to the framers of the First Amendment seems to have meant the opportunity to put before the public partisan political ideas without fear of government intervention. The issues of today are different: there were no mass media in 1791; there was no private monopoly power in the media. We are on our own in dealing with these issues, for little insight can be gained from the wisdom of the framers themselves.

Appropriate policy today seems to require that we minimize the economic and institutional barriers between potential speakers and their audiences. This is not by any means the same as ensuring that people are informed by agents of the government. It is not the same as ensuring that the media are balanced or "fair." Achieving this goal requires that the heavy hand of an increasingly paternalistic government be lifted from the controls of the editorial and creative stages of message production, and it requires new institutional structures surrounding access to the means of transmission of messages. What lies between speakers and their audiences are presses, cables, wires, and broadcast transmitters.

Just as it is inconsistent with competition and freedom for government to control who shall use these engines of mass speech, so it is inconsistent to allow them to fall into the hands of a few economic agents, however responsible they may claim to be. It is wrong for anyone but the individual editor to control individual editorial systems, but it is also wrong to allow the fortuitous monopolist of the printing press or the transmitter to be his own editor.

A right of access to the means of transmission may not be inherent in the constitution; perhaps it must be legislated.[a] Such a right does not require direct government supervision of the behavior of the owners of the means of transmission, but can be encompassed by structural reformation through legislation and antitrust activity. There is a significant difference between direct utility regulation and laws mandating certain kinds of behavior which can be enforced in the courts. The courts, despite the increasing burden they carry, are a far safer place for enforcement of First Amendment rights than are administrative agencies.

It is absolutely crucial, however, that both courts and legislators begin to understand the economics of media behavior. We have all listened too long to the so-called expert administrative and executive agencies in this field. These "experts" are in fact seldom expert at anything but retaining their own perogatives and jurisdictions, which depend on continued support from the industries whose economic interests they so consistently "protect" at the expense of the public's interest in competition and freedom.[b]

What has happened to the media over the years is this: thoughtful members of the industry have begun to realize that they are the arbiters of mass speech. They have reacted by institutionalizing their judicial role and by developing notions of fairness and responsibility. Due process has become part of the editorial process itself. In broadcasting, of course, due process has been institutionalized through the fairness doctrine and the license renewal procedures. But we need to reexamine the assumptions which lie behind this trend.

Granted that due process is better than arbitrary action, do we have to accept the notion that we must be at the mercy of a system requiring such institutional checks? It would be easy to attack the proposition that such procedural safeguards as exist are effective. But this is the wrong track. We do not want a fair and balanced press—we want a system of expression which is robust and partisan and impassioned. To be sure, there are economic as well as technological and social limits to our ability to achieve this, but we are a long way from doing as much as we can to achieve it.

The reaction of private and public individuals to the growing concentration

---

[a]One of the ways in which the word freedom has been used is in the sense of "a right to participate in the privileges attached to" as in the phrase, "He was granted the freedom of the city." It is in this sense that we might usefully read the constitutional injunction for "freedom of the press." (See the *Oxford English Dictionary*, "freedom," definition 13.)

[b]For an outrageous example, see the letter from the FCC to the Director of the Office of Management and Budget adopted October 3, 1974 (FCC #24100), commenting on the draft cable television legislation proposal by OTP.

in the mass media has been understandable. It is natural in our system to seek to attenuate arbitrary power by imposing procedual safeguards. Often this is just the right policy, particularly if one grants the necessity for the existence of the power in the first place. But in the First Amendment field this is just not good enough. We do not have to, and we should not, accept the premise that editorial monopoly is inevitable. The editorial process is not naturally monopolistic, though the means of transmission often are.

But the means of transmission are themselves affected with a public interest stemming from the First Amendment. No one would assert that paper factories or delivery trucks are infused with First Amendment immunities; the same is true of printing presses and broadcast transmitters. What the First Amendment does protect is the inviolability of the creative and editorial processes; what it seems to me to mandate under modern conditions is that these processes be given competitive access to the technical means of reaching the public.

I do not think it is necessary, from a practical standpoint, to make broadcast transmitters and printing presses into rate regulated common carriers like the telephone company, but such action *is* consistent with the First Amendment. At least it is much more consistent with the First Amendment than setting up the owners of these particular pieces of capital equipment as licensed arbiters of who shall speak and who shall not.

It may very well be that all of this is politically impossible. For that reason, we have to depend heavily on the advent of new technologies such as cable television to provide suitable and feasible opportunities for taking a more logical and consistent view of First Amendment freedoms. Some legislation affecting cable television regulation is perhaps inevitable. The opportunity this will afford to remedy our past mistakes should not be missed.

But we cannot go half-way. Cable will not grow to be a significant means of transmission unless consumers are allowed to pay for the information and other services it can provide. It is difficult to find a rationale in any of the theories of the First Amendment for our continued egregious kow-towing to the vested interests opposing pay television. That their power to influence political men stems in large part from widespread and emotional public misunderstanding of the consequences of pay television is little excuse for inactivity in such a crucial area of First Amendment concern. The modern equivalent of the Stationers Company must not be allowed to reinforce successfully the well meant paternalism of those who would suppress freedom in order to promote their personal vision of the public interest.

Notes

CHAPTER ONE

1. 326 U.S. 1 (1945); see also Judge Tamm's concurring opinion in *Hale v. FCC,* 425 F.2d 556 (D.C. Cir. 1970).

2. Equipment to start up a newspaper could be had, at the end of the eighteenth century, for well under $1,000 (Mott [57] p. 162). See generally pp. 37–43, *infra.*

3. Shannon and Weaver [83], Cherry [13].

4. See the surveys in Pool [68].

5. 418 U.S. 241 (1974), hereafter cited as *Tornillo.*

6. Adam Smith [85], and Koopmans [41].

7. See Spence [86], Hirshliefer [36], and Miller [53].

CHAPTER TWO

1. From the first issue in 1835 of Bennett's New York *Herald,* quoted in Tebbel [90], p. 97.

2. This section draws heavily on Roberts [72].

3. 394 U.S. 131 (1969).

4. 345 U.S. 594 (1953).

5. The census reports 319 such establishments in 1967, with revenues of $154 million, and 5,700 employees. *Statistical Abstract* (1973), p. 754, Table 1262.

CHAPTER THREE

1. See Barnouw [5], Minasian [54], and Herring and Gross [35] for early history of broadcasting regulations.

2. Interdepartmental Radio Advisory Committee—see Coase [16].

3. See Rostow Task Force Report, Staff Papers [70].

4. Coase [17]. The Coase Theorem says that, provided negotiation costs

are negligible, any definition of property rights is consistent with efficiency in the presence of external effects.

5. See Coase [15], De Vany [22].

6. See Owen, Beebe, Manning [62], Chapter 4.

7. See Epstein [25], Brown [9].

8. See Owen, Beebe, Manning [62], Chapter 4.

9. Owen, Beebe, Manning [62], Chapter 4.

10. *National Broadcasting Co. v. United States* 319 U.S. 190 (1943).

11. *Midwest Video Corp. v. FCC* 406 U.S. 649 (1972).

12. *Carroll Broadcasting Co. v. FCC* 258 F.2d 440 (D.C. Cir., 1958).

13. The anti-pay TV rules have been upheld in the courts. See *Fourth Report and Order* in Docket 11279 *Subscription Television* 15 FCC 2d 466 (1968); aff'd in *Nat'l Assoc. Theater Owners v. FCC* 420 F.2d 194 (D.C. Cir. 1969); *cert. den.* 397 U.S. 922 (1970). The rules, in section 73.643 of the FCC *Rules and Regulations,* were relaxed somewhat in 1975.

14. See Coase [15], De Vany [22].

15. All Channel Receiver Act 47 U.S.C. sec. 303(s), 330 (1970).

16. For the detent tuning rules, see 47 C.F.R. sec. 15.68(b) (1974).

17. See Cable Television Service, 47 C.F.R. sec. 76.1 ff. (1974).

18. The traditional literature on TV program patterns is found in Steiner [88], Rothenberg [73], Wiles [98], and Beebe [7]. For a critical summary see Chapter 3 in Owen, Beebe, and Manning [62].

19. See Barnouw [5], Herring and Gross [35].

20. See Communications Act of 1934 as amended, 47 U.S.C. sec. 315 (1970).

21. See FCC release 73-707 (7/2/73). The practice has recently been stopped.

22. See 43 FCC 2d 1-178.

23. But see such examples of FCC interference as the WUHY case, 24 FCC 2d 408 (1970).

24. See Whitehead [95].

25. See FCC 73-694 (Released 7/2/73) and FCC 72-967 (released 11/2/72), "In the Matter of Radio Reregulation." Also see Cheek [12].

26. Minow [55].

27. Carnegie Commission [11]; Public Broadcasting Act of 1967.

28. For discussion of the controversy, see Owen, Beebe, Manning [62], Chapter 7.

29. *Fortnightly Corp. v. United Artists Television, Inc.* 392 U.S. 360 (1968) and *Teleprompter Corp. v. Columbia Broadcasting System Inc.* 415 U.S. 394 (1974).

30. For a detailed history of cable regulations see Barnett [4]; for discussions of the 1972 rules see Park [66].

31. See Owen [63].

32. See Owen [64].

33. Epstein [25].

34. See Baker and Ball [3], Melody [51], Milgram and Shotland [52], Comstock and Rubenstein [19].

35. See Baer et al. [2], and Owen, Beebe, and Manning [62].

Bibliography

[1] Ayer, N.W. & Son. *American Newspaper Annual*. Philadelphia: Ayer, 1880–.

[2] Baer, Walter S., Geller, Henry, and Grundfest, Joseph A. *Newspaper-Television Station Cross-Ownership: Options for Federal Action*. Santa Monica: Rand Corp., 1974.

[3] Baker, Robert K., and Ball, Sandra J. "Violence and the Media." Staff Report to the National Commission on the Causes and Prevention of Violence, IX. Washington, D.C.: U.S. Government Printing Office, 1969.

[4] Barnett, S.R. "State, Federal, and Local Regulation of Cable Television." *Notre Dame Lawyer* 47 (April 1972).

[5] Barnouw, Erik. *A History of Broadcasting in the United States*, 3 vols. New York: Oxford University Press, 1966–1970.

[6] Barron, Jerome A. *Freedom of the Press for Whom?* Bloomington, Ind.: Indiana University Press, 1973.

[7] Beebe, Jack, H. "Institutional Structure and Program Choices in Television and Cable Television Markets." Research Memorandum #131. Stanford University: Research Center in Economic Growth, August 1972.

[8] Berstein, Carl, and Woodward, Robert. *All the President's Men*. New York: Warner Communications, 1975.

[9] Brown, Les. *Televi$ion: The Business Behind the Box*. New York: Harcourt-Brace-Jovanovich, 1971.

[10] Cabinet Committee on Cable Communications. *Report to the President*, (Whitehead Report.) Washington, D.C., January 1974.

[11] Carnegie Commission. *Public Television, a Program for Action*. New York: Bantam Books, 1967.

[12] Cheek, Leslie III. "An Analysis of Proposals to Deregulate Commercial Radio Stations." *Federal Communications Bar Journal* XXV (1), 1972.

[13] Cherry, Colin. *On Human Communication*. Cambridge, Mass.: MIT Press, 1971.

[14] Coase, Ronald H. *British Broadcasting: A Study in Monopoly*. Cambridge, Mass.: Harvard University Press, 1950.

[15] ———. "The Federal Communications Commission." *Journal of Law and Economics* 2 (October 1959).

[16] ———. "The Interdepartmental Radio Advisory Committee." *Journal of Law and Economics* 5 (October 1962).

[17] ———. "The Problem of Social Cost." *Journal of Law and Economics* 3 (1960).

[18] Collet, Collet, D. *History of the Taxes on Knowledge.* London: T.F. Unwin, 1899.

[19] Comstock, George A., and Rubenstein, Eli (eds.). *Television and Social Behavior.* Washington, D.C.: Report to the Surgeon General's Advisory Committee on Television and Social Behavior, 1972.

[20] Crandall, Robert W. "The Economic Case for a Fourth Commercial Television Network." *Public Policy* XXII (4) (Fall 1974).

[21] Demsetz, Harold. "The Private Production of Public Goods." *Journal of Law and Economics* XIII (October 1970).

[22] De Vany, Arthur S., Eckert, Ross D., Meyers, Charles J., O'Hara, Donald J., Scott, Richard C. "A Property System for Market Allocation of the Electromagnetic Spectrum: A Legal-Economic-Engineering Study." *Stanford Law Review* 21 (June 1969).

[23] Ephron, Edith. *The News Twisters.* Los Angeles: Nash Publishing, 1971.

[24] Emerson, Thomas I. *The System of Freedom of Expression.* New York: Random House, 1970.

[25] Epstein, Edward J. *News From Nowhere: Television and the News.* New York: Random House, 1973.

[26] Federal Communications Commission. *Detent Tuning Rules,* 40 FCC 2d 675.

[27] Federal Communications Commission. *Rules and Regulations,* Part 76: Cable Television Service. Washington, D.C.: September 1972.

[28] Festinger, Leon. *A Theory of Cognitive Dissonance.* Evanston, Ill.: Row, Peterson, 1957.

[29] Foster Associates, Inc. *The Impact of Proposed Postal Rates on Magazine Publications,* 1971, reprinted in U.S. Postal Service, *Postal Rate and Fee Increases,* Docket R71-1 1971 vol. 4 pt. 2, p. 4–895. Washington, D.C., 1971.

[30] Friendly, Fred W. "What's Fair on the Air?" *New York Times Magazine.* March 30, 1975, p. 11.

[31] Galbraith, John K. *American Capitalism: The Concept of Countervailing Power.* Boston: Houghton Mifflin, 1952.

[32] Greenberg, Edward. "Television Station Profitability and FCC Regulatory Policy." *Journal of Industrial Economics* 17 (July 1969).

[33] Harberger, Arnold C. "Three Basic Postulates for Applied Welfare Economics." *Journal of Economic Literature* IX (3) (September 1971).

[34] *Harvard Law Review.* "Morality and the Broadcast Media: A Constitutional Analysis of FCC Regulatory Standards." *HLR* 84: 664, 1971.

[35] Herring, James M., and Gross, Gerald C. *Telecommunications: Economics and Regulation.* New York: McGraw-Hill, 1936.

[36] Hirshliefer, Jack. "The Private and Social Value of Information and the Reward to Inventive Activity." *American Economic Review* LXI (4) (September 1971).

[37] Hofstadter, Richard. *The Age of Reform.* New York: Vintage Books, 1955.

[38] Hotelling, Harold. "Stability in Competition." *Economic Journal* 34 (March 1929).

[39] Innis, Harold A. *The Bias of Communication.* Toronto: University of Toronto Press, 1951.

[40] Kennedy, Jane. "Development of Postal Rates: 1845–1955." *Land Economics* 33 (2) (May 1957).

[41] Koopmans, Tjalling C. *Three Essays on the State of Economic Science.* New York: McGraw-Hill, 1957.

[42] Land, Herman W. and Associates, Inc. *Television and the Wired City.* Commissioned by the National Association of Broadcasters, July 1968, for the use of the President's Task Force on Communication Policy. Washington, D.C.: NAB, 1968.

[43] Lange, David L. "The Role of the Access Doctrine in the Regulation of the Mass Media: A Critical Review and Assessment." *North Carolina Law Review* 52 (1) (November 1973).

[44] Lee, Alfred McClung. *The Daily Newspaper in America.* New York: Macmillan, 1937.

[45] Levin, Harvey J. *The Invisible Resource.* Baltimore: Johns Hopkins University Press, 1971.

[46] ——. "Program Duplication, Diversity, and Effective Viewer Choices: Some Empirical Findings." *American Economic Review* 61 (May 1971).

[47] Levy, L.W. *Legacy of Suppression: Freedom of Speech and Press in Early American History.* Cambridge, Mass.: Harvard University Press, 1960.

[48] McAlpine, Dennis B. *The Television Programming Industry.* New York: Tucker, Anthony, Day, 1975.

[49] McLuhan, Marshall. *Understanding Media.* New York: McGraw-Hill, 1964.

[50] Mathematica, Inc. *A Study of the Demand for Advertising, Newspaper and Magazine Mail,* 1971, reprinted in U.S. Postal Service, *Postal Rate and Fee Increases,* Docket R71-1, 1971, vol. 4 pt. 2, p. 4-943. Washington, D.C., 1971.

[51] Melody, William. *Children's TV: The Economics of Exploitation.* New Haven: Yale University Press, 1973.

[52] Milgram, Stanley, and Shotland, R.L. *Television and Antisocial Behavior.* New York: Academic Press, 1974.

[53] Miller, Arthur. *The Assault on Privacy.* Ann Arbor, Mich.: University of Michigan Press, 1971.

[54] Minasian, Jora R. "The Political Economy of Broadcasting in the 1920's." *Journal of Law and Economics* 12 (October 1969).

[55] Minow, Newton W. *Equal Time: The Private Broadcaster and the Public Interest.* New York: Atheneum, 1964.

[56] Moore, Thomas G. "An Economic Analysis of the Concept of Freedom." *Journal of Political Economy* 77 (4) (July/August 1969).

[57] Mott, Frank Luther. *American Journalism.* New York: Macmillan, 1962.

[58] Noll, Roger, Peck, Merton J., and McGowan, John. *Economic Aspects of Television Regulation.* Washington, D.C.: Brookings Institution, 1973.

[59] Nozick, Robert. Anarchy, State, and Utopia. New York: Basic Books, 1974.

[60] Oakland, William H. "Public Goods, Perfect Competition, and Under-production." *Journal of Political Economy* 82 (5) (September/October 1974).

[61] Olson, Mancur, Jr. *The Logic of Collective Action.* Cambridge, Mass.: Harvard University Press, 1965.

[62] Owen, Bruce M., Beebe, Jack H., and Manning, Willard G. Jr. *Television Economics.* Lexington, Mass.: D.C. Heath, 1974.

[63] Owen, Bruce M. "Public Policy and Emerging Technology in the Media." *Public Policy* 18 (Summer 1970).

[64] Owen, Bruce M. "The Role of Analysis in the Formation of Cable Television Policy." R.E. Park (ed.). *The Role of Analysis in Regulatory Decision-Making: The Case of Cable Television.* Lexington, Mass.: D.C. Heath, 1973.

[65] Park, Rolla Edward. "New Television Networks." Rand Report R-1408-MF. Santa Monica: Rand Corp., December 1973.

[66] —— (ed.). *The Role of Analysis in Regulatory Decision-Making: The Case of Cable Television.* Lexington, Mass.: D.C. Heath, 1973.

[67] Peterson, Theodore. *Magazines in the Twentieth Century.* Urbana: University of Illinois Press, 1964.

[68] Pool, Ithiel de Sola, et al. (eds.). *Handbook of Communication.* Chicago: Rand McNally, 1973.

[69] Posner, Richard A. "Taxation by Regulation." *Bell Journal of Economics and Management Science* 2 (Spring 1971).

[70] President's Task Force on Communications Policy. "Staff Papers." Springfield, Va.: Federal Clearinghouse, June 1969.

[71] Rich, Wesley E. *History of the American Post Office to 1825.* Cambridge: Harvard University Press, 1924.

[72] Roberts, Keith. "Antitrust Problems in the Newspaper Industry." *Harvard Law Review* 82 (December 1968).

[73] Rothenberg, Jerome. "Consumer Sovereignty and the Economics of TV Programming." *Studies in Public Communication* 4 (Fall 1962).

[74] Rosse, James N. "Credible and Incredible Economic Evidence: Reply Comments in FCC Docket 18110 (Cross-Ownership of Newspapers and Television Stations)." Memorandum #109. Stanford University: Research Center in Economic Growth, April 1971.

[75] ——. "Daily Newspapers, Monopolistic Competition, and Economies of Scale." *American Economic Review* 57 (May 1967).

[76] ——. "Daily Newspapers, Monopolistic Competition, and Economies of Scale." Unpublished PhD dissertation, University of Minnesota, 1966.

[77] —— "Economic Limits of Press Responsibility." Discussion paper. Stanford University: Studies in Industry Economics, #56, 1975.

[78] ——. "On Estimating Cost Function Parameters Without Using Cost Data: Illustrated Methodology." *Econometrica,* April 1970.

[79] ——., Owen, Bruce M., and Dertouzos, James. "Trends in the Daily Newspaper Industry, 1923–1973." Studies in Industry Economics No. 57. Stanford, Calif., 1975.

[80] Rucker, Bryce, W. *The First Freedom.* Carbondale: Southern Illinois University Press, 1968.

[81] Schramm, Wilbur (ed.). *Mass Communications: A Book of Readings.* Urbana: University of Illinois Press, 1960.

[82] Schumpeter, Joseph A. *Capitalism, Socialism, and Democracy,* 3rd ed. New York: Harper & Bros., 1950.

[83] Shannon, Claude E., and Weaver, Warren. *The Mathematical Theory of Communication.* Urbana: University of Illinois Press, 1964.

[84] Shaw, Steven J. "Colonial Newspaper Advertising: A Step Toward Freedom of the Press." *Business History Review* 33 (1959).

[85] Smith, Adam. *An Inquiry into the Nature and Causes of the Wealth of Nations,* ed. by E. Cannan. New York: Modern Library, 1937.

[86] Spence, A. Michael. *Market Signalling.* Cambridge, Mass.: Harvard University Press, 1974.

[87] ———. "Product Selection, Fixed Costs, and Monopolistic Competition." Stanford: Unpublished draft (1974) forthcoming in the *Review of Economic Studies.*

[88] Steiner, Peter, O. "Program Patterns and Preferences and the Workability of Competition in Radio Broadcasting." *Quarterly Journal of Economics* 66 (May 1954).

[89] Stephenson, William. *The Play Theory of Mass Communication.* Chicago: University of Chicago Press, 1967.

[90] Tebbel, John. *The Compact History of the American Newspaper.* New York: Hawthorne Books, 1969.

[91] Thomas, Isaiah. *The History of Printing in America.* New York: Burt Franklin, n.d.

[92] Thompson, Earl. "The Perfectly Competitive Production of Public Goods." *Review of Economics and Statistics* 50 (February 1968), see comments and reply in vol. 51, November 1969.

[93] Weeks, Lyman H. *A History of Paper Manufacturing in the United States, 1690-1916.* New York: Lockwood Trade Journal Company, 1916.

[94] Weitzman, Martin L., "Free Access vs. Private Ownership as Alternative Systems for Managing Common Property," *Journal of Economic Theory* 8: 225 (1974).

[95] Whitehead, Clay T. "Remarks" before the IRTS, October 6, 1971. Reprinted as Appendix I to *The Politics of Broadcast Regulation,* M. Barrett (ed.). New York: Crowell, 1973.

[96] Whiteside, Thomas. "Annals of Television: The Nixon Administration and Television." *The New Yorker,* March 17, 1975.

[97] Whitney, Simon N. *Antitrust Policies* (2 vols.). New York: Twentieth Century Fund, 1958.

[98] Wiles, Peter. "Pilkington and the Theory of Value." *Economic Journal* 73 (June 1963).

[99] Willig, Robert. "Welfare Analysis of Policies Affecting Prices and Products." Memorandum #153. Stanford University: Center for Research in Economic Growth, September 1973.

[100] Wolff, Robert P., Moore, Barrington Jr., and Marcuse, Herbert. *A Critique of Pure Tolerance.* Boston: Beacon Press, 1965.

[101] Wroth, Lawrence C. *The Colonial Printer* (2d ed.). Charlottesville, Va.: University of Virginia Press, 1938.

Index

About the Author

Bruce M. Owen teaches economics at Stanford University, from which he received a PhD in 1970. Professor Owen has been an Economic Policy Fellow of the Brookings Institution and a National Fellow of the Hoover Institution on War, Revolution, and Peace. He was formerly Chief Economist of the White House Office of Telecommunications Policy. Professor Owen is co-author of the text *Television Economics*.